CODE
RED

CODE
RED

HOW PROGRESSIVES
AND MODERATES CAN UNITE
TO SAVE OUR COUNTRY

E. J. DIONNE, JR.

ST. MARTIN'S
PRESS
NEW YORK

First published in the United States by St. Martin's Press,
an imprint of St. Martin's Publishing Group

CODE RED. Copyright © 2020 by E. J. Dionne, Jr. All rights reserved.
Printed in the United States of America. For information, address St. Martin's
Publishing Group, 120 Broadway, New York, NY 10271.

www.stmartins.com

Design by Meryl Sussman Levavi

Library of Congress Cataloging-in-Publication Data

Names: Dionne, E. J., author.
Title: Code red : how progressives and moderates can unite to save our country /
E.J. Dionne, Jr.
Description: First edition. | New York : St. Martin's Press, 2020. | Includes bibliographical
references and index.
Identifiers: LCCN 2019043187 | ISBN 9781250256478 (hardcover) |
ISBN 9781250256485 (ebook)
Subjects: LCSH: United States—Politics and government—2017- | Progressivism (United
States politics) | Moderation—Political aspects—United States. | Political leadership—
United States. | Political culture—United States.
Classification: LCC E912 .D559 2020 | DDC 306.20973—dc23
LC record available at https://lccn.loc.gov/2019043187

Our books may be purchased in bulk for promotional, educational, or business
use. Please contact your local bookseller or the Macmillan Corporate and
Premium Sales Department at 1-800-221-7945, extension 5442, or by email at
MacmillanSpecialMarkets@macmillan.com.

First Edition: February 2020

10 9 8 7 6 5 4 3 2 1

For members of the rising generations who will restore
our democracy,
including James, Julia and Margot, and my students
and interns.
And for those in the older generation ready to lend
them a hand.

"This world demands the qualities of youth; not a time
of life but a state of mind, a temper of the will, a quality of
the imagination, a predominance of courage over timidity,
of the appetite for adventure over the life of ease."

ROBERT F. KENNEDY

And in grateful memory of
Cokie Roberts,
David Broder,
Flora Lewis,
and Michael Harrington

CONTENTS

CODE
RED

INTRODUCTION

THE OPPORTUNITY WE DARE NOT MISS

The Uprising Against Trump and the
Rendezvous with Dignity

WILL PROGRESSIVES AND MODERATES FEUD WHILE AMERICA burns?

Or will these natural allies take advantage of a historic opportunity to strengthen American democracy and defeat an increasingly radical form of conservatism?

The choice in our politics is that stark. This book is offered in a spirit of hope, but with a sense of alarm.

My hope is inspired by the broad and principled opposition that Donald Trump's presidency called forth. It is a movement that can and should be the driving force in our politics long after Trump is gone. His abuses of office, his divisiveness, his bigotry, his autocratic habits, and his utter lack of seriousness about the responsibilities of the presidency drew millions of previously disengaged citizens to the public square and the ballot box. The danger he represented inspired young Americans to participate in our public life at unprecedented levels. Tens of thousands of Americans, especially women, have gathered in libraries, diners, and church basements to share wisdom, to organize, and, in many cases, to run for office themselves. These newly engaged citizens have created an opportunity to build a broad alliance for practical

2 • *Code Red*

and visionary government as promising as any since the Great Depression gave Franklin Roosevelt the chance to build the New Deal coalition.

To seize this opening, progressives and moderates must realize that they are allies who have more in common than they sometimes wish to admit. They share a commitment to what public life can achieve and the hope that government can be decent again. They reject the appeals to racism that have been Trump's calling card and the divisiveness at the heart of his electoral strategy. Together, they long for a politics focused on freedom, fairness, and the future. This new politics would be rooted in the economic justice that has always been the left's driving goal and in the problem-solving approach to government that moderates have long championed.

It's true that these camps often battle over whether the nation should seek restoration or transformation in the years after Trump. In fact, our country needs both. To restore the democratic norms we have always valued, we must begin to heal the social and economic wounds that led to Trump's presidency in the first place. Yet there is resistance to common ground among progressives and moderates alike. They often mistrust each other's motives, battle fiercely over tactics, argue over how much change the country needs, and squabble over whether specific policy ideas go too far, or not far enough.

The moderate says: "Hey, progressive, you think that if you just lay out the boldest and most ambitious approach to any given problem, the people will rally to your side. Really? For one thing, people may like your objective but think you're changing things way more than we have to. And we can battle to the death over, say, a Democratic Party platform plank or the first draft of a bill, but without the hard negotiating and compromising that legislative politics requires, a bold idea will remain just a platform plank. That really doesn't do anyone any good. You subject everyone to so many litmus tests that we might as well be in chemistry class. And God save us from your abuse on Twitter if we disagree with you. You lefties have no idea how to win elections outside of Berkeley or Brooklyn, and some of your ideas are so sweeping that they will scare potential voters and allies away." At this point, the moderate is likely to wield the sturdy old punch line: "Don't let the perfect be the enemy of the good."

"But hold on," says the progressive, "you moderates spend so much time negotiating with yourselves that you compromise away goals and priorities before the real battle even begins. Your ideas get so soggy and complicated that they mobilize no one and mostly put people to sleep. Better to have the courage of your convictions, lay out your hopes plainly and passionately, and inspire voters to join you. Besides, you middle-of-the-roaders were so petrified of Ronald Reagan and the right wing that you caved in to the Gipper's economic ideas, let inequality run wild, and gave us a racist and grossly unfair criminal justice system. The extremists have pulled the political center so far right that the only way back to sanity is to show our fellow citizens what a real progressive program looks like."

At the risk of sounding like a perhaps unwelcome counselor attempting to ease a family quarrel, I would plead with moderates and progressives to listen to each other carefully. If the events since 2016 do not teach moderates and progressives that they must find ways of working together, nothing will. If they fail to heed each other's advice and take each other's concerns seriously, they will surrender the political system to an increasingly undemocratic right with no interest in any of their shared goals, priorities, and commitments.

Moderates are right about the complexity of getting things done in a democracy. Even when the boldest ideas have prevailed, they did so because complex coalitions were built, important (and, it should be said, often legitimate) interests were accommodated, and some lesser goals were left by the wayside, to be fought for another day. Moderates are also right that democracy requires persuading those who are open to change but worry about how this or that reform might work in practice or affect them personally. (Think: losing their private health insurance.) Disdaining as sellouts those who raise inconvenient questions or express qualms is not the way to build a majority for reform. Moderates are also right that Americans in large numbers are tired of a politics that involves more yelling than dialogue, more demonizing than understanding.

But progressives are right to say that for the last three decades, moderates *have* spent too much time negotiating with themselves. Consider all the effort Democrats put into wooing Republicans by responding to their proposals to amend Obamacare, only to have the GOP oppose it anyway and spend a decade trying to repeal it. Much the same happened with the 2010 Dodd-Frank financial services reform act. Moderates have too readily accepted the assumptions of their opponents, wasting energy and squandering opportunities by trying to accommodate a right wing that will never be appeased. Progressives are also right in saying that our political system tilts toward the wealthy and the connected. And whether they call themselves socialists or not, progressives have the intellectual high ground when they say that today's capitalism—a radical form of the market economy shaped in the 1980s that is quite different from earlier incarnations—is failing to serve the needs of Americans in very large numbers.

As I hope is already clear, this book does not make the standard centrist argument that progressives can't win unless they become more moderate. But neither does it make a claim, often heard among progressives, that moderation is hopeless and the only way to prevail in a deeply divided country is to mobilize your own base.

Each of these claims is incomplete. The problems with the first were underscored by the outcome of the 2016 election: Moderation alone does not guarantee victory, and the progressive critique of the center has become more persuasive as economic inequality has widened. The problem with the second is that every electoral contest involves *both* mobilization *and* persuasion. The important question is to establish where the balance between the two lies at a given moment. Neither can be ignored.

Democrats certainly got that balance right in the 2018 elections. Moderates and progressives came together behind a remarkably diverse set of candidates, winning important governor's races in states that voted for Trump and taking control of the House. It was this victory that enabled House Speaker Nancy Pelosi to begin a formal impeachment inquiry after it was learned that Trump tried to enlist the Ukrainian government in an effort to smear former vice president Joe Biden. A coalition for change produced a coalition for accountability. Maintaining and expanding this sense of unity, I will argue, requires a shared commitment to a set of goals and principles that I describe as a Politics of Remedy, a Politics of Dignity, and a Politics of More.

Remedy—solving problems, resolving disputes, moving forward—is the core purpose of democratic politics. Dignity is at the heart of demands for justice from long-marginalized groups as well as members of a once secure multiracial working class displaced by deindustrialization, trade, and technological change. And while moderates and progressives may differ on specifics (single-payer health care versus improvements on Obamacare, for example), they agree that energetic public action can provide more Americans with affordable health insurance, more with decent wages and benefits, more with family-friendly workplaces, more with good schools, more with affordable paths to college and effective training programs, more with unimpeded access to the ballot, more with adequate provision for retirement, more with security from gun violence. And, yes, we need to do much more to combat climate change.

But to forge the alliance American politics needs, moderates and progressives will have to abandon an unseemly moralism that feeds political superiority complexes.

Progressives are not the impractical visionaries many moderates suspect them to be, with no concern for how programs work or how change happens. On the contrary, there are times when progressives are *more* practical than their critics in seeing that piecemeal reforms can be too narrow to solve the problem at hand, too stingy to create systems that inspire broad-based political support, and too accommodating to narrow interest groups. It should always be remembered that without the vision progressives offer, many reforms would never have been undertaken. The abolitionists agitated against slavery when most of the country was indifferent, opening the way for more moderate and cautious politicians such as Abraham Lincoln to end the nation's moral scourge. Laws regulating wages and hours were viewed as violations of property rights—until they weren't. Racial equality was a radical demand until it became mainstream in the civil rights years. Gay marriage was opposed as recently as 2012 by a Democratic president.

Progressives continue to broaden a political debate long hemmed in by the dominance of conservative assumptions and the stifling of progressive aspirations. Bernie Sanders moved single-payer health care onto the political agenda, giving the lie to the idea that Obamacare was socialist and radical. Elizabeth Warren has suggested far-reaching reforms to capitalism, proposing aggressive action against monopolies and a wealth tax that would directly address concentrations of economic power. Warren, Sanders, and their supporters have thus expanded our policy imaginations. Ideas once cast as "leftist" (an increase in the capital gains tax comes to mind) were suddenly seen as "moderate" alternatives.

Moderates are not, as some progressives suspect, agents of influence for the status quo seeking to channel reformist energy into safe pathways that leave the powerful undisturbed. Moderates are often as fed up with existing distributions of power and ways of doing business as are their friends to their left. But, yes, moderates do counsel reformers to be on the lookout for the unintended consequences of their proposals. They hold out the hope that one step forward today can be followed by another step tomorrow—and they can point to Social Security and advances in health insurance coverage as examples of when modest first steps eventually led to more sweeping victories.

Moderation itself embodies specific virtues that any democratic system needs. The political scientist Aurelian Craiutu defines them well in his book *Faces of Moderation*. He notes that moderation "promotes social and political pluralism," has a "propensity to seek conciliation and find balance between various ideas, interests and groups," and does not assume there is "only one single correct (or valid) way of life on which we all might agree." Moderates recognize that "most political and social issues often involve tough trade-offs and significant opportunity costs, and require constant small-scale adjustments and gradual steps." Moderation is "a form of opposition to extremism, fanaticism and zealotry," teaches the virtues of "self-restraint and humility," and seeks to keep the conversation open with "friends, critics and opponents." All these are habits and dispositions that progressives and humane conservatives—no less than moderates themselves—value more highly than ever after our unfortunate national experiment with their opposite under Trump.[1]

Yes, moderates and progressives can drive each other crazy by being, respectively, too cautious and too rash, and I am not trying to wish away what are genuine differences between them. They can disagree over principle (how large a role should the state play?), over questions of political efficacy (which sorts of programs can draw majority support?), over practical concerns (do certain approaches work better than others?), and over the proper balance of influence in a democracy between experts and mass movements.

But what they share is, at this moment especially, more important: a deep belief in democracy and freedom, a commitment to public problem solving, a frustration over the collapse of norms that promote basic decency, and a desire for a fairer economy that allows all citizens to live in dignity and hope.

As I write, the Trump presidency confronts an impeachment crisis. Its causes were particular to his abuses—a hangover of deep mistrust created by Special Counsel Robert Mueller's findings, Trump's subordination of the country's interests to his own selfish needs in pressuring the Ukrainian government to help his reelection, and extravagant and dangerous claims of presidential immunity from any form of accountability. His refusal to separate himself fully from his own companies bred constant suspicion that his every action (including the profoundly destructive green light he gave Turkish President Recep Tayyip Erdogan to invade Syria and attack the Kurds) might be linked to his narrow economic interests. Until his efforts to get a foreign government to smear Joe Biden became public, moderate and progressive Democrats in the House were divided over whether to pursue impeachment. They came together in mutual revulsion. They were united by shared values and by a common strategic sense that only an impeachment inquiry would make clear to the country how aberrant and destructive his behavior was. The reluctance of most Republicans to take on Trump, in turn, underscored how deeply the party had been infected by Trumpism. A fear of the effects of speaking out gripped large parts of the party.

In the face of this radicalized and deformed Republicanism, the urgency of the progressive/moderate alliance I call for in these pages will long outlive the Trump presidency. The damage Trump has done to conservatism (and that conservatives have done to themselves) will not be suddenly repaired by his departure. Trump triumphed by exploiting public disaffection with a political system that many Americans saw as infested with sleaze and controlled by forces operating entirely for their own benefit. Rather than being the cure for such maladies, he was their apotheosis, the culmination of all that has gone wrong in our politics. Trump's presidency underscored how desperately our system needs reform and our country needs repair. In the post-Trump era, progressives and moderates must be prepared to take on these tasks—together.

Political labels are inherently vexing, especially since most voters don't care about them very much. They can also change meaning over time, and they go in and out of style. So a word on why I have chosen the terms I have.

I use "progressives" to refer to broad left-of-center opinion because that is the current term of choice among those who hold such views. I also use it because the word "liberal" is packed with many different meanings now, given, for example, the widespread use of "neoliberal" to refer to those who favor a less regulated economy. Broadly, progressives in these pages are those who favor far-reaching reforms to remedy inequalities related to class, race, gender, immigration status, and sexual orientation.

The word "moderate" is even more difficult to pin down, and a large share of the political science profession is skeptical that the word has any functional meaning in describing voters. Public opinion researchers have noted that those labeled as moderates are not necessarily middle-of-the-road. They often have a mix of views that can fall at the far ends of opinion on both sides of the conventional political spectrum. As the political scientist David Broockman told *Vox*'s Ezra Klein, a voter who favors single-payer health care and the deportation of all illegal immigrants might be deemed a "moderate" because the average of these two positions lands him or her at some midpoint on a scale. But neither position can be described as "centrist" or "moderate." Moreover, as Klein noted, voters who fall into the moderate category might well disagree with each other fundamentally. For the sake of simplicity, imagine one voter who favors legal abortion but strongly opposes labor unions and another who supports unions but would ban abortion. Two voters who hold very different worldviews might end up in the same hypothetical middle ground because neither is conventionally "liberal" or "conservative."[2]

While acknowledging these difficulties, I persist in using the word "moderate" not only because it has currency among politicians and other political actors but also because I still find it to be the best description of a significant swath of the electorate. Among Democrats and Independents, it would apply to those who see themselves as more on the center-left than the left. They might be more sympathetic to expanding health insurance coverage through reforms to the Affordable Care Act than to the creation of a single-payer system, or open to large-scale expansion of college access without making college free. Before the radicalization of the Republican Party, supporters of the GOP embraced the term "moderate" in significant numbers. They often found themselves in agreement with more liberal Democrats on reformist goals related to poverty, education, or neighborhood renewal but favored alternative solutions that they saw as more fiscally prudent or market friendly. That many of these onetime Republican moderates are now politically homeless is a central reason why they have far more in common with progressives than with a radicalized form of conservatism.

I prefer the term "moderate" to "centrist" not only because political moderation involves the dispositional virtues Craiutu describes but also because self-conscious "centrists" have often found themselves chasing a hypothetical middle ground that has shifted steadily rightward with the GOP's embrace of ever more extreme views. Principled moderates are now on the left side of politics because the right wing that controls the Republican Party gives them no quarter.

Which brings us to one thing this book is not: a call for a return to "bipartisanship." The rise of the radical right in the GOP means that, for now, the Democratic Party is missing a reasonable interlocutor. This shift toward a radicalized conservatism married to Trumpism up and down the party is also one reason why anti-Trump Republicans loomed larger among writers and commentators than among the party's politicians. Unlike GOP politicians, those honorable Never Trump conservative intellectuals and commentators didn't have to worry about primaries.

Democrats face formidable coalition-management challenges because they now provide a home to millions of voters (and scores of elected officials) who in earlier times might well have been moderate Republicans. This only increases the urgency of common action by progressives and moderates. They should welcome the rank-and-file defectors from the Republican Party as allies against Trumpian politics and a right-wing radicalism that has turned its back on many of the most constructive strains of the old GOP.

I am asking progressives and moderates to put aside their differences not just for one election, but for the larger purpose of moving the country forward.

My plea to progressives is to understand the difference between long-term goals and immediate needs, to see that Martin Luther King Jr.'s "fierce urgency of now" makes demands on all advocates of justice. At times, it is indeed a rebuke to those who evade the need for transformational change and are addicted to what King memorably called "the tranquilizing drug of gradualism." But at other moments, it is a call for negotiation and coalition building that focuses on the importance of making progress today—*now*—that can be built on tomorrow.[3]

We need, for example, to get affordable health insurance to all Americans as soon as possible, to move quickly to expand access to college or training after high school, and to raise incomes among the least advantaged. Progressives should be open to big steps toward all these goals, even steps that don't conform to their first-choice solutions (single-payer or free college, for example).

And we need, urgently, to end Trump's cruel border policies and the demonization of newcomers. We need immigration reform to give roughly 11 million undocumented immigrants a path to citizenship, and agreement on future immigration flows. We need our country to be open to refugees. Playing into Trump and his followers' hands by seeming to downplay the need for border security or offering proposals that make it easier for them to cast reformers—falsely—as advocate for "open borders" will make reaching agreement on such proposals far harder at a moment when morality demands action.[4]

In a democracy, persuasion is an imperative. Considering the views of your fellow citizens who might be on the fence is not timidity. It's a democratic obligation. And let's all face the obvious: Defeating Trumpism is a precondition to progress of any kind. Building the broadest possible coalition to bring this about means welcoming allies with whom we might have disagreements on matters that are important but, for now, are less urgent.

Moderates, in turn, need to acknowledge that in reacting to the long Reagan era, middle-of-the-road politicians (and liberals who wanted to look middle-of-the-road) made mistakes bred by excessive caution and, at times, abandoned principle.

As I will show in more detail, they were too quick to capitulate to the Reagan economic consensus, too eager to buy into the idea of market supremacy, too quick to deregulate financial markets, and too keen on winning the approval of financiers. Yes, the 1994 crime bill was a response to legitimate fears about a crime wave, but it was absurdly punitive and had disastrous consequences for African Americans. Along with similarly draconian laws at the state level, it helped lead us toward what Michelle Alexander has called "the new Jim Crow" and created, as Chris Hayes has written, "a colony in a nation." Moderates need to recognize that younger progressives are frustrated with liberals and Democrats who never quite got over the setbacks of the 1980s and now act, as K. Sabeel Rahman, the president of the think tank Demos, observed, from "a caution borne out of fear of the right and out of a progressivism chastened by recurring defeat."[5]

It is not an excess of wokeness to ask those who are privileged to ponder how their privilege influences the political choices they make. And pretending that achieving bipartisan outcomes is only a matter of will and better personal relationships is to ignore three decades of Republican obstruction and rejectionism.

Moreover, going big, as progressives typically suggest, can often be *more* politically effective than going small and careful. Big universal programs (think: Social Security, Medicare, and the GI Bill) often muster far more support than modest, targeted schemes. Acting boldly, even stubbornly, on behalf of the rights of the oppressed and excluded has often been the only way to sway public opinion in a new direction. History looks kindly on early advocates of abolition, labor rights, civil rights, and, more recently, LGBTQ rights.

If our country is to move forward, both sides must be willing to look to each other for guidance. The theologian Reinhold Niebuhr was right to teach us to seek the truth in our opponent's error, and the error in our own truth.

Both sides should also remember that successful political movements often define what they affirmatively believe after first coming together in opposition to a status quo they deplore. Call it the power of negative thinking.

Ronald Reagan used what he opposed—big government, taxes, and Soviet Communism—to develop his agenda for change: smaller government, lower taxes, and a forceful foreign policy. In doing so, he redefined our politics, and his ideas exercised broad sway for nearly three decades.

Trump similarly clarified what moderates and progressives alike abhor: racial and ethnic intolerance; a disdain for democratic values; corruption married to corporate dominance; and the pursuit of brutally divisive politics as a substitute for problem solving. As a result, Trump brought the left and moderates together in support of an open society and democracy, political reform, and limits on corporate power. Both favor forceful steps against rising inequality that are a necessary prelude to a more harmonious republic.

They also share something important with civil rights hero Fannie Lou Hamer: They are sick and tired of being sick and tired. They know the costs of remaining on our current path. They know this is a Code Red moment, for democracy and for decency. They must act—together—so we can put Trumpism behind us and build something better.

The political approach I describe is not a fantasy. The popular uprising against Trump led to the verdict American voters rendered in the 2018 midterm elections. Democratic candidates for the House of Representatives outpolled Republicans by nearly *10 million votes*—a margin roughly 7 million votes larger than Hillary Clinton's popular vote lead just two years earlier. As a revolt of progressive and moderate voters led by progressive and moderate candidates, 2018 offers the prototype of an enduring majority. This is why I devote chapter 1 to an analysis of what happened in 2018 and what it means for the future.[6]

In the following two chapters, I turn to history to explain how we reached this point. They examine the long-term forces at work in our politics pushing moderates and progressives together, and suggest lessons the left and the center can learn from the past.

The Democrats won in 2018 for the same reason that their party is the staging ground for nearly all of the difficult debates over pressing economic and social problems: The radicalization of the Republican Party has left moderates with no alternative but to find common ground with progressives. This is the focus of chapter 2, which looks at history to show how far the GOP has strayed.

I have dubbed chapter 3 "a short history of circular firing squads and enduring achievements." It looks at how liberals and progressives, moderate reformers and socialists, have alternately battled each other and worked together since the Progressive Era. The larger story of American reform helps explain both current tensions and the renewal of energy on the left. This history also points to earlier mistakes worth avoiding and successful strategies still worth pursuing.

Chapter 4 takes on what many might regard as the most unexpected development in American politics: the resurgence of democratic socialism. It turns out that what socialism means to many who embrace it is, not surprisingly, quite different from the caricature presented by the right. Its emergence reflects the collapse of the Reagan economic consensus, progressives' frustrations with neoliberalism, and the continued rise of inequality even after the Clinton and Obama years.

I will argue that while Republicans will seek to weaponize the S-word against Democrats (as the GOP has done since the days of the New Deal), the new interest in socialism reflects a larger yearning across a broad range of opinion for an economy in which morality plays a larger role, the powerful are held accountable, and wage and salary workers are protected.

Moving forward in politics requires coming to a settlement about the past—and, on the broad center-left, this means coming to terms with the legacies of Bill Clinton and Barack Obama. In chapter 5, I argue that they had important successes in grappling with the immediate problems facing the country, but neither overturned the broad assumptions that had governed American economic policy since the 1980s. The former is why most moderates and—especially in Obama's case—many progressives still honor their presidencies. The latter is why many progressives see both as falling short. It's essential, I argue, to see their presidencies whole: to recognize their achievements, and to turn now to the work they left unfinished. It is a political and historical error to leave their legacies undefended. It is also a mistake to ignore the reasons why they left many progressives frustrated.

Over the next several chapters, I deal with four issues that have been particularly vexing for progressives and moderates alike: the structure of the economy, the renewed political power of identity, the rise of nationalism, and the United States' role in the world. In all these areas, moderates and progressives have often allowed themselves to become too preoccupied with internecine battles, casting many issues as either/or choices that obscured more than they clarified, and privileged the hunt for heretics over the search for converts. In these chapters, I engage with the thinking of intellectuals, policy specialists, and activists, and also of politicians, including many of the 2020 Democratic presidential candidates, some of whom are no longer in the contest. This book is absolutely *not* an effort to pick winners or losers. The candidates I bring into the story are mentioned because their arguments and proposals help illuminate the debates I describe.

Chapter 6 shows how adventurous proposals—among them single-payer health care, free college, and the Green New Deal—have opened space for new policy advances. At the same time, I argue for a focus on goals rather than specific policies. Universal health insurance coverage is a legitimate litmus test, for example, but single-payer health care should be seen as simply one path toward achieving it. I also show that free college and the Green New Deal are not nearly as radical as you might think. And I make the case that dignity—a focus on empowering individuals in their professional, family, and community lives—should be the focal point of economic policy.

Donald Trump's explicit racism deepened conflicts around race, gender, religion, culture, and sexuality, with sharp divisions along generational lines. What would a constructive approach to what is often called "identity politics" (usually by its foes) look like? Can progressives link workers' rights with civil rights, racial and gender equality with social justice more broadly? Chapter 7 argues that there is no escaping the need for both a politics of distribution *and* a politics of recognition. They can and must be brought together as equally essential components of all struggles for social justice and enhanced democracy—and against bigotry, racism, and exclusion.

Chapter 8 explores the rise of nationalism, the advantage for progressives in advancing an inclusive patriotism as an alternative to Trump's narrow "America First" approach, and the role of immigration in fostering nationalist feeling. I also discuss how community and social breakdown have created fertile ground for ethno-nationalist appeals.

In chapter 9, I argue that the architects of a post-Trump internationalist foreign policy will have to pay far closer attention to the economic interests of average Americans, as Franklin Roosevelt and Harry Truman did in their time, and link the battle for democracy to the fight against kleptocracy and corruption. They should also revisit the idea of containment as an approach to China and Russia while acknowledging in China's case that a pure replay of the Cold War is neither in America's interests nor the world's. Our citizens will embrace an active American role in the world only if the stewards of foreign policy accept their own duties to those who do the nation's work and, when necessary, fight its wars. I argue that foreign policy is, perhaps surprisingly, an area of particular promise for synthesis and dialogue between moderates, who tend to support a traditional liberal internationalism, and progressives, who insist that economic justice and shared prosperity should be central goals of the United States' approach to the world.

The book concludes, in chapter 10, with a discussion of values that could bring Americans back together. It imagines what can be accomplished if progressives and moderates create a new politics. Politics alone certainly cannot cure all that ails us. But we have, at the least, a right to expect that it can do much less harm than it's doing now. And making politics less fractious and more welcoming could help restore our faith in the possibilities of mutual understanding and common action.

Donald Trump's misdeeds created an immediate crisis for the nation. But his rise also reflected a longer-term crisis of national self-confidence. Americans have drawn apart from one another politically, socially, and economically. It falls to progressives and moderates, working in concert, to find a path toward solidarity, empathy, and hope. They will meet this responsibility only by challenging themselves to act more strategically, think more clearly, and accept the responsibilities that history now imposes upon them.

ONE

THE POWER OF 60 MILLION VOTES

*Understanding What the 2018
Election Taught Us*

"DO WHATEVER YOU HAVE TO DO. JUST WIN, BABY."

Thus did soon-to-be House Speaker Nancy Pelosi grant absolution to any 2018 Democratic candidates who thought it would help them to say (or suggest) that they wouldn't support her return to her old job. Her comment, to a group of Harvard students three weeks before the election, signaled her confidence that no matter what Democrats said in 2018, she would find a way to earn enough votes in 2019 to wield the gavel again. And prevail she did, enhancing her standing by facing down an internal challenge to her leadership and immediately defeating Trump in an immigration showdown in January. What no one could have predicted on that fall day in 2018 is that once Pelosi was back in power, most of the criticism of her leadership would come not from her right but from her left. It was a sign of how much had changed in the Democratic Party.[1]

If Pelosi was sometimes frustrated with younger progressive House members, it was in large part because she understood what it had taken to win back the House in an astonishingly broad victory. Democrats flipped 43 previously Republican-held seats and lost only 3, for a net gain of 40. Their popular vote advantage across all House seats added up to 9.8 million. An Associated Press analysis found that absent partisan gerrymandering, they would have gained an additional 16 seats. Democrats managed a sprawling coalition while maintaining the enthusiasm of all its component parts.[2]

The margins were breathtaking. Democratic House candidates outpolled Republican House candidates 60,319,623 to 50,467,181, an 8.6 point lead. Compare this to the Republicans' midterm congressional showing in 2014: 39,926,526 for Republican candidates, 35,368,840 for Democrats. Republicans received 10 million more votes than they had won four years earlier. *Democrats received 25 million more votes than they had in 2014.*[3]

The 2018 alliance of progressives and moderates, of white and minority voters, of Americans ardently opposed to Trump and those primarily interested in protecting health care and reforming politics, is a model for the alliance that must come together again in 2020 and beyond. It was made possible by forbearance from all the components of the Democratic Party—and from all parts of the movement gathered against Trump.

Dozens of suburban Democrats prevailed in districts that were once hospitable to a moderate brand of Republicanism that was crushed in the Trump era. At the same time, urban progressives spurred new levels of participation among younger voters across the board, particularly among African Americans and Latinos. Some of the most important freshman members of the Class of 2018 came from this wing of the party, including Alexandria Ocasio-Cortez in New York, Ayanna Pressley in Boston, Ilhan Omar in Minneapolis, and Rashida Tlaib in Detroit. Their solidarity was such that they came to be known as "the Squad" for their persistent challenges to the party's leadership and their wide social media following. The Squad was joined by a much larger contingent of new moderates on the center-left. They had smaller social media followings but created the Democrats' majority by seizing formerly Republican territory. Their ranks included Abigail Spanberger, Jennifer Wexton, and Elaine Luria in

Virginia; Katie Porter in California; Mikie Sherrill, Andy Kim, Tom Malinowski, and Jeff Van Drew in New Jersey; Sharice Davids in Kansas; Xochitl Torres Small in New Mexico; Chrissy Houlahan and Susan Wild in Pennsylvania; Elissa Slotkin in Michigan; Kendra Horn in Oklahoma; and many others.

A presidential campaign is a more difficult coalition-building exercise because a party cannot run multiple candidates tailored to different parts of the country. (The Whigs actually tried this in 1836; it didn't work.[4]) Moreover, the hunger to rebuke Trump in 2018 was so strong across the party's wings that progressive voters were often willing to support more moderate House candidates in primaries to increase the party's chances in Republican-leaning districts. In a presidential nominating struggle, the trade-offs between "electability" and principle are more complicated.

The election of 2018 was thus only a first step toward reversing Trumpism and setting the country on a new course. But it was a necessary step that will make other steps possible. How did it happen?

The new majority of 2018 was the product of the highest midterm turnout since 1914. At 53.4 percent of all adults over the age of 18 (registered to vote or not), it was 11.5 points higher than in the 2014 midterms. Democrats won 62 percent of the ballots cast by those who told exit pollsters that 2018 was their first vote in a midterm election—and, in another sign of the new energy in politics, these new midterm voters cast one of every six ballots. Among those who did not vote in 2016 but turned out two years later, Democratic House candidates overwhelmed Republicans, 70 percent to 28 percent.[5]

The mobilization of young voters, African Americans, and Latinos far exceeded Democratic expectations. If their participation expands further in 2020, they would hasten the creation of the "coalition of the ascendant" that was the promise of Obama's victories. The energy on the left end of politics was an essential force behind this surge of ballots, but the new activism was not confined to any ideological sector. As the political scientist Theda Skocpol has shown in her research on the ground in Trump-leaning areas, the uprising against Trump transcended old ideological splits. There is promise in this, too.[6]

Equally heartening for those yearning for a new direction in politics were signs that "Trump Democrats" in the key 2016 swing states—Pennsylvania, Michigan, and Wisconsin—returned to the Democratic fold in significant numbers. In Wisconsin, exit polls showed that Senator Tammy Baldwin won not only virtually all of Clinton's 2016 voters but also 14 percent of Trump's. In Pennsylvania, Senator Bob Casey picked up 12 percent of Trump's backers, while Michigan's Senator Debbie Stabenow won 9 percent of their ballots. Democrats continued to struggle in Ohio, although Senator Sherrod Brown ran ahead of the rest of his party's ticket to victory, picking up 12 percent of Trump's voters in the process. Reflecting disillusionment with the president, exit polls suggested that Trump voters were less likely than Clinton voters to turn out in the midterms, which helped build the margins of all Democrats.[7]

Another measure of the comeback from 2016 and the consolidation of anti-Trump sentiment: In the new Congress, 31 House districts that had voted for Trump were represented by Democrats; only three districts that had voted for Clinton were represented by Republicans.[8]

It was not always appreciated that the ascendant coalition reflected in Barack Obama's twin victories required Democrats to win 40 to 50 percent of white voters in the old industrial states who did not attend college. Obama hit these levels. Clinton did not. The Democrats' success in reclaiming support in the heartland combined with the party's suburban surge holds the potential for creating a broader and even more durable alliance than Obama's 2008 and 2012 majorities.

Finally and crucially, many Republican-leaning suburban voters who had supported Hillary Clinton in 2016, particularly women, were changing their party allegiances altogether. Repulsed by the GOP leadership's embrace of Trump—his white ethno-nationalism, his lies, his extremist rhetoric, his self-centered irrationality—they proved willing to vote for Democrats up and down the ticket in 2018. Democrats had been picking up metropolitan and suburban votes since Bill Clinton's election in 1992, but the 2018 gains were deeper and broader, extending even into such core Republican states as Oklahoma, Kansas, and Texas. If the Republican leadership remains loyal to Trumpism, this trend will continue.

Long before Trump, Republicans had moved much further to the right than Democrats had to the left. Research on congressional votes cast from the late 1970s to 2013 by the political scientists Keith Poole, Nolan McCarty, and Howard Rosenthal, summarized by the journalist Michael Tomasky, found that Democrats had moved 33 percent more left while Republicans moved *150 percent* more right.[9]

The 2018 election pushed the GOP even further away from moderation. Classifying incumbents by the measures developed by Poole and his colleagues, the political scientist Alan Abramowitz found that the more moderate a Republican was, the more likely he or she was to be defeated in 2018. This is not surprising, since moderates tend to represent more competitive districts. The outcome was nonetheless devastating for what remained of the Republican center. Of the 199 Republican incumbents on the 2018 ballot, 39 were moderates—and 9 of them, 23 percent, were defeated. Mainstream conservatives accounted for 90 GOP members of Congress on the ballot; 16 of them—18 percent— lost. The remaining 70 were classified as "extreme conservatives," and only four, 6 percent, lost. The most right-wing Republicans were largely sheltered from the anti-Trump storm because they represented the most pro-Trump parts of the country.[10]

Lest anyone miss the degree to which the 2018 outcome was a revolt against Trump, *The Atlantic*'s Ronald Brownstein noted that the president's drag on Republican candidates was the strongest in 36 years. Typically, Brownstein noted, "between 82 and 84 percent of voters who disapproved of the president voted against his party's candidates for the House." In 2018, that number soared: "Fully 90 percent of Trump disapprovers said they voted for Democrats for the lower chamber." It was the worst performance for an incumbent's party since 1982, when Ronald Reagan was presiding over a steep recession that saw unemployment top 10 percent just weeks before Election Day.[11]

The Trump effect was, in fact, without any recent precedent. In a careful postelection analysis of midterm outcomes since the 1940s, the political scientist Gary Jacobson found that "the congruence" between attitudes toward the president and the party chosen in House races was the highest it had ever been, up from "about 70 percent from the 1940s through the 1970s" to 93 percent in 2018. Trump likes everything to be about him. The 2018 midterms really were.[12]

Another sign of how Trump doomed Republican chances: The network exit poll found that only 26 percent of voters said they cast ballots in House races to support Trump, while 38 percent said they voted as they did to oppose Trump. That was decisive. Similarly, Democratic pollster Stan Greenberg reported in his book *R.I.P. G.O.P.* that "the top reason Democratic House voters gave to vote *against* the Republican and *for* the Democrat . . . was to have leaders who would be a check on President Trump."[13]

These figures underscore a paradox of the Democrats' 2018 strategy: If many of the party's candidates in swing districts refrained from making Trump the centerpiece of their campaigns—they talked far more about health care, jobs, education, and infrastructure—*it was because they didn't have to.* To pretend that Democrats won the House because of health care or infrastructure alone is to miss the underlying power of the anti-Trump dynamic. Many of the arguments they did make—about problems that were still festering or the nasty tone of politics—were implicit critiques of Trump's approach to his job. And for all the talk about candidates not making Trump the issue, there were plenty of ads touting how often a given Republican incumbent had voted with Trump, especially in districts that had backed Clinton. Then there was Trump himself, who, as Greenberg noted, "succeeded in making himself the most important factor in people's vote, though not with the intended result."[14]

Understanding 2018's bottom line is essential for grasping what will be required in 2020: The election was *about* Trump—but the House was *won* by a coalition of moderates and the left. Winning the White House will require the same alliance.

The exit poll found that 27 percent of the electorate identified themselves as liberal, 36 percent as conservative, and 37 percent as moderate. Democratic House candidates, not surprisingly, won 91 percent of the ballots cast by liberals, but they also won 62 percent from moderates. This underscores the futility of debates over whether electoral victory can be achieved primarily by "mobilizing the base" or by bringing around "persuadable voters." Because partisan polarization runs so deep, mobilization is more important now than it was in the past. Still, persuasion—especially of middle-ground voters who are not particularly partisan—remains indispensable.[15]

Progressives have rightly noted that the electorate has moved leftward over the last quarter century, in significant part because younger voters now lean far more in a liberal direction than their elders. This long-term change in ideological identification is playing an important role in our politics, and its effect is especially strong in Democratic primaries.

A report by Gallup in January 2019 (using a slightly different approach than the exit poll) dramatized the shift. While in the country as a whole, "conservatives continue to outnumber liberals, the gap in conservatives' favor has narrowed from 19 percentage points in Gallup's 1992 baseline measurement to nine points" in its 2017 and 2018 surveys. Over a quarter century, the country as a whole had drifted toward the left, not the right.

In 1992, the year of Bill Clinton's first election, 43 percent of Americans identified themselves as moderate, 36 percent as conservative, and just 17 percent as liberal. Is it any wonder that Clinton pursued his New Democrat strategy to distance his party from liberalism? By 2018, the country painted a different ideological self-portrait: 35 percent of Americans called themselves moderate, 35 percent conservative, and 26 percent liberal.

The shift among Democrats was especially striking. The percentage of Democrats identifying as liberal averaged 51 percent in Gallup's 2018 surveys, up from 25 percent in 1994. In other words, *the proportion of self-identified liberals in the Democratic Party has more than doubled since the Clinton era.*

The Democrats are still far more ideologically diverse than the Republicans. In keeping with arguments that polarization is asymmetric, Gallup found that the share of Republicans who described themselves as conservative rose from 58 percent in 1994 to 73 percent in 2018. The proportion of Republican liberals fell from 8 percent to 4 percent in the period, and the proportion of moderates in the GOP fell from 33 percent in 1994 to 22 percent in 2018.[16]

The bottom line: *Even in an increasingly liberal Democratic Party, fully half of its supporters do not think of themselves as liberal. In the GOP, only a quarter fail to identify as conservative.*

Ideological shifts were less dramatic among those who describe themselves as independent, although there has been a modest movement toward liberalism.

These transformations have important implications for the battles that will take place both inside the two parties and between them. Progressives have more power to win fights inside the Democratic Party but still need the votes of moderates to prevail in general elections. The moderates, in the meantime, will not find a comfortable home inside the Republican Party until the electorate gives the GOP a decisive rebuke.

And it is impossible to understand 2018 without taking note of Trump's alienation of women. Female voters backed Democratic House candidates by a 19-point margin, overwhelming the Republicans' narrow 4-point margin among men. White men voted Republican by 21 points; white women split their ballots evenly. This underscored the importance of the Democrats' margins among African Americans (9 to 1 Democratic), Asian Americans (better than 3 to 1 Democratic), and Latinos (roughly 7 to 3 for the Democrats).

The elections confirmed the continued movement of young voters toward the Democrats. Voters under 30 voted Democratic by 2 to 1. While 54 percent of whites overall voted Republican, 56 percent of whites younger than 30 voted Democratic. The outcome underscored the GOP's long-term demographic problem: Republicans barely carried voters over 45 (50 percent to 49 percent), while voters younger than 45 gave 61 percent of their ballots to the Democrats.

The election confirmed a decisive shift in a progressive direction on three important issues: health care, guns, and taxes.

One measurable outcome of the first two years of the Trump presidency was the triumph of Obamacare, the unintended consequence of the GOP's repeal effort. A losing cause in 2010—many Democrats then were afraid even to mention it—the Affordable Care Act became the centerpiece of the battle against Republicans across the country eight years later.

When Obamacare first passed, it was an abstraction that merely *promised* new benefits. By the time Trump and his party mounted their repeal campaign in earnest, millions of Americans had benefited from the plan. Much of the news coverage during the original Obamacare debate focused on the messy congressional politics that pushed it into law. Reporting on the GOP's effort to scrap the Affordable Care Act, by contrast, focused on the effects of the law itself. It highlighted how many Americans would lose health coverage if Republicans had their way, the damage repeal would inflict on local health systems, and the devastating consequences scrapping the law would have for Americans with preexisting conditions. A majority came to value both the law's expansions in coverage and its protections of those with private insurance.[17]

The Affordable Care Act now defines the minimum standard for what Americans expect from their government when it comes to health benefits, and this became obvious in 2018. When asked to name the most important issue facing the country, the largest share of voters, 41 percent, picked health care—and they voted 3 to 1 for their Democratic House candidate. Asked which party would better protect those with preexisting conditions, voters again overwhelmingly picked the Democrats over the Republicans, 57 percent to 35 percent.

Historically, guns had motivated the minority of voters who strongly opposed all forms of regulation far more than the majority who supported additional restrictions on firearms. Not in 2018. Among voters who listed gun policy as the most important issue, Democrats overwhelmed Republicans, 70 percent to 29 percent. The outcome reflected innovative organizing efforts by young Americans, backed by older gun control groups but led by the students of Marjory Stoneman Douglas High School in Parkland, Florida, where a gunman killed 17 students and staff members on February 14, 2018.

Even taxes, the GOP's stock-in-trade, failed the party. The corporate tax cut signed by Trump in 2017 was a political flop. Only 29 percent of voters told the exit pollsters that it had helped their family finances, 22 percent said it was harmful, and 45 percent said it had no impact. The latter two groups voted overwhelmingly for Democrats.[18]

If exit polls provide one measure of the dramatic shift between 2016 and 2018, the election returns from the nation's counties provide another. Although Clinton carried the popular vote, the vast majority of her ballots came from larger metropolitan counties. Small-town and rural counties went overwhelmingly to Trump. Thus, Trump won 2,584 counties nationwide, while Clinton carried just 472.[19]

In efforts to decipher what had happened in 2016, much attention was paid to "pivot counties" that shifted from Obama to Trump. The website Ballotpedia identified 206 counties that backed Trump in 2016 after voting for Obama in both 2008 and 2012. Its analysis found that in 2018 Democratic House candidates won 113 of these pivot counties and cut Republican victory margins in 71 more, leaving only 22 pivot counties where the Republican maintained or improved the party's share. "In [pivot] counties where a Democratic candidate won," Ballotpedia concluded, "the Republican candidate performed worse than Trump's 2016 numbers by an average of 21 percent. In counties where a Republican candidate won, they underperformed Trump's 2016 numbers by an average of 6.9 percent."[20]

In another careful analysis, William H. Frey of the Brookings Institution found that Democrats gained ground in 78.6 percent of the nation's counties, and that "83 percent of the voting population lived in counties where support for the Democrats . . . improved since 2016."[21]

Frey found that Democrats, not surprisingly, substantially increased their already significant margins in counties he described as "urban core." But large suburban counties moved from a narrow margin for Trump in 2016 to a somewhat larger Democratic margin in the 2018 House races. This was one of the many indicators that suburbs were an essential building block of the

Democratic victory. Democrats also cut Republican margins in smaller metropolitan areas and in nonmetropolitan (essentially rural) counties, although they continued to lose both.

Frey's analysis concluded that the Democrats posted their largest gains in counties with "Republican leaning" attributes—greater shares of noncollege whites and persons over age 45, and smaller shares of minorities and persons who were foreign born. This, he wrote, "suggests that there was a shift toward Democratic support in counties that helped elect Donald Trump in 2016." This is consistent with Greenberg's findings that while Democrats continued to lose rural areas, they gained more ground there than in either urban or suburban areas.

When Frey applied the House returns statewide, five states—Iowa, Wisconsin, Michigan, Pennsylvania, and Arizona—moved from support for Trump to Democratic majorities. Assuming Democrats held all the states Clinton won, these shifts would give the party's nominee 293 electoral votes and victory in the Electoral College.

None of this should be assumed, of course, and even this margin leaves little room for error. Despite Democratic gains in what had been Trump Country, the party's share of the popular vote in House races was boosted substantially by landslide margins in states (such as California) that Hillary Clinton carried in 2016.

Nonetheless, the House breakthrough laid the groundwork for a new coalition on behalf of decency, dignity, and remedy. And behind 2018's numbers were the personal stories of candidates who reflected both the philosophical diversity and the unity of purpose powering the anti-Trump wave.

Listening to the conversation at Robert Jones's Parkside Barber Shop & Grooming Lounge in Glen Allen, Virginia, on a Saturday night a little over a week before Election Day, you would not have imagined that we live in a deeply divided country incapable of discussing everyday challenges.

Jones, a successful local entrepreneur, hosted a group of business leaders and educators in his suburban Richmond establishment to discuss how to prepare the new workforce for meaningful jobs. Paying close attention were Senator Tim Kaine, a Democrat who was up for reelection, and Abigail Spanberger, a Democratic congressional candidate challenging a Republican incumbent in a longtime GOP stronghold.

The conversation avoided the obsessions of cable news or Twitter, concentrating instead on an issue at once old-fashioned and oriented toward the future: how educational institutions at all levels—and employers themselves—could endow students with the skills to succeed while providing enterprises large and small with the well-trained labor they need to thrive. The dialogue was detailed and practical. Jones could well have hung a banner that night declaring "We're all in this together."

"I think you're more likely to pull people together in the context of solving problems," Kaine said in an interview after the session. He predicted a wave in the coming election, but he didn't talk about a party. It would be, he said, "a wave of dignity and compassion and respect and community."[22]

For her part, Spanberger said that voters had tired of politicians "who are just ideologues, and trying to stop things." It was a quiet jab at her opponent, Republican congressman Dave Brat. Brat made national headlines as an uncompromising Tea Party candidate by defeating Eric Cantor, then the Republican Majority Leader, in a 2014 primary.[23]

The 39-year-old CIA veteran and mother of three didn't mention Trump. But it was impossible to miss the subtext when Spanberger said that if she and other Democrats around the country prevailed, the victory would "be about decency, modeling good behavior, being enthusiastic about who we are as a people and what this country has to offer. It will be," she added, "about solving problems and working with other people and working across party lines."

Notice how similar her language was to Kaine's. Both were making an argument that in 2018, only one party was actually bipartisan. Spanberger spoke of a voter who had echoed what many others had told her: "I've always been a Republican, but the party's left me. I don't know what I am anymore." The coalition of 2018 was built in part by Republicans who had lost their political home.

This was already clear during the summer when I met 36-year-old Andy Kim at a diner in Bordentown, New Jersey. It was the best place to meet, he said, because he had to pick up his 3-year-old son at the daycare center next door. Kim was a decided underdog in his race against two-term incumbent Republican Tom MacArthur in a district that had resisted the Democratic landslide in the 2017 off-year election for governor.

Yet Kim was upbeat because the mobilization of political energy in response to Trump was as strong in his area as in the bluest of blue districts. "The amount of political engagement that we see on a daily level is extraordinary," said the former Obama administration official who returned home after Trump's victory. MacArthur's vote to repeal Obamacare was very unpopular in his district, Kim said, because of its impact on those with preexisting medical conditions. And the incumbent's vote for the Republican tax bill was anathema in high-tax New Jersey because it sharply reduced the deductibility of state and local taxes.

Kim's approach to Trump was, like Spanberger's, indirect but pointed nonetheless: "The way that I kind of sum it up is: 'Do you feel like there is a steady hand at the wheel? Do you feel like you're in good hands right now?' And those questions are ones that cut through."[24]

They did. Kim defeated MacArthur, 50 percent to 48.7 percent—a margin of 3,973 out of more than 300,000 votes cast on a day when Democrats won all four of New Jersey's swing seats. Spanberger defeated Bratt by 6,784 votes out of some 350,000 cast, a margin of 1.9 percent. She was one of three Virginia Democrats to take a seat from the Republicans.[25]

The freshman class that included Spanberger and Kim also counted Ayanna Pressley in its ranks, and her path to Washington was as different from theirs as inner-city Boston is from suburban Virginia and New Jersey. A 44-year-old African American Boston City Council member, Pressley rattled national Democrats in September by overwhelming Representative Mike Capuano, a popular 20-year incumbent in a high-turnout primary.

Pressley's campaign slogan, "Change Can't Wait," reflected the principled impatience of the new progressive breed. She built her alliance of voters of color and younger professionals across racial lines by going beyond opposition to Trump with a call to move politics, including the Democratic Party itself, in a more progressive direction. She argued again and again that the problems of racial and economic inequality long predated Trump's rise, making clear that many in the party were not interested in a simple return to the pre-Trump status quo. Hers was a campaign of insurrection, not restoration.

I caught up with Pressley at her Jamaica Plain campaign headquarters the night before she won. She had brought her youthful canvassers there to fire them up for the final offensive, and her speech also had the benefit of explaining, in one sentence, why she would win the next day: "The district has changed," she said, "the needs have changed, and given what's happening in Washington, the job description has changed."

Pressley didn't just win. She swamped Capuano, 59 percent to 41 percent, and her success was quickly compared to Ocasio-Cortez's defeat of Democratic representative Joseph Crowley in New York earlier in the summer. Echoing Ocasio-Cortez's appeal, Pressley expressed her determination to speak for "communities that far too often go unseen and unheard." But unlike

Ocasio-Cortez, Pressley had deep roots in local politics, had served on former senator John Kerry's staff, and had endorsed Hillary Clinton, not Bernie Sanders, in 2016.[26]

So Democratic was her district that Pressley would be elected unopposed. This marked an important dividing line in the new Congress's freshman class. The staunchest progressives had little to worry about in a general election, but Kim, Spanberger, and moderates from other swing districts did. The new Democratic coalition cannot work unless these two groups find common ground and understand that their ability to wield power depends upon respect for each other's constituencies.

But tensions were inevitable, and the opening year of the new Congress saw regular skirmishing between the young progressives in "the Squad" (Pressley, Ocasio-Cortez, Omar, and Tlaib) and moderate members such as Spanberger and Chrissy Houlahan of Pennsylvania. "We come from places where different ideologies live side by side," Houlahan told *The Washington Post*, "and we have a real responsibility to legislate that way. I feel like the narrative is that the Democratic Party has been hijacked by the left."[27]

Nobody ever said that sustaining a diverse majority would be easy, a truth Pelosi would confront day after day.

The campaigns Democrats ran in 2018 reflected the twin yearnings Trump inspired: for a robust opposition and for a radically different approach to politics. Spanberger summed up her version of the new civility by speaking of "a responsibility to honor the opinions and ideas of people that you disagree with, and who didn't vote for you."[28]

It's obvious that a candidate with the political views of Pressley or Ocasio-Cortez could not have prevailed in the districts won by Kim, Spanberger, or dozens of other Democrats who took seats from Republicans to give Pelosi the gavel. It was less obvious but also true that the moderates, in turn, would not have prevailed without the energy of the anti-Trump movement and the party's left. Kim, for one, knew this. "This is the most important election our district has ever been a part of," he said, "and people here are fighting like it is."[29]

Many Democrats found ways of turning moderation itself into explicit or implicit reproaches to Trump that appealed simultaneously to the president's angriest critics and to the middle-ground voters they were trying to woo. Tom Malinowski, who served in the State Department during the Obama administration, narrowly defeated incumbent Republican Leonard Lance in a district near Kim's in New Jersey by defining what he called "the all-American middle-ground issues that the Trump Republicans" had ceded to Democrats.[30]

"We're now the party of fiscal responsibility in America. We didn't just add $2 trillion to the national debt for that tax cut that Warren Buffett didn't want," he said, referring to the legendary investor. "We're the party of law enforcement in America; we don't vilify the Federal Bureau of Investigation every single day. We're the party of family values. We don't . . . take kids from their parents at the border."

Was this moderate or progressive? Might it have been both?

In an interview in the spring of 2019, Malinowski nicely captured the dual nature of his campaign message, which paralleled the overall message of the election. He was resolute in supporting his party's practical, targeted initiatives but equally resolute in promising to hold Trump accountable. "I ran on health care and infrastructure and getting things done for our district and our country," he said in an interview, "but I never hesitated in talking about checks and balances, decency, and the rule of law."[31]

When the allegations that Trump used foreign aid to pressure the Ukrainian government to dig up dirt on former vice president Joe Biden first emerged, seven freshman Democrats with national security backgrounds, including Houlahan, Sherrill, Slotkin, and Spanberger, wrote a *Washington Post* op-ed declaring that if true, "these actions represent an impeachable offense." Despite the political risks this step entailed, all understood their obligations, as they wrote, "to our oaths to defend the country" and "to uphold and defend the Constitution." Their intervention was the prelude to Pelosi's decision to launch a formal impeachment inquiry.[32]

In the meantime, Democrats in blue-collar areas were acutely aware of the need to win back voters who had supported Trump. Ohio's Senator Sherrod Brown faced what many thought would be a difficult reelection campaign because of his state's sharp swing toward Trump in 2016. The centerpiece of Brown's campaign was "the dignity of work." "People who get up every day and work hard and do what we expect of them should be able to get ahead," Brown said. "I don't think [we] hear that enough from Republicans or national Democrats."[33]

In an otherwise disappointing election night for Democrats in Ohio—of the midwestern swing states, it was the one where the Trump effect was strongest and where his turnout efforts seemed to be most effective—Brown prevailed over Republican representative Jim Renacci by just under 7 percentage points. In the process, he kept his blue-collar base intact. Mahoning County, home of blue-collar Youngstown, delivered one of the country's larger swings against the Democrats in 2016. It gave Obama 63 percent of its vote in 2012, but just 50 percent to Hillary Clinton four years later; Brown prevailed with 59 percent in the county, very close to his showing six years earlier.[34]

Brown offered a model for winning back Trump voters without giving ground on social issues or racial justice concerns. The other Democratic Senate victors in the industrial-belt states Trump had carried—Casey in Pennsylvania, Stabenow in Michigan, and Baldwin in Wisconsin—underscored the fragility of Trump's 2016 achievement.

The year's key gubernatorial contests pointed in a similar direction. Democrats picked up seven governorships, two of them in the key 2016 Trump states of Wisconsin and Michigan, another in traditionally Republican Kansas. Democrats also took state houses from the GOP in Illinois, Nevada, Maine, and New Mexico. (Republicans posted a single gain, in Alaska, from a retiring Independent.)

The victorious Democrats combined elements of progressivism with pragmatism. The emphasis on practical governance was puckishly and effectively captured by Gretchen Whitmer's successful battle cry in Michigan: "Fix the damn roads." Democratic consultants, concerned that the word "damn" might offend some general election voters, tested it with focus groups after the primary. It turned out they were more offended by the condition of the roads.

In Wisconsin, Tony Evers, the state's superintendent of public instruction, defeated Republican governor Scott Walker, a national hero to conservatives for his wars on unions, taxes, and education. Walker seemed to have nine political lives, surviving a recall and easily winning reelection in 2014. But Evers highlighted health care, especially the Democrats' staple of protections for people with preexisting conditions, along with taxes, school spending, and economic development.

The most dramatic example of the potential reach of alliances between the center and the left was the Democrats' successful fight for the governorship of Kansas. The Republican nominee was the state's hard-right secretary of state, Kris Kobach, who had made a career championing voter suppression efforts and warning of the dangers posed by "illegal aliens." Democratic state senator Laura Kelly targeted not only Kobach's extremism but also former governor Sam Brownback's deep tax cuts, which were supposed to be a grand experiment in the wonders that low taxes could do for the state's economy. In practice, they produced budgetary chaos and crippled the schools, driving the Republican from office. Brownback resigned, accepting an ambassadorship from Trump.[35]

Even before the election, moderate Republicans and Democrats formed a bipartisan alliance in the state legislature to repeal most of Brownback's tax program. Kelly widened the split in the state's Republican Party, winning endorsements from venerable Republican figures including former governor Bill Graves and former senator Nancy Kassebaum.

Her victory reflected the power of the four building blocks of progressive politics in moderate states: schools, roads, health care, and opposition to right-wing radicalism. Kelly campaigned relentlessly on the need to restore support for public education and to spend more on infrastructure. She followed a formula described by former Iowa governor and U.S. agriculture secretary Tom Vilsack that captured the year's underlying dynamic: For Democrats, Vilsack said, the key was to be "moderate in tone but progressive in thinking."[36]

A pair of narrow gubernatorial losses, however, took some of the joy out of the Democrats' jubilant night. That two African American candidates came so close to being elected governor in two states in the Deep South might, at another time, have been a source of encouragement, a harbinger of changes in the political map that would benefit progressives and moderates in the long run. But since both Stacey Abrams in Georgia and Andrew Gillum in Florida had realistic chances of victory, their very narrow defeats were genuine disappointments.

I spent time with Abrams in late October when her protests against voter suppression in the state were at full cry. Her Republican opponent, Georgia secretary of state Brian Kemp, happened to be the man overseeing the election. Abrams, the first African American woman in any state to be nominated for governor, charged that Kemp had taken steps—including leaving 53,000 voter registrations in limbo—to keep minority voters from casting ballots and to persuade others that even trying to vote would be difficult. "The reality is, voter suppression is not simply about being told no," Abrams said. "It's about being told it's going to be hard to cast a ballot."[37]

The Yale Law School graduate's campaign was a reminder of how important control over the rules of the game is to gaining and

holding power—and of how urgent structural, democratizing reform has become. In the end, she lost by only 54,723 votes out of
3.9 million cast. She received nearly 800,000 more votes than Democratic nominee Jason Carter, the grandson of former president
Jimmy Carter, had four years earlier. "If we turn out unlikely voters,
if we turn out those who aren't typically seen as part of the midterm
electorate," she had told me in an interview on her campaign bus,
"then I will win this election." She very nearly did exactly that.[38]

Abrams also represented something different from both the
suburban moderation of candidates like Spanberger, Malinowski,
and Kim and the northern urban progressivism of Pressley and
Ocasio-Cortez. As a Democratic legislative leader in a southern
state where pro-business attitudes are deeply embedded and
where conservative Republicans still hold sway, Abrams was un-
apologetic about embracing the word "pragmatism."

"People who want to make a good living need good jobs, and
that means you have to work with business if you want to be progressive," she told me during my visit. "And [when] you live in
a state where Republicans control every mechanism of politics,
then you've got to be able to work with everyone. And the ability to work with everyone is sometimes cast as being moderate. I
consider it pragmatism. I can't win by myself." She called herself
"a progressive with Georgia values." A hero to progressives around
the nation, she understood the centrality of coalition building.

If Abrams was a key figure in one intra-progressive debate,
she provided a model of how another might be resolved. In a
party where many white liberals are firmly secular, she showed
how African American politicians with close church ties might
provide a bridge between the party's secular and religious
voters—and between progressives and the broader religious
community. It was a sign of her standing that Democratic legislative leaders chose Abrams to reply to Trump's 2019 State of
the Union address, and she went out of her way to refer proudly
to the Methodist home in which she was raised. "These were our

family values: faith, service, education and responsibility," she declared, praising the "uncommon grace of community."

She drove the point home by reciting the creed of the coalition builder—and of all who prefer a healthy but tempered individualism over the narcissistic kind: "We do not succeed alone."[39]

It was a measure of his gift for denial that Trump chose to play down the Democrats' sweep of the House races and instead bragged at his postelection news conference about Republican gains in the Senate. It was equally predictable that he ascribed the victories to his own campaigning, which focused on the invented threat of an immigrant "caravan" making its way to our southern border.[40]

The impact of Trump's campaigning should not be dismissed. Republican turnout was up, and Trump loyalists were certainly key to the defeats of incumbent Democratic senators in Indiana, Missouri, and North Dakota. Democrats in Ohio reported that GOP turnout in pro-Trump rural and exurban counties also increased, to the detriment of all the party's candidates except Brown.[41]

But the GOP's Senate gains also underscored the retreat of the Republican Party to its conservative bastions. In the process, they made clear the long-term problem for democracy posed by what *New York Times* columnist Jamelle Bouie called the Senate's "highly undemocratic and strikingly unrepresentative" character. It is a body where the two Dakotas (population 1.6 million) have equal representation with New York and California (population 59.1 million). Only one of the Republican Senate pickups, Florida governor Rick Scott's victory over Democratic senator Bill Nelson (by 10,000 votes out of more than 8 million cast), came in a large swing state.[42]

The limits of the Republican gains defined the limits of Trump's strategy and the problems his coalition confronts— especially since Democrats gained Senate seats in Nevada and Arizona, confirming the steady shift of both increasingly diverse states away from the GOP.

Even as Trumpism was receding in swing areas and among moderate and suburban voters, his party was being more and more defined in his image. Trump made clear that he would have it no other way. A president whose extremism led to the defeat of many moderate and moderately conservative Republicans stood before reporters and spitefully trashed vanquished GOP candidates who had wisely chosen to distance themselves from him.

The elections held in November 2019 only reinforced the messages sent by voters a year earlier. They showed that even in Trump strongholds, right-wing Republicanism, and the president himself, were no longer selling.

In Kentucky, a state that had given Trump a 30-point margin over Hillary Clinton in 2016, Democrat Andy Beshear ousted Republican governor Matt Bevin, despite an election eve trip by Trump on Bevin's behalf. Both the demographics of the outcome and the issues that made it possible were instructive.

Bevin did the three things he needed to do. Turnout in Kentucky's urban Democratic strongholds was through the roof for an off-off-year election. Beshear flipped many rural counties that had backed Trump overwhelmingly while cutting Republican margins in others. And he continued the Democrats' march through the suburbs, reflected in his success in taking two key northern Kentucky counties, Campbell and Kenton, in the Cincinnati suburbs that voted for Bevin in 2015 and for Trump a year later.

Beyond suburban alienation from Trump, two powerful issues motivated the outcome in a clear echo of 2018. Bevin's efforts to scale back the Medicaid expansion under Obamacare undertaken during Beshear's father's term in office played badly in rural areas whose hospitals and residents alike depended on funding from the program. And Bevin had clashed, sharply and at times rudely, with public school teachers. The teachers and public schools themselves proved far more popular than Bevin did.

On the same day, Democrats took control of both houses of Virginia's state legislature, turning the state government entirely blue for the first time since 1994. The flight of suburban voters from the GOP was again a key to the Democrats' triumph, and the gun issue was decisive. Supporters of gun safety laws rallied against a GOP legislative leadership that had blocked legislation to control firearms even after a May 2019 mass shooting in Virginia Beach that left 12 dead. If there was any doubt about the degree to which the politics of guns had changed, the Democratic victories in the home of the National Rifle Association's headquarters laid them to rest.

In the Deep South, Republicans did hold on to the governorship in Mississippi. But Trump and his party suffered another setback later in November when Governor John Bel Edwards, the incumbent Democrat, defeated Republican Eddie Rispone in Louisiana, a state that had gone to Trump by 20 points. Trump flew to Louisiana two days before the election to pull Rispone through, but—as in Kentucky—his efforts failed, and may have backfired.

"The point of a last-minute presidential rally, after all, is turnout," wrote the Washington Post's Philip Bump. Turnout was indeed up over the first round of voting—but it was up far more in Democratic areas than in those dominated by Republicans. Bump reported that in the parishes (Louisiana's name for counties) that backed Edwards, 97,000 more voters came to the polls for the final than in the first round. In Rispone counties, the increase between rounds was just 68,000.[43]

In both 2018 and 2019, the political energy was with the center and the left, not the right. Voters in Clinton and Trump areas alike expressed dismay with the president, but also with right-wing radicalism. Trump's hold on his own voters was weakening even as many of them expressed a yearning for government-supported problem solving in areas such as education and health care. This pointed to a challenge for Republicans that encompassed but went beyond Trump, because the GOP's flight from public remedy began long before he seized control of the party.

TWO

MISSING IN ACTION

Radicalized Republicans and the
Problem with Bipartisanship

LET'S IMAGINE A DIFFERENT REPUBLICAN PARTY INSPIRED BY a different kind of conservatism.

This GOP would still be broadly pro-business. It would extol freedom, entrepreneurship, and inventiveness. It would stress the important role of nongovernmental institutions in solving problems—community groups, houses of worship, and families. It would be skeptical of sweeping plans to transform society because it would be conservative in the true sense of that term. It would argue that safeguarding fundamentally admirable institutions is the first task of politics. Among other things, it would not launch attacks on the FBI or the CIA. It would be intent on keeping taxes low, but not so low as to make it impossible to finance needed government initiatives without enormous deficits.

Like conservatives in the past, members of this party would understand that institutions cannot be saved without reform and that new problems require rethinking old dogmas. This forward-looking conservatism would promote higher education and believe in the wide diffusion of wealth and property ownership. It would see conservation—of our land, our water, our air, and the planet itself—as central to the conservative task, the two words sharing the same root.

The Republican Party I have in mind would honor capitalism, but it would also accept that the market—like all human institutions—has flaws and limitations. (A skepticism about human nature and its deficiencies is about as conservative an idea as there is.) It would see, for example, that the housing market often fails to provide decent, affordable shelter to all our families and that the private market in health insurance leaves millions without coverage. In both cases, it would acknowledge that government is the only institution available to correct the market's shortcomings.

Such a Republican Party would also accept that the market needs adequate regulation, since every game requires sensible rules. Friends of capitalism know that monopolies are a problem and that companies hoping to act in the interests of employees can be pushed by worries about competitive pricing to cut corners and shortchange their workers. Sensible regulation can allow the market to work within social and moral constraints, thereby serving the common good.

This conservative Republican Party would acknowledge that certain public goods can only be provided by government, starting with good roads, good public schools, and good mass transit. Sensible investments in such amenities would be seen as good for capitalism because they provide the transportation networks businesses need and the skilled workforce they require.

The Republican Party I am envisioning would unflinchingly support civil rights and voting rights and civil liberties. Slogans about "freedom" mean nothing if it is not guaranteed to all our citizens. This Republican Party would honor religion and its public role while insisting that religious freedom must encompass all Americans, including Muslims, Jews, and those with no religious faith at all. And it would not pressure foreign governments to intervene in our election campaigns.

This brief description is not an invention. It describes the

Republican Party that existed for well over a century. The GOP has certainly long had a staunchly conservative wing, and many of the right-wing slogans of today were first mobilized against FDR's New Deal. But the party was, in the past, both more ideologically diverse and more open to the good that government can do. To understand how and why the GOP radicalized is to see that Trumpism did not come from nowhere. This transformation means that those who see themselves as moderates must, for the foreseeable future, ally with progressives to turn back a reactionary tide that is antithetical to progress, to governance, and to what was historically best in the conservative disposition.

At its origins, as the historian Heather Cox Richardson showed in her valuable revisionist history of the Republican Party, *To Make Men Free*, the GOP believed that only a strong federal government could guarantee freedom—beginning with, but not limited to, freeing the slaves from bondage.[1]

Consider that within 48 hours in 1862, Abraham Lincoln signed the Pacific Railroad Act and the Land-Grant College Act. The former was one of the great infrastructure subsidy bills of all time. The latter, often known as the Morrill Act after its sponsor, Vermont Republican congressman Justin Morrill, provided states grants of land to finance colleges that specialized in "agriculture and the mechanic arts." Higher education, it should be noted, was not seen as "elitist." The spread of knowledge was, on the contrary, seen as powerfully democratic and conducive to economic growth. The legacy of this one piece of legislation is staggering. From the University of Maine to the first University of California—and, in between, to name a few, Penn State, Ohio State, Michigan State, and the Universities of Wisconsin, Minnesota, Georgia, Florida, Missouri, Arkansas, Wyoming, Arizona, and Nevada—over 100 institutions owe their existence to Morrill's dream and Lincoln's action.[2]

Lincoln also signed the Homestead Act, turning midsized plots of government land over to farmers. This could be seen as a supremely socialist endeavor (a massive exercise in wealth redistribution) or as a quintessentially capitalist enterprise (turning government land over to private use and creating a new class of owners and entrepreneurs). Such labels did not trouble the program's sponsors.

The first two great national parks were created under Republican presidents, Yosemite in 1864 and Yellowstone in 1872. Theodore Roosevelt vastly increased the acreage of land under federal protection, naming Gifford Pinchot, one of the most energetic environmentalists in our history, to oversee his conservation program. Of course, Roosevelt was also known as a trust-busting foe of monopoly. "Corporations, and especially combinations of corporations, should be managed under public regulation," he said. His administration argued that antitrust law should be "aimed at what we certainly know to be unreasonable practices directly restrictive of freedom of commerce." Revisionist historians would note that TR was friendlier to business than his reputation suggested, and there's truth to this—he was, after all, a Republican, not a socialist, and was highly critical of the rising socialist movement of his day. But his attitude toward regulation and monopoly was decidedly different from the approach his party would take decades later.[3]

During most of the 1930s and 1940s, Republicans were critical of the New Deal, yet their presidential nominees—Alf Landon, Wendell Willkie, and Thomas E. Dewey—all spoke for a more progressive brand of Republicanism. As governor of New York, Dewey compiled a broadly liberal record and offered a pithy summary of the moderate Republican creed. "It is our solemn duty," he said, "to show that government can have both a head and a heart, that it can be both progressive and solvent, that it can serve the people without becoming their master."[4]

Even Dewey's conservative archrival in that period, Senator Robert A. Taft of Ohio—known as "Mr. Republican"— acknowledged that government had a role to play in the capitalist economy he so energetically embraced. He cosponsored the Housing Act of 1949 with two Democrats, Senators Robert Wagner and Allen Ellender, that financed slum clearance and created 810,000 public housing units. "We have long recognized the duty of the state to give relief and free medical care to those unable to pay for it," Taft said, "and I think shelter is just as important as relief and medical care."[5]

But Taft repeatedly lost his party's nomination to more moderate candidates, culminating with his defeat at the deeply divided 1952 Republican National Convention to Dwight Eisenhower. Ike prevailed with strong support from Dewey, who had defeated Taft in 1944 and 1948.

Eisenhower was viewed as a conservative by the liberals of his day. He was both frugal and pro-business. Ike liked to say that his approach was to "apply common sense—to reach for an average solution." But as the historian Stephen Ambrose noted, "when basic decisions affecting the economy were involved, his average solutions usually came down on the side of business."[6]

Yet Ike mistrusted his party's right wing and sought to define what he called a "Modern Republicanism" that came to terms with the New Deal. Eisenhower offered the best summary of his approach in a 1954 letter to his brother Edgar. Note the attack on H. L. Hunt, the right-wing oil billionaire who helped finance the subsequent conservative takeover of the GOP:

> Now it is true that I believe this country is following a dangerous trend when it permits too great a degree of centralization of governmental functions. I oppose this—in some instances the fight is a rather desperate one. But to attain any success it is quite clear that the Federal government cannot avoid or escape responsibilities which the mass of the people firmly believe should be undertaken by it. The political

processes of our country are such that if a rule of reason is not applied in this effort, we will lose everything—even to a possible and drastic change in the Constitution. This is what I mean by my constant insistence upon "moderation" in government. Should any political party attempt to abolish social security, unemployment insurance, and eliminate labor laws and farm programs, you would not hear of that party again in our political history. There is a tiny splinter group, of course, that believes you can do these things. Among them are H. L. Hunt (you possibly know his background), a few other Texas oil millionaires, and an occasional politician or business man from other areas. Their number is negligible and they are stupid.[7]

The program put forward by the first Republican president since the New Deal built on the GOP traditions established by the very first Republican president. Lincoln, like his Whig hero Henry Clay, was committed to "internal improvements," which meant using government to build the country's transportation network and educate its people. So was Ike. He signed the Federal Aid Highway Act, creating the Interstate Highway System now responsible for over 46,000 miles of road. And the National Defense Education Act in 1958 stood firmly in the tradition of the Morrill Act—strengthening science curriculums across the country (at a time when the United States feared it was falling behind the Soviet Union) and providing loans to millions of students (I'm one of them). The NDEA built on the vast expansion of educational opportunities afforded by the GI Bill, which, while passed under a Democratic president, had broad Republican support.

It is fascinating to ponder the possibility that modern Republicanism might have defined the Republican Party for decades if Richard Nixon, Eisenhower's vice president, had prevailed over John F. Kennedy in 1960. The Nixon of 1960 was a thoroughly moderate Republican, and his policy differences with Kennedy were rather modest, especially by later standards. Nixon's defeat opened the way for the nomination of Barry Goldwater in 1964, setting the party on the conservative path that would reach its culmination with Ronald Reagan's election 16 years later.

It would be a long transition, and both moderate and liberal Republicans continued to thrive in the intervening period. The 1966 Republican midterm victory was at least as much a triumph of the Republican center as of its right. The new GOP senators included Edward W. Brooke of Massachusetts, the first African American elected to the Senate since Reconstruction, and a long list of others who could be classified as moderate or even liberal. With the singularly important exception of Ronald Reagan in California, the 1966 class of Republican governors was broadly progressive.

In this period, Republicans played leadership roles in passing both the Civil Rights Act of 1964 and the Voting Rights Act of 1965. (Goldwater was in the minority in his party in voting against the 1964 bill.) During the flood of Great Society legislation under Lyndon Johnson, Republican leaders felt an obligation to offer what they called "Constructive Republican Alternatives." And Republicans in significant numbers joined Democrats in supporting LBJ's programs: 10 of the 32 Republicans in the Senate voted for the president's signature Economic Opportunity Act of 1964 that authorized many of the anti-poverty programs for which Johnson is known. Although Republicans in the House overwhelmingly opposed it, it still received 22 GOP votes.[8]

The Richard Nixon who won the Republican nomination in 1968 was still in the center of his party, but it was a center that Goldwater had moved well to the right. Nixon accepted what Goldwater had shown: that the conservative South was destined to become the foundation of a new majority. Nixon thus developed his "Southern Strategy." Once a strong supporter of civil rights, Nixon maintained a general commitment to racial equality and spoke of creating a "black capitalism." But he campaigned hard against crime and for "law and order," and he excoriated liberal Supreme Court decisions, long a cause of the far right—the John Birch Society had sponsored "Impeach Earl Warren" billboards—and southern segregationists.

Yet Nixon was a paradoxical figure. If he courted white backlash and spoke for a "silent majority" that rejected the 1960s left, he also worked closely with a Democratic Congress that set the tone in many areas of domestic policy. He signed into law a staggering number of progressive achievements, including bills creating the Environmental Protection Agency, the Occupational Safety and Health Administration, and the Consumer Product Safety Commission. He signed the Clean Air Act of 1970 and approved the law indexing Social Security benefits to inflation, guaranteeing senior citizens steady increases in benefits without a vote by Congress. He established affirmative action and proposed a health insurance plan more aggressive than Obamacare. (Years later, Ted Kennedy would say that not working with Nixon to pass this bill was one of the biggest mistakes of his career.) The all-volunteer military force was created under Nixon, and he proposed a universal basic income through his Family Assistance Plan, though he later backed away.

This is a partial list, but it explains why the columnist Mark Shields, writing in 1996, declared Nixon "the last liberal American President." In 2012, *New York Times* economics writer Eduardo Porter reached a similar judgment. After listing all of Nixon's achievements, Porter concluded: "Americans today might not elect somebody as liberal as Richard Nixon."[9]

Among the ironies of Watergate is that Nixon's fall hastened the end of both the liberal and moderate Republican traditions. Had Gerald Ford, Nixon's successor, won a term of his own in 1976 (after narrowly defeating Ronald Reagan in a highly contested Republican presidential primary), what remained of modern Republicanism might have won a reprieve. Reagan's victory in 1980 confirmed the shift rightward that began with Goldwater. And steadily, moderate and liberal Republicans were driven from office. Some lost primaries to conservatives, the fate of two of the Senate's most liberal Republicans of the post–World War II period, New Jersey's Clifford Case in 1978 and New York's Jacob Javits in 1980. Others were defeated in general elections. Many voters who had once embraced progressive Republicanism as reflecting their own broadly middle-ground attitudes gradually turned to Democrats out of frustration over the GOP's rightward drift.

One of Ronald Reagan's most celebrated quips——it always drew laughter and applause from appreciative conservative audiences——captured the transformation of Republicanism better than many a manifesto or policy paper: "The nine most terrifying words in the English language are: 'I'm from the government, and I'm here to help.'"[10]

One should certainly not romanticize the Republican Party of old or pretend that the seeds of Reaganism had not been planted long before. The party's long-term course was set by the defeat of Theodore Roosevelt for the 1912 Republican presidential nomination by the conservative forces who rallied to William Howard Taft. Many progressives who bolted the party with TR that year never came back, and many who did became New Dealers in the 1930s. Progressives would never again have the same role in the party, and Republicans in large numbers gave no quarter to FDR. As the historian Kim Phillips-Fein demonstrated, many of the ideas and organizational habits of the right took root in the business-financed conservative war on the New Deal in the 1930s—including, as we will see later, the habit of labeling all efforts at social reform as dangerous incarnations of "socialism." While some progressive Republicans supported New Deal programs, most of the party rallied against FDR. After the 1938 elections, Republicans and most southern Democrats joined in a "conservative coalition" in Congress that blocked further reform while rolling back some of the earlier progressive victories.

Nonetheless, from Lincoln through Nixon, the Republican Party had often seen government in precisely the terms that Reagan mocked: as a means of helping people and the country as a whole through reform, public investment, and sensible rule-making. It sought to create a public sector that operated, in Dewey's terms, with both a head and a heart. The rise of Reaganism marked the end of all that.

To suggest any links between Trump's presidency and the Republican presidencies that came immediately before him would seem unfair to his predecessors. It was not uncommon after Trump's rise to hear Democrats express nostalgia for Reagan and the Bushes, father and son.

In fact, all three contributed to the trends in conservative politics that helped make Trumpism possible. But let's look first at the important ways in which they differed from Trump.

Reagan's sunny approach to politics—his 1984 advertising spoke of "Morning in America"—could not be further removed from Trump's "American Carnage." Nowhere were the two more at odds than in their respective approaches to immigration. Many a Democrat has quoted Reagan on the subject, including Nancy Pelosi in her first speech upon taking over as Speaker in 2019. She tweaked Trump and the Republicans by citing words Reagan spoke the day before he left office in 1989: "If we ever closed the door to new Americans, our leadership in the world would soon be lost."[11]

When Reagan mentioned walls, they were an unfortunate necessity, not a central goal of his administration. In his Farewell Address, Reagan reached back to his old reference to "a shining city on a hill," and he described this city as a place "teeming with people of all kinds living in harmony." He added: "And if there had to be city walls, the walls had doors and the doors were open to anyone with the will and the heart to get there."[12]

It's hard to think of a president more different from Trump than the first President Bush. Indeed, his death in 2018 became an opportunity not only to celebrate an honorable life but also to offer, as *Washington Post* columnist Dana Milbank put it, "an implicit rebuke of everything Trump is." Milbank cited former Canadian prime minister Brian Mulroney's compact and devastating condemnation of the sitting president that never had to mention Trump's name: "When George Bush was president," Mulroney said, "every single head of government in the world knew that they were dealing with a gentleman, a genuine leader, one who was distinguished, resolute and brave." Nearly every word was a dagger aimed at Trump.[13]

Although he loyally served Reagan as vice president, Bush was a partial throwback to pre-Reagan Republicanism. He adjusted his politics to the new conservatism, but never fully converted. He was by instinct a follower of Edmund Burke, the British philosophical founder of conservatism who saw change and reform as necessary to the work of conserving what he believed to be a fundamentally good society.[14] A fierce partisan when necessary, Bush refused to see cooperation with political adversaries as a form of ideological treason. A product of the World War II generation, he did not dismiss government as merely a necessary evil. He ran on promises to be an "environmental president" and an "education president." His two main domestic achievements, a new Clean Air Act and the Americans with Disabilities Act, were broadly progressive and passed with Democratic support.

He cared about deficits—in fact and not just rhetorically. So he was willing to violate his politically opportunistic 1988 "No new taxes" pledge to get a responsible budget deal two years later. Conservatives never forgave him, although his tax increase was smaller than one Reagan had signed when deficits began soaring. Conservatives forgave their hero—if the Gipper agreed to raise taxes, it must have been because he had no choice. The right gave Bush no benefit of the doubt, and its hostility helped fuel a 1992 primary challenge from right-wing commentator Pat Buchanan. It was a wounded Bush who faced Bill Clinton that fall. More enduringly, the rebellion against the Bush tax increase led by Speaker-to-be Newt Gingrich marked the transformation of tax cutting from a preference to dogma on the right.

As for his son, George W. Bush ran in 2000 as "a uniter, not a divider." He tried to define a new, "compassionate conservatism," pledged to rally "the armies of compassion," and spoke warmly of the work of faith-based institutions in lifting up the poor. He went far enough out of his way to distance himself from the anti-government formulas of the hard right—"Government cannot be replaced by charities," Bush insisted—that many in the party's ranks accused him of being a "big government conservative." Unusually for a Republican, he made education a central cause. His No Child Left Behind Act proved controversial over time. But it used the strong arm of the federal government to impose standards on local schools. He also pushed through a prescription drug benefit under Medicare (which, in its use of private insurance, bore a family resemblance to Obamacare). Both initiatives became part of the right-wing critique. Bush's quest for a "compassionate conservatism" was largely pushed aside after the attacks of September 11, 2001, but even before that, many on the right bridled at the idea that conservatism even needed an adjective. For its critics on the right, compassionate conservatism was a treasonous acknowledgment that normal, garden-variety conservatism lacked a heart.

In two areas, the contrast between Bush 43 and Trump could not be starker. One of the most deeply honorable acts of the younger Bush's presidency was his visit to the Islamic Center in Washington six days after 9/11. His condemnation of any American

who held Muslims as a group responsible for the attacks on the
World Trade Center and the Pentagon was unambiguous:

> Muslims are doctors, lawyers, law professors, members of
> the military, entrepreneurs, shopkeepers, moms and dads.
> And they need to be treated with respect. In our anger and
> emotion, our fellow Americans must treat each other with
> respect. . . . Those who feel like they can intimidate our fel-
> low citizens to take out their anger don't represent the best of
> America, they represent the worst of humankind, and they
> should be ashamed of that kind of behavior.[15]

Bush's stance on immigration, like Reagan's, was diametrically
opposed to Trump's. The forty-third president and Karl Rove,
his top political adviser, understood that a Republican coalition
dependent solely on white, non-Hispanic voters would not long
endure as an electoral majority. Bush had successfully wooed
Latino voters in his two campaigns for governor of Texas, and he
would do the same in his presidential races.

Rove was an admirer of Republican president William McKinley, his respect rooted partly in McKinley's refusal to cater to his
own party's nativists, who preferred to write off votes of new immigrants. After his White House years, Rove's passion led him to
write *The Triumph of William McKinley: Why the Election of 1896
Still Matters*. Rove was quite explicit about the echoes between that
campaign and the present. "To prevent Democrats from achieving
a durable advantage in battleground states," he wrote, "McKinley
would have to expand the GOP coalition by recruiting new allies,
including industrial laborers, Catholics and immigrants. For the
general election, he needed to show these Americans that they had
a place in the GOP's vision of the nation's future."[16]

This is what W. did with Latinos, winning over 40 percent of
their ballots in both 2000 and 2004. His language was warm and

Reaganesque. He called for steps toward legalizing the status of most immigrants who had entered the country illegally, but also offered what in retrospect can be read as a sharp riposte to how Trump would demagogue on the immigration issue. "America needs to conduct this debate on immigration in a reasoned and respectful tone," he said in his 2006 address calling for immigration reform. He continued:

> Feelings run deep on this issue, and as we work it out, all of us need to keep some things in mind. We cannot build a unified country by inciting people to anger, or playing on anyone's fears, or exploiting the issue of immigration for political gain. We must always remember that real lives will be affected by our debates and decisions, and that every human being has dignity and value no matter what their citizenship papers say.

He closed with a classic presidential tribute to the heroic role of newcomers to our shores. "Our new immigrants are just what they've always been," he said, "people willing to risk everything for the dream of freedom. And America remains what she has always been—the great hope on the horizon, an open door to the future, a blessed and promised land."[17]

It might be said that the 2006–7 immigration debate was the beginning of Trumpism. Bush's immigration reform effort failed not because of opposition from Democrats but because it was scorned by Republicans. The battle against the bill was led by Senator Jeff Sessions, later Trump's first attorney general. On the key procedural vote in June 2007 to move the immigration bill forward, only 12 of the Senate's 49 Republicans stuck with their own president. By contrast, two-thirds of the Democrats (including Senator Barack Obama) voted yes. The bill was defeated, and Sessions explained why its opponents wanted a long debate while its supporters favored an earlier vote. The Bush side wanted to pass the bill quickly, Sessions explained, "before Rush Limbaugh could tell the American people what was in it."[18]

This was no joke, and the immigration debate was one of the earliest indicators of the hold talk radio hosts and Fox News had over the Republican Party. Banu Akdenizli of the Project for Excellence in Journalism pointed to the substantial role played by conservative media in killing Bush's effort in a study that found a vast disparity in the coverage given the issue by conservative outlets on the one side and both mainstream and liberal media on the other. "Conservative radio hosts devoted 31% of their newshole to the coverage of immigration," Akdenizli found, "while their liberal counterparts paid little attention."[19] The conservative coverage was overwhelmingly hostile. A similar pattern was visible on cable television, with Lou Dobbs (then of CNN and later an ardent Trump supporter on Fox) and Bill O'Reilly giving the bill heavy negative coverage, even as it received limited notice on MSNBC.

A study of blogs by Roberto Suro, a professor at the University of Southern California's Annenberg School for Communication, found a similar left/right difference:

> On the liberal side of the spectrum, "Talking Points Memo" barely took note of the debate while the "Daily Kos" did increase its coverage but peaked at 9 percent in June. "Instapundit," which is usually identified as libertarian in spirit, spiked coverage but only to 6 percent. Meanwhile on the right, "Michelle Malkin" showed a jump to 20 percent in May and 40 percent in June. Similarly, "Powerline," another conservative blog, surged to 13 percent in May and 17 percent in June.

Summarizing the impact of all media on the bill, Suro concluded that "the advocacy journalists on cable and radio talk and in the blogosphere mirrored what was happening in Washington's more formal political arena. Most liberals and progressives backed the Senate legislation but with a variety of reservations about its major provisions. Meanwhile, most conservatives opposed it adamantly. Weak support met fierce resistance and the bill was defeated."[20]

Eight years before Trump declared that Mexican immigrants were "rapists," the energy on the Republican right against immigration was obvious.

Yet if both Bushes and Reagan were on the opposite side of the immigration issue from Trump, many of the other trends that led to Trump's ascendancy began on their watch. As important as anything else was the transformation of the GOP into a party dominated by older, white conservative voters. The younger Bush did well among Latino voters, but he did not convert them to Republicanism. After the defeat of the immigration bill at the hands of Republicans, many of the Latinos Bush had won over fled the party. Thus, despite his own staunch support for immigration reform, John McCain ran far behind Bush's Latino numbers in 2008, and the party hemorrhaged support from Asian Americans as well. Muslim voters who had backed Bush in 2000 fled after the invasion of Iraq.

Reagan, for all his sunniness, consciously built upon Richard Nixon's Southern Strategy. He opened his fall 1980 campaign with a speech extolling "states' rights" at a county fairground seven miles from Philadelphia, Mississippi, the site of the notorious murder of three civil rights workers in the 1960s. He thrived on the term "welfare queen" and was certainly aware that, like Nixon before him, he stood to profit from the white backlash vote. His Justice Department backed away from tough enforcement of civil rights laws, and conservatives waged war on affirmative action. In the summer of 2019, Reagan's partisans were embarrassed when the historian Timothy Naftali published racist comments that Reagan had made in a conversation with Richard Nixon in 1971: "To see those, those monkeys from those African countries—damn them, they're still uncomfortable wearing shoes!" Many liberals said the uncovered tape simply confirmed what the country had known about Reagan and his party all along. "It's irrefutable evidence that racial animus was rooted within the GOP decades before Trump descended a Trump Tower escalator and slandered Mexican immigrants as 'rapists' and 'criminals,'" wrote Renée Graham in *The Boston Globe*. "It's always been too easy for Republicans to pretend that Trump is a defect in their conservative machine."[21]

Reagan's larger ideology was just as important: Not only did his attacks on government break with the tradition of Republican activism; his campaigns in 1976 and 1980 coincided with and helped fuel successful conservative efforts to take control of major institutions. White evangelical churches swung right with the formation of the Moral Majority before the 1980 election, while the Christian Coalition was born in the 1990s out of televangelist Pat Robertson's 1988 presidential campaign. In 1977, gun rights radicals took over the National Rifle Association and turned it into one of the most feared lobbies in Washington— and an ally to all anti-government conservative causes. As Joel Achenbach, Scott Higham, and Sari Horwitz wrote in *The Washington Post*, "The NRA didn't get swept up in the culture wars of the past century so much as it helped invent them—and kept inflaming them."[22]

The business community shifted rightward in the 1970s, too, in reaction to a growing consumer movement and new forms of government regulation. From World War II through the late 1960s, as John Judis recounted in *The Paradox of American Democracy*, significant parts of the business sector, while decidedly conservative, leaned toward a middle-of-the-road, consensual approach to public life. Then, in the years leading up to Reagan's presidency and especially during the 1980s, "corporate leaders and bankers abandoned their commitment to disinterested public service" and "turned against union organizers, environmentalists and consumer activists with the same resolve that an older generation of business leaders had turned against the AFL, the IWW and the Socialist Party." This had important implications in the Trump era. Many individual business leaders were privately horrified by Trump's behavior. But their support for his tax and deregulatory policies and the pro-business judges he named largely kept them on his side.

For his part, George H. W. Bush was not shy about using unsubtle racial appeals to win the election in 1988 against Governor Michael Dukakis of Massachusetts. Bush attacked a Dukakis-era prison-furlough program, and his criticism of the program was linked to the release of Willie Horton, an African American serving a life sentence for murder, who raped a white woman and stabbed her husband while on a weekend furlough. Years later, when Bush's wily, engaging, but also ruthless campaign manager, Lee Atwater, was facing death from cancer, he apologized for having said he would "make Willie Horton [Dukakis's] running mate."[23]

The flight of African Americans from the Republican Party reshaped the GOP in fundamental ways. In 1960, running against John F. Kennedy, Nixon secured a third of the black vote; in 1972, an election he won by a landslide, his share fell to 18 percent—and, compared with subsequent years, that turned out to be a high point for the Republicans. In the seven presidential elections between 1980 and 2004, Republicans averaged just over 9 percent of the African American vote. (It fell further in 2008 and 2012 as black voters were nearly unanimous in supporting Barack Obama as the first African American president.)

A party competing for black voters would be wary of racial appeals and make some effort to build a passable civil rights record. To some degree, George H. W. Bush did this. But on the whole, the GOP did what the Southern Strategy suggested it should: It moved right on civil rights and turned the white South into the party's most loyal constituency. Between 1980 and 2004, the GOP averaged 63.5 percent of the white southern vote—and this number is slightly depressed by the showing of Independent Ross Perot in 1992 and 1996. If those elections are excluded, the average Republican share of the white South stood at 67 percent. Whites elsewhere were somewhat less Republican, particularly in the Northeast, where Democrats won a plurality or a majority of the white vote from 1992 forward. Still, beginning in 1992, Republicans won the white vote nationwide in every election.

The growing homogeneity of the GOP explains why George W. Bush's strategy of appealing to Latinos and embracing immigration reform was ultimately spurned by most in his party. Outside of Florida, where Cuban Americans, inspired by anti-Castro politics, played a central role in the GOP, Republican politicians depended on an overwhelmingly white electorate. White voters dominated GOP primaries, and Barack Obama's rise only reinforced this. In 2012, 88 percent of the voters who supported Mitt Romney were white.[24]

Romney's defeat inspired the party's Growth and Opportunity Project, otherwise known (even in Republican circles) as "the autopsy," a strange word since autopsies usually follow death, not defeat. Its report insisted that the party needed to reach out, especially to Latinos, and was specifically critical of Romney's response to the immigration issue, which turned, in his memorable formulation, on "self-deportation." The autopsy concluded:

> If Hispanic Americans perceive that a GOP nominee or candidate does not want them in the United States (i.e. self-deportation), they will not pay attention to our next sentence. It does not matter what we say about education, jobs or the economy; if Hispanics think we do not want them here, they will close their ears to our policies. . . . We are not a policy committee, but among the steps Republicans take

in the Hispanic community and beyond, we must embrace
and champion comprehensive immigration reform. If we
do not, our Party's appeal will continue to shrink to its core
constituencies only.[25]

The Growth and Opportunity report proved to be no more
effective in changing the party's course than the pleading of Bush
and Rove. In fact, Obama's election and reelection, far from moving the party to a degree of moderation, pushed it back on itself
and moved it further to the right. A backlash against Obama,
aggravated by the economic catastrophe that began in the Bush
years, gave rise to the Tea Party. Its supporters opposed taxes and
government—except for Social Security and Medicare, since Tea
Partiers were on the older side—and fiercely resisted immigration. If it would be wrong to say that the reaction to Obama was
fueled only by race, it would be equally wrong to deny powerful
racial—and racist—motivations. How else to explain the success
of the birther movement inspired by lies about where Obama
was born? The birther movement's liar-in-chief was Donald
Trump. If the forces that led to Trump began coming together
with the defeat of immigration reform in 2007, he staked his
claim to leading them during Obama's presidency.

The behavior of Republicans in Congress during the Obama
years reflected the narrowing of the GOP's field of policy vision
that began under Reagan. His opposition to taxes, government,
and regulation had a long-term effect. Being Republican no
longer meant favoring innovative, market-friendly government
programs. Instead, it meant disdain for government programs
altogether, reflecting how Reagan's laugh line was in fact a rigid
ideological commitment.

This left broad running room for Democrats, an opportunity
both Bill Clinton and Barack Obama seized by occupying the
middle ground of politics. But the retreat to the right also meant
that Republicans—except during brief moments in Clinton's

second term—rebuffed any olive branches the two Democrats in the White House offered. Obama, for example, carefully constructed his health care proposal around ideas conservatives had offered in the past, from the creation of market-friendly health care exchanges (first proposed by the Heritage Foundation) to an emphasis on subsidies to help Americans with lower incomes buy private insurance (the thrust of Romney's successful Massachusetts project). Not only did Republicans reject his overtures, they denounced Obamacare as "socialist." This came as a surprise to actual democratic socialists like Bernie Sanders, for whom government-run, single-payer health care, not Obamacare, deserved to be called socialist—which was, for Sanders, an adjective of honor. Trump and his party were unrelenting in their efforts to repeal it, trying to achieve in court what they failed to achieve in Congress.[26]

Similarly, Obama's thoroughly conventional efforts to boost a collapsing economy with large-scale government spending won near-uniform opposition from Republicans who denounced big deficits—even though big deficits were precisely what a collapsing economy required. House Republicans voted unanimously against Obama's stimulus plan. Only three Republican senators supported it, and at the price of cutting back on the spending required.

Republicans' takeover of Congress in 2010 during the Tea Party wave and their subsequent congressional victories in 2012 and 2014 effectively blocked any further Democratic initiatives. What is striking about the GOP's stewardship in that period is the cramped nature of their agenda. Their major initiatives, unfulfillable as long as Obama was president, were Paul Ryan's budgets, pushed before and after he became Speaker. All focused on cuts in taxes and government spending (except for defense).

Citizens did not have to worry any more about Reagan's helpful federal bureaucrat. If the Republicans had their way, the federal government would not be making any new offers to help you—unless you were looking for lower taxes. The days of Justin Morrill and Dwight Eisenhower were over.

Despite George W. Bush's honorable attitudes toward immigrants and America's Muslims, it's important to recognize that his presidency also reinforced and aggravated other tendencies among Republicans that Trump exploited. In some cases, Bush did so unintentionally. In others, it was by design.

The Iraq War involves elements of both. The long, frustrating conflict—and the administration's misbegotten promises of how easy the project would be ("we'll be greeted as liberators")—certainly heightened anti-interventionist tendencies among the Republican rank and file. Although Trump was lying when he said during the 2016 campaign that he had always opposed the Iraq War, his ex post facto critique of the war resonated with primary voters and differentiated him from his rivals, particularly Jeb Bush. Yet the Bush administration's celebration of unilateralism fit well with Trump's nationalism. So did criticisms of the war's opponents by Bush's supporters that often fell into a form of demagoguery that divided the country.

After initially bringing the country together across party lines after the 9/11 attacks, Bush launched what became a partisan effort to build support for the invasion of Iraq—and he was scornful of any suggestions that the war might be problematic. When Democrats argued that such an adventurous endeavor required broad international backing, Bush mocked them as too weak to act on their own. In September 2002—two months before the midterm elections—Bush characterized those in Congress who wanted UN support for any war as saying, "I think I'm going to wait for the United Nations to make a decision." He went on: "It seems like to me that if you're representing the United States, you ought to be making a decision on what's best for the United

States. If I were running for office, I'm not sure how I'd explain to the American people—say, 'Vote for me, and, oh, by the way, on a matter of national security, I'm going to wait for somebody else to act.'"[27]

It was disgraceful to imply that those who wanted to follow Bush's father in building a broad coalition to back what would inevitably be a difficult endeavor were simply afraid to make "a decision on what's best for the United States." The notion that seeking approval from allies or the UN was the same as waiting "for somebody else to act" was a remarkable distortion of the Democrats' arguments.

Attacks on the opposition's patriotism and its resolve against terrorism were central to Bush's reelection strategy. At the 2004 Republican National Convention, Bush-supporting Democrat Zell Miller was unrestrained: "Today's Democratic leaders see America as an occupier, not a liberator. In their warped way of thinking, America is the problem, not the solution."[28]

A popular form of Republican mockery against John Kerry, Bush's 2004 Democratic opponent, was to declare him "French." Since France had refused to support the Iraq War, this was a way of saying Kerry was squishy soft, and pretentious to boot. Radio hosts gleefully referred to "Monsieur Kerry" and "Jean Cheri." Commerce Secretary Don Evans said that Bush's opponent "[is] of a different political stripe and looks French." House Majority Leader Tom DeLay took to beginning his speeches by saying hi to the crowd and adding, "Or, as John Kerry might say, 'Bonjour.'"[29]

Thus was one party cast as championing salt-of-the-earth American patriotism and the other as locked in an embrace with foreign elitism and timidity. The effort continued after the election was over, with Rove telling the New York State Conservative Party convention in 2005, "Perhaps the most important difference between conservatives and liberals can be found in the area of national security." He went on: "Conservatives saw the savagery of 9/11 and the attacks and prepared for war; liberals saw the savagery of the 9/11 attacks and wanted to prepare indictments and offer therapy and understanding for our attackers." The word "therapy" did a lot of work here. Even more offensive were his insinuations about a speech by Democratic senator Richard Durbin criticizing the treatment of prisoners at Guantanamo. "Al Jazeera now broadcasts the words of Senator Durbin to the Mideast, certainly putting our troops in greater danger," Rove said. "No more needs to be said about the motives of liberals." Rove's words said a lot about the motives of conservatives.[30]

Bush counted on cultural conflict to help him win reelection in another sphere: Early in 2004, he endorsed a constitutional amendment that would have banned gay marriage by defining marriage as being between a man and a woman. Rove had calculated that millions of conservative white evangelicals had stayed home in 2000, and he was determined to rally their votes for Bush. The president said the amendment was necessary "to prevent the meaning of marriage from being changed forever," and Rove encouraged state referenda on the issue to draw social conservatives to the polls. The strategy worked on Election Day, but the amendment fell by the wayside.[31]

Linking patriotism, culture, and religion with efforts to cast one region of the country against another all came together in another GOP trope popularized in the Bush years: that only conservatives and Republicans represented "the real America." The Northeast, the West Coast, and Democratic-voting midwestern states—and pretty much anyone who, for example, believed in gay marriage or reasonable restrictions on firearms—became part of an "un-real" America, or not part of America at all. At times, defensive Democrats seemed to accept this definition of reality, looking faintly ridiculous as they struggled to become fluent in NASCAR talk, discussed religion with the inflections of a white southern evangelicalism foreign to most of them, or demonstrated how well they knew their way around guns.

Trump would nuclearize the notion that conservatives were

the only "real Americans," but the ground was well prepared for him. Campaigning as John McCain's running mate in 2008, Sarah Palin defined who constituted the authentic nation. "We believe," Palin told a rally in North Carolina, "that the best of America is in these small towns that we get to visit and these wonderful little pockets of what I call the real America, being here with all of you hard-working, very patriotic, very pro-America areas of this great nation."[32]

The places Palin extolled would be central to Trump's success.

Over the last half century, Republicans have driven out the moderate forces that might have provided more robust resistance to Trump, turning themselves into an almost uniformly white party in the process. This led to the regular use of often coded racial appeals by Republican candidates that crossed into explicit racism with Trump. It also meant that the party became increasingly resistant to immigration. And, beginning in 2013—after a Republican majority on the Supreme Court eviscerated the Voting Rights Act so many in the party had championed in 1965—Republican-controlled states began passing measures (disguised as efforts to stop "voter fraud") that impeded access to the ballot by racial minorities and younger voters.

The Republican agenda steadily narrowed, following the inexorable logic of Reagan's anti-government appeal. The two Bushes made some effort to buck the trend, but it was too strong, and their own approaches to politics strengthened it in other respects. By 2009, the Tea Party made clear that it could not abide anything resembling Big Government conservatism beyond supporting programs for the elderly. During the Obama years, the GOP Congress was almost entirely obstructionist. Their central causes were unsuccessful efforts to repeal Obamacare, deep program cuts (largely resisted by Obama), and endless investigations (particularly into Hillary Clinton).[33]

Culturally, Republicans moved steadily rightward, depending more and more on white conservative evangelical voters and Americans living outside big metropolitan areas. The Trump coalition was only a slightly purer strain of this alliance. Together with business groups, evangelicals made Supreme Court appointments their highest priority. As young people moved left, older cultural conservatives and opponents of government regulation realized they would need a right-wing Court to nullify the decisions of an emerging progressive majority.[34]

For all the talk that Trump was an alien force in his own party, the old coalition rallied to him on Election Day. He won 88 percent of the votes cast by self-identified Republicans, 81 percent of conservatives, and 80 percent of white evangelicals. These were little different from the proportions Mitt Romney had won in 2012 (93 percent of Republicans, 82 percent of conservatives, and 78 percent of white evangelicals). Long before Trump's inauguration, Republican leaders had fallen into line. Senate Majority Leader Mitch McConnell blocked a bipartisan statement before the election denouncing Russian interference to protect Trump, and he would continue to act as Trump's shield after the release of Special Counsel Robert Mueller's report on the issue.[35]

But capitulation was a two-way street: Trump did his part, too. In a strange echo of Bush's compassionate conservatism, Trump suggested during the campaign that he was not like other, presumably heartless, Republicans. He promised he would get health care to everyone, praising the system in "Scotland," which of course was British socialized medicine. He said he would make no cuts in Medicare, Medicaid, or Social Security, and he would get tough on trade.[36]

Once elected, he threw most of his heretical ideas over the side, except on trade policy. The results of his verbal toughness on trade were ambiguous, although he relished unilaterally imposing tariffs. On everything else, he behaved as a standard-issue corporate Republican. He supported a straight-out repeal of the

Affordable Care Act without putting forward an alternative, Scottish or otherwise. He proposed cuts in Medicare and Medicaid and sharp reductions in spending on other social programs. For all his talk about standing up for American workers, he regularly sided with business over unions and workers on regulatory decisions, and he was never serious about his promises to create jobs through a big infrastructure program. One of the signature headlines of the Trump era appeared in the print edition of *The New York Times* in late July 2019: "Despite Rhetorical Appeals, Trump Has Accomplished Little for Working Class."[37]

His main achievements were rooted in thoroughly conventional conservative Republicanism. He signed a tax cut tilted heavily toward corporations and Americans with high incomes that cost the Treasury an estimated $1.5 trillion over a decade. He appointed conservative judges, including two justices of the Supreme Court, Neil Gorsuch and Brett Kavanaugh.

Trump, however, was innovative in the barbarity of his policies toward immigrants, refugees, and asylum seekers, culminating in his administration's policy of separating children from their parents at the border. He broke all precedents on the separation of powers by declaring a phony national emergency so he could finance part of his border wall after Congress refused to fund it. Here, at least, there was some Republican resistance—12 Republican senators supported a resolution rejecting the emergency claim—but enough Republicans went along to sustain Trump's veto. After the release of the Mueller report, and again after Trump's efforts to secure Ukraine's help against Joe Biden became public, Trump engaged in across-the-board resistance to the Democratic House's efforts to hold him and his administration accountable. His obstruction efforts—inventing phony privileges to keep members of his administration from testifying before Congress, having his White House counsel issue a letter filled with partisan language denying any administration responsibility to respond to the House's impeachment inquiry—went far beyond anything attempted by previous administrations, Republican or Democratic.

In the spring of 2019, two decisions underscored the transformation of the on-your-side populist into a radical conservative budget-cutter. His budget proposed eliminating federal support for the Special Olympics—a decision from which Trump divorced himself after an outcry from left, right, and center. And he enthusiastically supported a legally flimsy lawsuit that would have destroyed the Affordable Care Act. Democrats were furious about the substance and elated about the politics. Trump picked the one issue above all others that allowed them to retake the House.

Ross Douthat, the conservative *New York Times* columnist, was disgusted. A longtime advocate of a GOP agenda that would take the needs of its working-class supporters seriously, Douthat concluded in late March 2019 that Trump's choices made him "look like a guy who didn't keep his promises, who promised to be a different kind of Republican and then kept trying to defund the Special Olympians and throw people off their health care coverage. That's the most unpopular version of Trumpism, which is saying something."[38]

It is indeed. The country ended up with the worst of all possible Trumps.

The divisive demagogue who regularly attacked African American members of Congress, especially members of the Squad, and incited extremists with talk of an immigrant "invasion" was consistent with the man who ran in 2016. But in embracing a brand of Republicanism far removed from the problem solving that Lincoln, Eisenhower, and even Nixon had embraced, Trump confirmed he was very much part of the contemporary Republican Party from which he had once distanced himself. Trump had joined those who abandoned efforts to use government to improve lives, make the market work better, protect the environment, invest in the future, or redress the economy's injustices.

The stewards of America's progressive tradition could once be found in both parties. Now they did their work in only one of them. When it came to reform, Democrats had cornered the market. This was a great opportunity, but it also made their party the staging ground for all the arguments over what reform meant and what it would require.

THREE

PROGRESSIVISM'S CROOKED PATH

*A Short History of Circular Firing
Squads and Enduring Achievements*

LIBERALS AND PROGRESSIVES HAVE BEEN ARGUING ABOUT
who they are since those two words came into general circu-
lation after the turn of the last century. These debates often involved dialogue with those who called themselves socialists and
social democrats, moderates and centrists. Governing liberal
establishments and rebellious outsiders struggled—sometimes
in alliance, often against each other—in search of paths toward
reform and revitalization.

There has never been an obvious way to draw clean lines
across all these contending groups. The populism of William
Jennings Bryan, the progressivism of Theodore Roosevelt and
Woodrow Wilson, the socialism of Eugene V. Debs—all jostled
and interacted to produce what came down to us as the foundation for the New and Fair Deals, the New Frontier, the Great
Society, and the programs of Bill Clinton and Barack Obama.
This intellectual effervescence on the broad left and center-left
was not confined to the United States. As the historians James
Kloppenberg and Daniel T. Rodgers showed in their respective
books, *Uncertain Victory* and *Atlantic Crossings*, American progressives and their counterparts in Europe—including socialists

and those known as "New Liberals" in Britain—engaged in a rich two-way traffic of ideas. Transatlantic political interchange continues to this day, on the nationalist right no less than among progressives, greens, and liberals.[1]

Adding to the confusion, liberals in the 1950s often claimed that they were the true conservatives. They cast Republicans like Joe McCarthy as right-wing radicals eager to tear down established institutions and the socially stabilizing programs of the New Deal.[2]

At a time of tension and conflict across the spectrum of progressive thinking, from the more moderate to the more adventurous, it's especially useful to remember this history. The successes of the reformers of the past are instructive. So are the failures—and so, too, the times when early defeats enabled later victories.

Coalition politics can be frustrating because allies often disagree and come to their commitments from very different political pedigrees and philosophical starting points. They may agree on a course of action, but not on the reasons for pursuing it. Political establishments, even when they are inclined in a progressive direction, often need to be pressured into embracing reform. Insurgent groups, in turn, need allies among traditional leaders to achieve their goals. These are the lessons of the socialist movement at the turn of the last century, the labor movement in the New Deal era, and the civil rights movement in the 1960s. Understanding that today's battles have echoes in arguments of the past is a precondition to avoiding a repetition of earlier mistakes.

The words "progressive" and "liberal" have gone in and out of style, with one replacing the other, usually as a matter of political convenience. From the time of TR to the era defined by his cousin Franklin's presidency, "progressive" was the term of choice among reformers. "Liberal" was claimed as the true title of the movement by FDR, and "progressive" largely fell by the wayside (although some Republicans, recalling Theodore Roosevelt's glory days, still liked the word in the 1930s and 1940s).[3]

The New Deal was made possible when unregulated capitalism and capitalists themselves lost popular esteem and public legitimacy after the crash of 1929 and the deepening of the Great Depression in the early 1930s. But the New Deal did not come from nowhere. Many of the ideas that animated it were first fought for by progressives in Congress and in the states during the conservative 1920s. Their efforts prepared the way for much of what Roosevelt did. Fiorello LaGuardia of New York illustrates the transition from a defeated progressivism to a victorious New Deal. LaGuardia was an anomalous figure, a nominal Republican who was once reelected on the Socialist ticket and gained fame in the 1930s as New York City's New Deal mayor. In his insightful *LaGuardia in Congress*, Howard Zinn argued that LaGuardia was "a vital link between the Progressive and New Deal eras" because he "represented a gradual departure from the atmosphere of respectable middle-class reformism that characterized the Progressive movement and toward the less genteel working-class elements that helped form the New Deal coalition." The older progressive spirit infused the New Deal, yet it would not have succeeded without the alliance with the new urban immigrant and working-class voters mobilized by Roosevelt and urban politicians of LaGuardia's stripe.[4]

The New Deal was shaped by these new forces, and also empowered them. By signing the Wagner Act, Roosevelt galvanized the labor movement and thus fundamentally altered the nation's structure of power. The unions, in turn, developed a usefully complicated relationship with Roosevelt, supporting him against his conservative enemies but also pushing him leftward on social and economic questions. Sidney Hillman, the mastermind of the Congress of Industrial Organization's political strategy, exemplified this approach, and Roosevelt himself regularly counseled his allies to bring pressure on him. The story is widely told of a meeting FDR had with A. Philip Randolph, the labor and civil rights leader who was urging FDR to act against racial discrimination. Roosevelt, it's said, declared: "I agree with you, now go out and make me do it." The same productive interaction between power and dissidence asserted itself in the 1960s when Martin Luther King Jr. and the movement he led pushed John F. Kennedy to endorse civil rights and Lyndon B. Johnson and Congress to enact the Civil Rights and Voting Rights Acts.[5]

Roosevelt needed all the pressure labor and the left could bring to bear because he had to move his program through a Congress in which southern segregationist Democratic committee chairs wielded enormous influence. As a result, many New Deal programs explicitly excluded African Americans, as Ira Katznelson detailed in his revelatory book *When Affirmative Action Was White*. This was true, for example, of Social Security, which did not cover workers in many job categories that were largely the province of African Americans. It was not until the 1950s that Congress included household employees and hotel, laundry, and agricultural laborers in the system.[6]

There are important messages here for our time. Advocates of racial equality are right to point us to the many moments in American history when even progressives capitulated to racism. The structure of the political system can rig it against oppressed minorities. Jim Crow laws in the South radically distorted representation and thus legislative outcomes. At the same time, continuing pressure from champions of racial equality led to the expansion of the system over time. The Affordable Care Act, which fell short of covering everyone (though not for the racially motivated reasons that initially limited Social Security's reach), may yet prove to be another program that begins in compromise but culminates in fundamental reform.

The New Deal underscored the paradoxical interactions between the politics of class and race. Despite his concessions to southern segregationists, Roosevelt converted a majority of black voters from the Party of Lincoln to the Democrats because many of the New Deal's programs benefited them as *workers,* if not explicitly as African Americans. Most African Americans who had access to the ballot lived in the North, and they became important components of Democratic political organizations— and, despite ongoing discrimination, the labor movement. These new members of the party's coalition pressured northern Democratic politicians to move the party to embrace civil rights. The result: Harry Truman's dramatic endorsement of racial equality in 1948 that led southern segregationists to bolt and set in motion the realignment that would shape the next 70 years of our politics.

It was in Truman's time that the onset of the Cold War brought the words "progressive" and "liberal" into conflict. Democratic advocates of Truman's hard line toward the Soviet Union put themselves firmly in the "liberal" camp, while Henry Wallace, a proponent of peaceful accommodation with the Soviets, embraced the word "progressive." It became the name of the other Democratic breakaway party that year, whose standard Wallace bore. That Wallace had the support of Communists meant that many Cold War liberals mistrusted the word "progressive" for a generation. For many of them, "progressive" was a synonym for Stalinism.

We might be tempted to think of the long New Deal era between 1932 and 1968 as a glorious liberal time when the L-word went largely uncontested. But even before the rebellion and reaction of the 1960s, the word "liberal" had already taken on politically troublesome baggage. John F. Kennedy was alive to the L-word's downsides when he accepted the endorsement of the New York State Liberal Party in the 1960 election. Under New York's unusual election law, candidates can run on more than one ticket, which encourages the creation of ideological third parties—these days represented by a Conservative Party and the union-oriented Working Families Party. In Kennedy's era, most Democrats ran on both the Liberal Party's ticket and their own.

But Kennedy knew there were potential costs to embracing the L-word, as his speech accepting the Liberal nomination in September 1960 made clear:

> What do our opponents mean when they apply to us the label, "Liberal"? If by "Liberal" they mean, as they want people to believe, someone who is soft in his policies abroad, who is against local government, and who is unconcerned with the taxpayer's dollar, then the record of this party and its members demonstrate that we are not that kind of "Liberal." But if by a "Liberal" they mean someone who looks ahead and not behind, someone who welcomes new ideas without rigid reactions, someone who cares about the welfare of the people—their health, their housing, their schools, their jobs, their civil rights, and their civil liberties—someone who believes that we can break through the stalemate and suspicions that grip us in our policies abroad, if that is what they mean by a "Liberal," then I'm proud to say that I'm a "Liberal."[7]

Kennedy went on to extol liberalism "as it is an attitude of mind and heart, a faith in man's ability through the experiences of his reason and judgment to increase for himself and his fellow men the amount of Justice and freedom and brotherhood which all human life deserves." But his defensiveness is telling. No doubt with an eye on the electoral votes he needed to win from still-segregated southern states, Kennedy was careful to distance himself from attitudes liberalism's enemies had associated with the word—being "soft in his policies abroad," "against local government," and "unconcerned with the taxpayer's dollar." The echoes of what conservatives would say about democratic socialists during the Trump years are easy to hear. It was already hard enough to be a liberal in 1960. It would get tougher as the decade rolled forward because the sixties were a time not only of liberal triumph but also of liberal catastrophe.

The years between 1963 and 1966 saw the most extraordinary outpouring of liberal legislation since the New Deal. "In few periods in our history has reform been so concentrated and far-reaching," G. Calvin Mackenzie and Robert Weisbrot wrote in *The Liberal Hour*, their definitive account of the victories. America has experienced nothing like that liberal hour since. Until the 1966 midterm elections put an end to lopsided Democratic majorities in Congress and strengthened conservative voices in the congressional GOP, an era of consensus enabled a large and confident majority to embrace national action expanding opportunities and alleviating needless suffering. The Civil Rights and Voting Rights Acts, Medicare, Medicaid, federal aid to education, new environmental laws, Head Start, the Job Corps, immigration reform—these are among the achievements of a period when the country still knew how to "reason together," the prophet Isaiah's call that Lyndon Johnson often invoked.[8]

But it was also a time of coming apart. At the moment of its greatest victories, liberalism found itself under assault from the right and from the left. The left referred derisively to "establishment liberals," the problem being that liberals had become the *establishment*. The right referred to "the liberal establishment," the problem being that the establishment had become *liberal*.[9]

The most durable attack came from the Republican right, with Barry Goldwater's takeover of the GOP and the onset of a new intellectual vitality on the right led by the writer and editor William F. Buckley Jr. But young dissenters on the left were increasingly impatient with conformity, bureaucracy, accommodation of corporate power, and a spiritual vacuum created by a prosperous, materialistic society. Inspired by the civil rights movement, revolutions for independence among the formerly colonized, and fear of nuclear annihilation, a New Left arose to challenge the comfortable liberalism that dominated Washington.

The Port Huron Statement, issued by the Students for a Democratic Society in 1962, eloquently (if at times grandiloquently) captured the frustrations bred by a consensus politics rooted in affluence:

> Beneath the reassuring tones of the politicians, beneath the common opinion that America will "muddle through," beneath the stagnation of those who have closed their minds to the future, is the pervading feeling that there simply are no alternatives, that our times have witnessed the exhaustion not only of Utopias, but of any new departures as well. Feeling the press of complexity upon the emptiness of life, people are fearful of the thought that at any moment things might be thrust out of control. They fear change itself, since change might smash whatever invisible framework seems to hold back chaos for them now. For most Americans, all crusades are suspect, threatening.[10]

In its impatience with status quo politics, this language may seem familiar to the rising young left of the Trump era.

The civil rights victories of 1964 and 1965 were accompanied by a growing sense of aggrievement in the black community—again, especially among younger activists—because legal and legislative victories were not accompanied by a transformation of conditions on the ground, particularly in northern cities. The word "ghetto," recalling historical restrictions on Jews that turned deadly in the Holocaust, came into wide use. The rise of the Black Power movement and the urban riots beginning in 1964 carried a double message. From the point of view of progressives, they reflected the breakup of the liberal consensus and the broad civil rights coalition. For fearful whites, they deepened the anxieties the Port Huron rebels described: Many in the middle and working classes really did see the new disorder that played out on their television screens as an effort to "smash whatever invisible framework seems to hold back chaos."

The Vietnam War definitively ended the Liberal Hour. It radicalized the New Left, split the Democratic Party and the liberal movement, and destroyed Lyndon Johnson's presidency.

Johnson decided not to seek reelection after he was nearly defeated in the New Hampshire primary by Minnesota senator Eugene McCarthy. McCarthy's New Hampshire showing brought Robert F. Kennedy into the contest, and there was a historically instructive divide between the Kennedy and McCarthy camps. It was defined less by ideology than by sensibility—a largely white, educated, reform-minded, and often suburban middle-class constituency that rallied to McCarthy; a multiracial, cross-class, urban-inflected constituency that embraced Kennedy. Variations on that divide would haunt progressive politics for the next half century.[11]

Briefly, Kennedy's gift for drawing votes from both African Americans and the white working class seemed to point to a new path forward for liberals. But the assassinations of Martin Luther King Jr. in April and Kennedy in June delivered decisive blows to what Todd Gitlin, an early New Left leader and premier chronicler of the sixties, mourned many years later as "the wild hope, or the impossible dream, that equality could, without much interruption, continue its onward march through the institutions of American life."[12]

Antagonisms from that campaign would live on for decades. There was what can be seen in retrospect as a tragic divide between anti-war Democrats and supporters of Vice President Hubert Humphrey. As a young Minneapolis mayor, Humphrey had called his party to the cause of civil rights at Harry Truman's 1948 convention. But in 1968, he was Johnson's man and a supporter of the Vietnam War until very late in the campaign. He won the Democratic nomination without contesting Kennedy and McCarthy in the primaries under a system that still gave party leaders (including machine bosses) control over the presidential nomination process. Their choice of Humphrey carried a stain of illegitimacy, a factor in his narrow defeat by Nixon.

Humphrey's nomination in defiance of the primary results led to a reform of Democratic Party rules, which had a ripple effect on the Republicans. From 1972 forward, the role of party warhorses in picking nominees would be sharply limited. The voters would choose through a much-democratized process. Senator George McGovern of South Dakota, the lead architect of those rules and an early foe of American intervention in Vietnam, emerged as the leading anti-war candidate.

McGovern won the nomination, but the party was badly splintered. Using a phrase initially coined by a Democrat, Republicans demonized McGovern as a radical who stood for "acid, amnesty and abortion," neatly parodying his liberal views on drugs, amnesty for draft resisters, and abortion rights. It was Nixon in 1972, not Reagan in 1980, who pioneered the new conservative coalition. He united traditionally Republican voters with most of those who had supported Alabama governor George Wallace's third-party segregationist campaign in 1968. And he made deep inroads in the white working class. The Reagan Democrats were Nixon Democrats first.[13]

Watergate seemed to give liberalism a reprieve. Democrats swept the 1974 midterm elections, picking up 49 seats in the House for what today seems an astonishing 291–144 majority over the Republicans. Equally striking was the party's 16.8 percent popular vote lead. The Class of 1974 was a vast assemblage: 91 new members, all but 16 of them Democrats, many of whom had been inspired by the campaigns of Kennedy, McCarthy, or McGovern.[14]

The Democrats' sweep presaged Jimmy Carter's 1976 victory, but as longtime Capitol Hill aide John Lawrence argued in *The*

Class of '74, it also "created an unwarranted confidence in the sustainability of Democratic hegemony, which contributed to the failure to recognize the growing GOP threat." It took only six years for the Democratic coalition to fall apart—again.[15]

In light of Carter's overwhelming defeat in 1980, it's easy to forget that his victory presented Democrats with a historic opportunity. His status as the first southern president since Woodrow Wilson gave him credibility with the southern whites who had been fleeing the party since Goldwater, yet he embraced civil rights and had support from many African American leaders. As a result, he was the only Democrat since 1944 to achieve a virtual sweep of the South. (Among the old Confederate states, only Virginia eluded him.) He built the alliance between African Americans and lower-income whites that was the coalitional dream of the early populists. Both Clinton and Obama would make inroads in the South, but their successes fell far short of Carter's.

As the political scientist William Schneider has observed, Carter defeated candidates representing each faction of the party, one by one: George Wallace, back in the Democratic fold, representing racial reaction on the party's right; Senator Henry M. "Scoop" Jackson, representing the Cold War liberals and neoconservatives; and Representative Morris K. Udall and former senator Fred Harris, representing left-liberalism—a more reform-minded variety in Udall's case, a more populist strain in Harris's. Briefly, Carter could boast of the ultimate achievement for a politician: He managed to be all things to all people. At one point in the campaign, a *New York Times*/CBS News poll found that Carter was regarded as a liberal by liberals, a moderate by moderates, and a conservative by conservatives.[16]

But it was not to last. Carter's lack of a firm base in any part of the party meant that loyalty to him across the party was thin. In 1980, Senator Edward M. Kennedy challenged him from the left in the Democratic primaries. While Carter prevailed, many of

Kennedy's working-class supporters became Reagan Democrats. Carter's southern white evangelical supporters, goaded on by the newly founded Moral Majority, defected in large numbers. But in the end, facts on the ground were more important to Carter's defeat than factionalism or ideology. The Iranian hostage crisis and the stagflation of the late 1970s doomed Carter and elected Ronald Reagan.

Reagan's impact was nearly as profound on the Democrats as on the Republicans.

It was during the Reagan years that the word "liberal" was definitively demonized, and Reagan's political revolution was accompanied by what was both an intellectual and a moral revolution. Sluggish growth and inflation at the end of the Carter years discredited Keynesian economics and the welfare state in much the same way that the Great Depression had discredited unregulated capitalism. Reagan and conservative intellectuals led a counterrevolution. Radically pro-market economics from the pre-Depression Era came back into vogue. Reagan supporters proudly wore Calvin Coolidge ties and pronounced the New Deal a collection of old, irrelevant nostrums.[17]

The new morality of the period linked traditional values— marriage, family, conservative theology, and an individualism rooted in hard work—with a glorification of entrepreneurs and investors. The most comprehensive and eloquent expression of this worldview was George Gilder's *Wealth and Poverty*, published the month Reagan took office.

If the 1930s left had lifted up the worker as the hero of economic development, Gilder saw the entrepreneur as society's moral exemplar. In the year that would usher in what others would see as "the decade of greed," Gilder wrote, counterintuitively: "Capitalism begins with giving. Not from greed, avarice, or even self-love can one expect the rewards of commerce, but from a spirit closely akin to altruism, a regard for the needs of others, a benevolent, outgoing and courageous temper of mind." Suddenly, those who made great fortunes were saintly, other-regarding souls who took risks the timid avoided and who understood the future in ways the captives of conventional thinking could not.

In arguing that greed was not the point of market economics, Gilder linked faith in the capitalist future with faith in God Himself. "Our greatest and only resource is the miracle of human creativity in a relation of openness to the divine," he wrote. "It is a resource that above all we should deny neither to the poor, who can be the most open of all to the future, nor to the rich or excellent of individuals, who can lend leadership, imagination and wealth to the cause of beneficent change."

As Gilder told it, egalitarian liberals were the true enemies of the poor because they destroyed traditional institutions and preached the futility of individual effort. "The irony of this position," he wrote, "is that the influences that the egalitarians would vitiate—home, family, church and ethnic community—are the only influences that work." And it was "economic futility—not capitalist growth—that gives license to a culture of hedonism and sensuality."[18]

In fact, the pervasive eroticism of modern advertising and the "leave us alone" culture of libertarianism may have done as much to destroy "traditional values" as anything preached by the prophets of sexual freedom. Gilder was nevertheless an important figure for the right because he took the hard edge off arguments for laissez-faire and offered a moral basis (however flimsy it seemed to his critics on the left) for a return to the economics and values of the pre–New Deal era. As an electoral matter, he provided an intellectual and moral basis for the alliance between ardent capitalists and the equally fervent supporters of the religious right that proved decisive in the 1980s—and into our day.

The Italian Marxist thinker Antonio Gramsci argued that the

true power of a ruling group came not simply from ownership of the means of production but from its control over a society's ruling ideas and moral values. "Common sense," he wrote, "is not something rigid and stationary, but is in continuous transformation." In the 1980s, the right seemed to be paying far more attention to Gramsci than the liberal-left. Conservatives succeeded because they transformed the "common sense" of the country. "The terms that had dominated post–World War II intellectual life began to fracture," wrote the historian Daniel T. Rodgers. "One heard less about society, history and power and more about individuals, contingency and choice." When Margaret Thatcher declared that "there is no such thing as society," she captured the moment's ethos with near perfection.[19]

This meant that Democrats and large parts of the center-left (along with the British Labour Party) found themselves losing the initiative and reacting to the conservatives' new moral and intellectual hegemony.

The liberalism-is-so-yesterday response came in two stages. First came the "Atari Democrats." The phrase, Randall Rothenberg reported in his book *The Neoliberals*, was coined at a Washington Sunday brunch in January 1982 by Chris Matthews, then an aide to House Speaker Tip O'Neill and later a prominent television commentator. The innovative game company became, in Matthews's formulation, a stand-in for all that was new and technological. It was a time when the "neoliberal" moniker was worn with pride by Democrats who not only had high hopes for high tech but also understood themselves as having a properly up-to-date view of what liberalism needed to become. They would often criticize the power of "special interests" in the Democratic Party, but the interest that seemed to bother them most was organized labor. This was not surprising, Rothenberg wrote, because "the structure of the American union movement seems to be antithetical to the organization of postindustrial society."[20]

In their praise of tech, the neoliberals sounded a whole lot like Gilder, who saw scholars of the left neglecting "the most dynamic industries." And in fairness to both Gilder and the Atari Democrats, they were prophetic in understanding how revolutionary the tech future would be. Gilder's list of coming technologies that critics of capitalism's dynamism were missing is genuinely impressive in its foresight: "They ignore the surge in informatics and telecommunications and the myriad new energy technologies. They pay little attention to the revolutionary developments in microbiology, the breakthroughs in the production of glass products, the innovations in copying, printing and photography." In later life, Gilder became popular on the high-tech circuit as a kind of techno-utopian.[21]

Like Gilder, the neoliberals laid heavy stress not on the technology itself but on the entrepreneur who brought it to life. This, Rothenberg noted shrewdly, was part of their problem with unions. "If, as the neoliberals state, the future depends not on the technostructure but on the entrepreneur," he wrote, "it is difficult to see how organized labor, as it now exists, fits into their political economy." The unions returned the favor, despising the neoliberal turn from the start.

Gilder was prepared to let the market rip; the neoliberals were more ambivalent. They tended, as Rothenberg noted, to criticize traditional liberals for not appreciating risk and for favoring market-distorting government programs. But they also took conservatives to task for failing to recognize the need for a degree of security, adequate safety net programs, and enhanced job training. If the neoliberals never fully succeeded, their policy prescriptions would have an impact on Democrats for decades to come.

The hunger for the new among Democrats created a surge for Gary Hart's presidential candidacy in the 1984 Democratic primaries. In the New Hampshire primary, the Colorado senator trounced Walter Mondale, Jimmy Carter's vice president, who was well loved among liberals and respected across the party.

Hart made his name as an opponent of "old arrangements" and a champion of "new ideas." Mondale eventually came back to defeat him, only to lose 49 states to Reagan.[22]

Hart was the early front-runner for the 1988 nomination, but was knocked out of the race by a sex scandal that, in light of what came after, now seems rather tame.[23] When Massachusetts governor Michael Dukakis emerged as the Democratic nominee in 1988, the neoliberal phase ended, even though Dukakis, a practical budget hawk, had much in common with the Atari Democrats. "Few figures better personified the new orientation," the historian Lily Geismer argued, pointing out that by 1985, "Massachusetts had the highest percentage of service-sector workers and the highest average per capita income of any state in the country." But Dukakis was easily parodied as a "Massachusetts Liberal," given his opposition to the death penalty and his past as "a card-carrying member of the ACLU," a phrase George H. W. Bush never tired of using.[24]

Dukakis's defeat led to a renewed effort by centrist Democrats to transform the party, but this time, the renovators would speak with a southern accent and focus on culture, race, work, and crime. While the Atari Democrats reacted primarily to Reaganomics and the turn toward entrepreneurship and individual enterprise, the New Democrats of the Democratic Leadership Council, led by an Arkansas governor named Bill Clinton, were reacting more to Reagan's cultural turn and his emphasis on "family, work, neighborhood." There was certainly overlap with the neoliberals. The New Democrats stressed their support for markets, capitalism, and entrepreneurship, too, and critics of the DLC would joke that the organization's initials stood for "Democratic Leisure Class." But the DLC's stress was on winning back the white working-class voters, north and south, whom Democrats had lost in the Nixon and Reagan years.[25]

Thus, the DLC's slogan: "Opportunity, Responsibility, Community." Equality was defined in terms of "opportunity, not results," as the organization's partisans would say again and again. Opportunity, in turn, was to be seized through responsible behavior, although the DLC would often argue that it was speaking of the need for responsible corporate behavior as well. "Community" had a double purpose: as an answer to the radical individualism of the right, but also as a signal that progressives, too, accepted the importance of the traditional solidaristic institutions—"home, family, church and ethnic community"—that Gilder had lauded.[26]

Specific policies addressed the concerns of the fleeing Nixon-Reagan Democrats. Clinton called for welfare reform that emphasized work, responding to the racially charged conservative argument that welfare promoted sloth. A persistently tough message on crime culminated in the 1993 crime bill. (In Britain, Tony Blair's ideologically balanced formulation cast New Labour as "tough on crime, tough on the causes of crime.") Clinton's open support for the death penalty, including his decision to fly back to Arkansas during the campaign to oversee the execution of a man of limited mental ability, sent the signal that he was no Michael Dukakis.

Yet despite the pride New Democrats took in his campaign, Clinton was a protean figure who had historic ties to the liberal wing of the party (he had been a young McGovern organizer in 1972) and a populist streak. Clinton understood that he had to hold on to traditional Democrats even as he sought to augment the party's vote. He thus attacked "the forces of greed" and argued that government had been "hijacked by privileged, private interests." He said Bush had "raised taxes on the people driving pickup trucks, and lowered taxes on people riding in limousines." He insisted that "American companies must act like American companies again, exporting products, not jobs."[27]

Once in office, Clinton made good on his pledges to raise taxes on the wealthy, establish family leave laws, and expand access to college. In so doing, he not only closed the deficit but created surpluses in the fiscal years 1998 to 2001. This had not happened since 1969 and has not happened since. He fought for but failed to enact a universal health plan—a far more comprehensive proposal than Obama would offer that reflected an approach that was more traditionally liberal than "Atari." Economic growth averaged 4 percent annually during the Clinton years, and a record 22.7 million jobs were created while he was in office. While incomes at the top continued to rise, it was also a time when growth reached down the ladders of class and race. By 2000, 56 percent of African American households had incomes of $35,000 or more, compared with just 26 percent in 1969. Nearly 14 percent of African American households had incomes of over $100,000, compared with just 3 percent in 1967.[28]

The 1990s are thus remembered broadly as a decade of contentment. When Hillary Clinton ran for president in both 2008 and 2016, she would regularly ask of her husband's legacy, "What didn't you like, the peace or the prosperity?"[29]

The New Democrats had hoped to reduce ideology's role in American politics, depolarize the country, and anchor a new Democratic majority in the broad political center. But exactly the opposite happened during the Clinton years. Despite Clinton's reelection in 1996, it was not a time of either Democratic or progressive consolidation. On the contrary, in 1994, Republicans took control of the House of Representatives for the first time in 40 years and also won the Senate, which they had lost in 1986. The House Republicans were led by Newt Gingrich, the most partisan Speaker of the postwar period. Republicans would control Congress for the rest of Clinton's term, as well as governorships in states critical to Democratic Electoral College majorities: Illinois, Wisconsin, Michigan, and Pennsylvania.[30]

Republicans profited from the failure of the economy to recover robustly until later in Clinton's term, from the collapse of the health reform effort, from aggressive campaigning by the gun lobby, and from a dispirited Democratic base. Clinton's push for

the North American Free Trade Agreement, against the wishes
of much of his own party and in the face of vociferous opposition
from the labor movement, contributed to disillusionment and
disengagement among the party's loyalists.[31]

As important, the 1994 election marked a consolidation of
conservative voters into the Republican Party. This was especially
true in the South. Districts that for decades had voted for Republican presidential candidates while sending moderate or, in many
cases, conservative Democrats to Congress rationalized their
political behavior by switching to the GOP in House races as
well. In 1994, "Republicans won every open Congressional seat
in districts that had a Republican presidential majority in 1988
and 1992," wrote Stanley Greenberg, Clinton's 1992 pollster, in
1995. "They won only 35 percent of open seats where there had
been no Republican majority." Democratic incumbents in districts that had voted Republican for president "were three times
as likely to lose" as Democrats in other seats. Greenberg noted
that "particularly in the South, an energized conservative bloc
rebelled against the direction of Democratic politics. . . . Strong
supporters of the Clinton agenda in the South faced three times
as much erosion as weak supporters did."

Yet Greenberg foresaw the strategy that would allow Clinton to come back two years later. While Democrats were "ideologically diverse," 70 percent of Republicans were self-identified
conservatives. This, he said, put Clinton "in a position to benefit from the reaction to a reign of conservative orthodoxy." He
added: "The challenge for Democrats is *how to rally the liberals
and moderate center and create an energy that erodes the conservative bloc*" (emphasis added). Remember, Greenberg was writing in 1995. Although liberals loom larger in the electorate now
than they did in the Clinton years, his words are a fair description of the strategy Democrats would pursue successfully in the
2018 House races.[32]

The Clinton years saw the beginning of several trends that

would sharpen in 2016. Greenberg pointed to a 12-point increase in conservative identification among white voters with high school educations, and a 13-point shift to conservatism among white men without college degrees. Older voters also became markedly more conservative in this period. In a sense, 1994 was a prequel to the breakthroughs Trump would make to secure his 2016 Electoral College victory.

Clinton's 1996 reelection pointed to a countertrend that would help Democrats: He presided over a successful Democratic push in suburbs across the Northeast, the Midwest, and on the West Coast. If 1994 foreshadowed where Trump would be strong, Clinton's reelection in 1996 presaged the broad suburban gains Democrats would make in 2018 House races. The flip side of the realignment of southern conservatives to the GOP was a slow but steady counter-realignment of liberal and moderate Republicans to the Democrats outside the South, particularly in the Northeast and on the West Coast.

Washington Post political reporter Dan Balz was one of the first analysts to spot what would be a two-decade-long transformation. In suburban Detroit, he noted, Clinton was the first Democrat to carry McComb County since 1968 and the first to carry nearby Oakland County since 1964. "The same pattern held true throughout the states that in past elections were considered the prized battlegrounds of presidential elections," Balz wrote. Among Clinton's suburban breakthroughs: Bergen and Monmouth counties in New Jersey, and Lake County, east of Cleveland. All three had supported George H. W. Bush in both 1988 and 1992. Clinton, as Balz noted, also "expanded his victory margins of four years [earlier] in three counties surrounding Philadelphia: Montgomery, Bucks and Delaware. Bush carried all three in 1988." All three counties were the sites of important Democratic breakthroughs in 2018.[33]

Any judgments about the Clinton political project are shadowed by the Monica Lewinsky scandal and the House impeachment vote at the end of 1998. Clinton survived, and over the short term, the GOP's impeachment threat hurt the party in a country broadly satisfied with Clinton's tenure and uneasy about turning a president's sexual behavior into a reason for ousting him from office. Republicans suffered unexpected losses in the 1998 midterm elections, driving Gingrich from power.

But over the longer run, the bitterness of the controversy hobbled the 2000 campaign of Clinton's vice president, Al Gore. George W. Bush capitalized on the quiet backlash against Clinton without making it a central issue. (He learned from the electoral failure of the House Republicans' head-on approach.) He would simply repeat, over and over, a promise to "restore honor and dignity to the White House."[34]

Gore never let go of his rage over the impossible position Clinton left him in. To send a strong message that voters should not judge him by Clinton's very personal failures, the man who had been Clinton's loyal partner picked one of the harshest critics of the president's sexual transgressions as his running mate. Voters knew exactly what Joe Lieberman's presence on the ticket meant.

More revealing for the longer run, Gore was conflicted about whether to run on Clinton's record—prosperity was near its peak in 2000—or to wage a more populist campaign by way of appealing to voters still left out of the great boom. This argument would arise again during Obama's term. It spoke to differences between progressivism's center and left—between Democratic left-populists and the party's supporters in business, on Wall Street and in the Silicon Valley.

In his acceptance speech at the Democratic National Convention, Gore tried to split the difference. He declared that "millions of Americans will live better lives for a long time to come because of the job that's been done by President Bill Clinton." To applause, Gore spoke of "the biggest surpluses, the highest home ownership ever, the lowest inflation in a generation" and, of course, those "22 million good new jobs" and "higher family incomes."

But then Gore pivoted. "Now we turn the page and write a new chapter," he said, signaling that he was not really running on Clinton's record. He continued:

> This election is not an award for past performance. I am not asking you to vote for me on the basis of the economy we have. Tonight, I ask for your support on the basis of the better, fairer, more prosperous America we can build together. Together, let's make sure that our prosperity enriches not just the few, but all working families.

He went on to assail "powerful forces and powerful interests" standing in the way of working families, "the skyrocketing costs of prescription drugs," "big drug companies [that] run up record profits," "crumbling schools," "bean-counters at HMOs," and "Big tobacco, big oil, the big polluters."[35]

At the time, journalists understandably made much of Gore's complicated personal dance with Clinton. But Gore's speech also reflected ongoing conflicts within the broader Democratic and center-left coalition. Even after the undeniable success of Clinton's economic policies in balancing the budget and spurring growth and job creation, many on the left were still restive over the administration's free trade policies, the embrace of globalization, and the deregulation of financial markets.

As a political matter, Gore's advisers were concerned that the Green Party candidacy of consumer advocate Ralph Nader would draw votes away from Gore on the left, and their fears proved well placed. Nader's vote far exceeded Bush's ultimate margin in New Hampshire and his disputed lead in Florida. Either state would have given Gore an Electoral College majority— taking the election out of the hands of five conservative Supreme

Court justices, who, in the unprincipled *Bush v. Gore* decision, handed George W. Bush the presidency.

The implicit argument with Clintonism, reflected in Gore's populist turn, became more explicit over time—and dramatically so after the economic meltdown in 2008 and the rise of Occupy Wall Street and the Sanders movement. There was always a tension in Clintonism between its populist side and its centrist side, between Clinton's support for free trade and deregulation and his embrace of redistributive measures, including more progressive taxes and large increases in the Earned Income Tax Credit for the working poor. As long as the economy was soaring, a majority of Americans were quite content with the Clinton blend. As late as 2012, when Clinton's systematic defense of Barack Obama's record was the most effective speech at the Democratic National Convention, the man from Hope and his time in office remained broadly popular with Democrats. But by 2016, and especially after Trump's victory, Third Way politics was judged more and more by its failure to reverse the long rise of inequality and its accommodation of conservative economic policies.[36]

The fallout from the Clinton and Obama years defines and explains much of the turmoil on the broad center-left and is the focus of chapter 5. For now, it is important to underscore that the left has always displayed impatience with administrations that govern in the name of progressivism but take pragmatic (or, as their critics often see them, opportunistic) turns driven by practical necessity, electoral concerns, the need for compromise, or failures of nerve.

In the most successful reform periods, the left found ways of bringing pressure to bear on mainstream liberal leaders without undercutting them. This was especially true during the New Deal and in the years leading up to the civil rights victories. Left, labor, and liberal groups kept one foot inside the establishment and one foot outside.

The crisis of the 1960s led to a breakdown of this arrangement. It's plausible in retrospect to criticize the New Left and parts of the anti-war movement for failing to realize that a successful left needs a healthy liberal establishment. It's axiomatic that mainstream liberals in power are far more likely than a conservative regime to respond to pressure from the left.

It's also true that many of the differences between the moderate and more adventurous wings of the progressive movement are more of degree than of kind. Both support policies that would move the country in an egalitarian direction. The left would be more aggressive, more inclined to disrupt existing structures of power, less fearful of reaction. The proper test for whether a partnership between the left and moderates is fruitful lies in whether an early round of modest reform can lead to more fundamental change down the road.

Yet the left's opposition to the liberal establishment in the 1960s was not simply a matter of temperament or youthful impatience. A very specific issue, the Vietnam War, blew up the liberal consensus. And on the war, the left was right. The Vietnam intervention ended in failure—a failure that led to as many as 2 million deaths, among them 58,318 American service members. The cultural changes of the 1960s also put liberalism under pressure and are a source of moral and intellectual strife to this day. But do we regret the era's push for racial and gender equality or the advancement of the rights of LGBTQ people that grew out of new sexual freedoms? The struggles that undercut liberalism at the time also transformed it for the better over the longer run.[37]

The New Deal era also taught an underappreciated lesson: that progressives need to be more attentive to how structural changes can redistribute power. The Wagner Act is perhaps the best example of legislation that not only improved the economic bargaining power of American workers but also enhanced their political power. The Voting Rights Act had a similar effect for African Americans.

Contrast these advances with the setbacks of recent years. The decline of the union movement—the product of both economic change, including the decline of manufacturing work, and active measures taken against unions by the political right—has sharply shifted power away from working people. A conservative Supreme Court decision undercutting the Voting Rights Act and the voter suppression laws this enabled are rolling back gains that African Americans have made; it is a double whammy, because once these changes happen, the ability of African Americans to fight them at the ballot box is impaired. When these steps are considered in tandem with the *Citizens United* decision empowering big money in politics, it becomes clear that the Court is waging a campaign to limit rather than expand democracy's reach. And the pace of the Court's anti-democratic interventions is only likely to quicken with the addition of two Trump appointees. Its decision in the *Rucho* case in June 2019 to let gerrymanders plainly rooted in race and partisanship stand was a sign of things to come.[38]

Going forward, both progressives and moderates must attend to the importance of fostering democratizing changes in the structure of political power even as they prepare themselves for battles over the judiciary itself. Expanding the Court has been out of favor since FDR's failed attempt to do so in the 1930s. But in the wake of the refusal of Senate Republicans even to give a hearing to Merrick Garland, President Obama's nominee, what might once have been seen as "court packing" can now be viewed simply as redressing an earlier abuse of power.[39]

The progressive century that began in 1900 demonstrated the value of boldness and vision, but also the importance of patience, persistence, and hope. In a democracy, there are no final victories—or defeats. Programs and breakthroughs for new rights have to be defended. Reconstruction empowered African Americans in the South, and Jim Crow took those rights away. Only the Second Reconstruction of the 1960s restored them— and particularly when it comes to access to the ballot, they are under attack again.

But defeats can also be preludes to later victories if advocates of change continue to build support for reform. This is the significance of 1920s progressives like LaGuardia and Nebraska's Senator George Norris. Fighting for public power on the Tennessee River, Norris lost to vetoes from Coolidge and Herbert Hoover, but he triumphed in the 1930s with the creation of the Tennessee Valley Authority under Franklin Roosevelt.

Two weak civil rights bills passed in the 1950s fell far short of the civil rights movement's goals, yet they prepared the way for the large breakthroughs of the 1960s. Medicare was defeated in 1962 before it became law in 1965. In 2019, comprehensive political reforms—for broad access to the ballot, public financing to promote small political contributions, and tougher ethics laws— passed by the House as HR 1 with virtually no chance of enactment in the Senate. But the bill's supporters understood that theirs was only the beginning of a long effort that they hoped would lead to change in the 2020s. All of HR 1's proposals would democratize the political system structurally, from protecting and expanding the right to vote to challenging the power of big money.

It is not surprising that the political right is eager to roll back so many of the advances progressives made in the twentieth century. Yet as the examples of Medicare and Social Security show, some reforms become irreversible. Obamacare is showing signs of having similar staying power. Despite efforts by the Trump administration to curb environmental and economic regulations, the abolition of the Environmental Protection Agency, the Federal Trade Commission, the Food and Drug Administration, and comparable agencies is unthinkable. In a time of reaction, it's important to recognize the durability of so many progressive achievements.

Yet this story is often read differently by progressivism's center and its left. The moderate interpretation is primarily one of success brought about by broad coalitions and incremental change. Progressives are often inclined to speak of surrender by the center-left to conservative narratives and assumptions, beginning in the Carter years but accelerating in the 1980s and reaching a culmination in the accommodations of the Clinton and even Obama years. Moderates see the left as unwilling to acknowledge genuine constraints and the need to adjust to strong currents of opinion. The left sees moderates as too timid to change the direction of popular opinion and too eager to accommodate political and economic structures tilted against workers, people of color, and women.

Each version of the story contains truth. Each is incomplete. Can they be harmonized to enhance the possibility of progressive change?

In fact, this process has already begun. One of the most surprising developments in American politics, the resurgence of democratic socialism, is part of the larger collapse of the Reagan-era consensus. This opens possibilities not only for progressives but also for moderates who are coming to terms with the failures of the long Reagan era. They have an opportunity to move away from political approaches that were primarily reactive and defensive. The new socialism can be seen primarily as a threat to the center-left's electoral prospects, or as a sign of a broadening of a political conversation long hemmed in by conservative assumptions. Which is it?

FOUR

ARE THE SOCIALISTS COMING?

*The Collapse of the Reagan Consensus
and the Urgency of Economic Renewal*

IF REPUBLICANS HAD THEIR WAY, THEY WOULD RUN AGAINST Socialists, not Democrats.

Trump certainly felt that way. "We are alarmed by new calls to adopt socialism in our country," Trump declared in his 2019 State of the Union address. "America was founded on liberty and independence—not government coercion, domination, and control. We are born free, and we will stay free. Tonight, we renew our resolve that America will never be a socialist country."[1]

You expected Lee Greenwood to pop onto the podium and break into "I'm Proud to Be an American," his Reagan-era hit. Trump cast himself as Horatius at the bridge standing against the Red Menace.

Ronna McDaniel, the chair of the Republican National Committee, later made clear that this was all about 2020 politics, and that the entire GOP would make opposition to socialism its battle cry. "Whichever Democrat wins the nomination will have to own their party's socialist agenda," she told the *New York Times*' Jeremy Peters in April 2019. "That's a debate that President Trump is eager to have and knows he can win."[2] When threatened with impeachment in late 2019, Trump was, indeed, eager to turn to attacks on "socialists" and "radicals."

Trump's approach did not come from nowhere. He was drawing on an old conservative tactic of casting any and all measures to enhance social welfare or regulate corporate power as a form of socialism, creeping or otherwise.

During the New Deal, the Liberty League and other conservative business groups saw the dark hand of the socialistic planner or, worse, Moscow itself behind FDR's alphabet agencies and relief schemes. Al Smith, Roosevelt's erstwhile friend and ally, sounded the alarm in a League-sponsored speech: "There can be only one Capital—Washington or Moscow. . . . There can be only one flag, the Stars and Stripes, or the red flag of the godless union of the Soviet. There can be only one national anthem, the Star Spangled Banner or the Internationale."[3]

As Ian Millhiser pointed out on the *ThinkProgress* blog, the attack by the man Roosevelt had once hailed as "the Happy Warrior" carried a certain irony. When Smith was the Democratic nominee against Herbert Hoover in 1928, Hoover had accused Smith of favoring "State Socialism" and of abandoning "the tenets of his own party" in favor of "paternalistic and socialistic doctrines."[4]

Seeing socialism in the workings of Democratic administrations in the 1960s was a habit of Ronald Reagan's. His speech on behalf of Barry Goldwater's presidential candidacy in 1964 made the Gipper a hero to conservative activists, his first big step on the road to the presidency. It was called "A Time for Choosing," and Reagan defined the choice dramatically, quoting Norman Thomas—"six-times candidate for President on the Socialist Party ticket," Reagan explained helpfully—as having complained, "If Barry Goldwater became president, he would stop the advance of socialism in the United States." Reagan's next line would long be remembered among conservative loyalists: "I think that's exactly what he will do."

Demonstrating how conservatives could hold a rather elastic view of socialism's meaning, Reagan argued that "it doesn't require expropriation or confiscation of private property or business to impose socialism on a people . . . if the government holds the power of life and death over that business or property." The threat was clear: "Our natural, unalienable rights are now considered to be a dispensation of government, and freedom has never been so fragile, so close to slipping from our grasp as it is at this moment."[5]

By this definition, almost anything government required business to do was a form of socialism that carried the risk of confiscation—which, of course, was the entire point of Reagan's polemic. This approach would define the tone for conservative anti-government politics for the next half century. Fortunately for conservatives, the country would get through the fragile moment Reagan described and preserve its freedom long enough to send him to the White House 16 years later.

And it's easily forgotten that Bill Clinton, the man conservatives now often cite as a model of pro-capitalist moderation, did not escape being painted dark pink.

It was a sign that we will be hearing a lot about socialism from the right that *National Review*, the flagship magazine of American conservatism, devoted its June 3, 2019, number to an "Against Socialism" special issue. The man conservatives had once tried to impeach won the highest form of conservative praise from the magazine's editor, Rich Lowry. "Bill Clinton," he wrote, "operated within the broad economic consensus established by Ronald Reagan." A few months earlier, the conservative writer David French had taken to the magazine's pages to offer the remarkably expansive claim that Clinton's "social and economic policies . . . would make him right-leaning even within the modern *Republican* party."[6]

Liberal writer Jonathan Chait fired back at the conservatives' historical revisionism. Bill Clinton, he noted, "raised taxes on the rich, increased the Earned Income Tax Credit, raised the minimum wage, and attempted to pass universal health care, all of which are heretical positions within the GOP and were hysterically labeled as socialism by the GOP at the time Clinton did all these things." No, Clinton would not be "right-leaning" in the modern Republican Party.[7]

Finally, who can forget the many denunciations of Barack Obama as a socialist and how often his market-oriented health plan was labeled "socialized medicine." To this day, many conservatives hold tight to this idea. Obama, wrote *Wall Street Journal* columnist Daniel Henninger in February 2019, "held the door open for the socialists with his endless speeches about 'the wealthiest' and 'the 1%.' Arguably Mr. Obama was our first Pop Marxist president, obsessed with class issues."[8]

But if Trump was operating within conservatism's long tradition of seeing socialism in everything liberals undertook, he was right about one thing: "socialism" is no longer a dirty word for a large section of the Democratic Party. Running proudly as a democratic socialist, Bernie Sanders won 13.2 million votes in the 2016 Democratic primaries. As we've seen, another democratic socialist, Alexandria Ocasio-Cortez, became the social media star of the Democrats' Class of 2018 and, as only a first-term member of Congress, a dominant voice on the left who tangled frequently with the party's leadership.[9]

Nor was the growing popularity of socialism merely a fad prompted by the success of two savvy political figures. The economic catastrophe that followed the collapse of the financial markets in 2008 began a slow unraveling of the prestige and moral authority that capitalism had enjoyed since the 1980s. This has made attacks on socialism far less effective than they used to be.

During the Cold War, the Union of Soviet *Socialist* Republics offered a powerful example of the oppression that state control of all of the means of production could unleash. But the Soviet Union has been dead for nearly three decades. China is communist on paper but a wildly unequal crony capitalist dictatorship in practice. Young Americans especially are far more likely to associate "socialism" with generous social insurance states than with jackboots and gulags. Sweden, Norway, and Denmark are not frightening places.[10]

The problem with "socialism," as we'll see throughout this chapter, is that it has many meanings—and can be invested by its critics with many more. As recently as the early 1950s, democratic socialism really did involve direct government takeovers of major industries. The Labour government elected in Britain in 1945 was proud of its nationalization policies, and the German Social Democrats were committed to a broadly Marxist understanding of the economy until the SPD's 1959 Bad Godesberg Program redefined it from being a "party of the working class" to a "party of the people." And lest socialism be seen as purely a foreign idea, consider all the forms of "socialism" that exist in the United States right now. Medicare and Social Security can fairly be seen as socialist by definition. So are our public schools, universities, and community colleges, our water supplies and sewers, and our mass transit systems. Municipally owned and built sports stadiums are forms of socialism, of a corporate sort. North Dakota still has a state-owned bank, created in 1919, a time when agrarian populism and socialism overlapped.

But since the 1960s—and, in many cases, much earlier than that—virtually all European parties calling themselves socialist have largely abandoned state ownership as a goal, focusing on greater social and economic equality as their central mission. They are not socialist but social democratic, accepting a large role for the market (i.e., capitalism), tempered by energetic government regulation, a large social insurance state and, in most cases, a strong labor movement that bolsters the rights of wage and salary earners. The line between social democracy and progressive forms of capitalism is thin to the point of vanishing.

It may be a sign of socialism's growing popularity that many conservatives who once saw Scandinavian economies as "sclerotic" now want to claim them as vibrant exemplars of capitalism. This is fine, said Harold Meyerson, the (as it happens) socialist writer, as long as these newfound friends of social democracy on the right are willing to buy the whole package. "Yes, the Nordic nations are capitalist social democracies," he wrote, "but the reason they are capitalist is that their Social Democratic parties created unprecedented levels of worker power, social welfare and income equality as far back as the 1930s, and had the power to maintain those levels to this very day."[11]

Polling in the United States makes very clear how much times have changed. The 2018 PRRI American Values Survey offered respondents two definitions of socialism. One described it as "a system of government that provides citizens with health insurance, retirement support and access to free higher education," essentially a description of social democracy. The other was the full Soviet dose: "a system where the government controls key parts of the economy, such as utilities, transportation and communications industries."

You might say that socialism is winning the branding war: 54 percent said socialism was about those public benefits, while 43 percent picked the version that stressed government domination. Americans ages 18 to 29, for whom Cold War memories are dim to nonexistent, were even more inclined to define socialism as social democracy: 58 percent of them picked the soft option, 38 percent the hard one.

Gallup has been polling on socialism for a long time. In a 1949 survey, a plurality of 34 percent of Americans saw socialism as meaning government ownership or control. (Since more than a third of those surveyed had no opinion at all on the subject back then, this finding meant that more than half of those who did have a view saw socialism as entailing government ownership.) By 2018, the proportion seeing socialism as synonymous with government ownership or control had been cut in half, to 17 percent, and just over a fifth of those who held an opinion.[12]

With socialism now viewed by a majority as synonymous with a strong social safety net, not as a system of centralized state power, it's not surprising that its standing has improved, especially among Democrats. Thus, a 2018 Gallup poll found that more Democrats held a positive view of socialism (57 percent) than of capitalism (47 percent). Republicans were in another place altogether: 71 percent viewed capitalism favorably; only 16 percent had a positive view of socialism. There were also enormous generational differences. Among Americans under 30, 51 percent viewed socialism favorably; among those aged 50 to 64, only 30 percent did, a figure that dropped to 28 percent among Americans 65 and older. Stronger Cold War memories meant greater hostility to socialism.

Still, attacking socialism was a reasonable strategic bet for Trump and his party. His attacks not only rally Republicans but also speak to a majority of Americans. Overall, Gallup found, 56 percent of Americans viewed capitalism favorably while only 37 percent rated socialism positively. It's no wonder that Democrats elected from swing districts in 2018 were wary of the S-word. "I have a confession to make," Representative Max Rose, a Staten Island Democrat who won in a heavily Republican district, told a group of constituents packed into a church in the spring of 2019. "I'm not a socialist." Similarly, Florida Representative Stephanie Murphy described herself as a "proud capitalist" and said she was "offended by this whole conversation about socialism."[13]

If the Sanders campaign was the proximate cause of socialism's new popularity in other parts of the party, it inspired grassroots enthusiasm because a substantial and increasingly impatient young left was already there to be rallied. The Great Recession was the formative experience for the young adults who form the political base of the new socialist outlook. The younger working class entered a job market that provided far fewer stable opportunities than their parents had enjoyed. Facing falling revenues, many state governments slashed public support for higher education, forcing public colleges and universities to raise tuition sharply. Students had to abandon college hopes or take out larger loans that would consume a substantial portion of their future incomes. They became increasingly open to the idea that only transformational systemic change could get the job done, and many saw socialism as the available alternative to the failed model of contemporary capitalism.

Socialism's champions were disillusioned by what they saw as betrayals by New Democrats and neoliberals, seeing recent Democratic history as one long saga of kicking away opportunities for more fundamental change. "Our current politics don't seem to offer much of a future at all," wrote Bhaskar Sunkara, the editor of the popular left-wing magazine *Jacobin*, in his thoughtful and often lively 2019 book *The Socialist Manifesto*. "The choice before us appears to be between, on the one hand, a technocratic neoliberalism that embraces the rhetoric of social inclusion but not equality, and, on the other, a right-wing populism channeling anger into the worst directions."[14]

But what does "socialism" really mean for the politicians who embraced the word? Ocasio-Cortez is inclined to define socialism in relationship to capitalist countries with generous social insurance programs. "So when millennials talk about concepts like democratic socialism, we're not talking about these kinds of Red Scare boogeymen," she told Nisha Stickles and Barbara Corbellini Duarte of *Business Insider*. "We're talking about countries and systems that already exist that have already been proven to be successful in the modern world. . . . We're talking about single-payer health care that has already been successful in many different models."[15]

Hers is a labor-oriented creed, and she offered her own version of the labor theory of value. "At the end of the day, as workers, and as people in society, we're the ones creating wealth, not a corporate CEO," she said. "It is not a CEO that is actually creating billions of dollars a year, it is the millions of workers in this country . . . creating billions of dollars in economic productivity every year, and our system should reflect that."[16]

Sanders's definition similarly made him far more a reform-minded social democrat shaving off capitalism's rough edges than a revolutionary. In a 2015 speech at Georgetown University, he explicitly disowned radical interventions by the state:

> I don't believe government should own the means of production, but I do believe that the middle class and the working families who produce the wealth of America deserve a fair deal. I believe in private companies that thrive and invest and grow in America instead of shipping jobs and profits overseas. I believe that most Americans can pay lower taxes—if hedge fund managers who make billions manipulating the marketplace finally pay the taxes they should. . . . I don't believe in some foreign "ism," but I believe deeply in American idealism.[17]

It was solid, progressive stuff, but nothing outside the range of traditional New Deal liberalism. In fact, a large chunk of Sanders's speech was in praise of New Dealism itself.

For his June 2019 speech on democratic socialism—his definitional forays, it seemed, had become quadrennial events—Sanders traveled across town to George Washington University, where he was, again, more New Dealer than collectivist. He quoted FDR's attack on "government by organized money," which Roosevelt saw as being "just as dangerous as government by organized mob." Sanders clearly identified with his hero's pride in the opposition he inspired from the megarich of an earlier era, citing one of Roosevelt's most famous and most insouciant lines:

"They are unanimous in their hate for me—and I welcome their hatred." Once again, democratic socialism became New Dealism as Sanders promised to "take up the unfinished business of the New Deal and carry it to completion."[18]

Sunkara, for one, acknowledged that Sanders's program was social democratic, not socialist, but argued that, like Jeremy Corbyn in Britain, he was engaged in "class-struggle social democracy" involving "confrontation with elites" and was using electoral campaigns as a way of "generating working class strength." As a committed socialist, Sunkara sees social democracy as a way station on the path to socialism. Because "the social democratic compromise is inherently unstable," he argued, "the route to a more radical socialism will come from the crisis of social democracy our very success initiates."[19]

Of course, Sunkara is at the left end of the Sanders movement. Most progressives, while accepting that social democracy is under new pressures in a globalized economy, do not see "the social democratic compromise" as "inherently unstable." They are more likely to look back, as Sanders does, to the New Deal's success in demonstrating that expanding social justice and widening the distribution of income and wealth are essential to capitalism's health.

Sanders has already succeeded in getting the idea of socialism back on the mainstream political agenda to an extent not seen since Eugene V. Debs won 6 percent of the presidential vote on the Socialist Party ticket in 1912—a genuine achievement. A related breakthrough was reminding Americans that socialism is a genuine part of the American political tradition, a story well told by John Nichols of *The Nation* in his 2015 book *The "S" Word*. As the historian Christopher Lasch noted, the year Debs ran, Socialists held 1,200 offices in 340 American cities, their ranks including 79 mayors.[20]

Today's socialists may do for progressives what an earlier generation of socialists did in the New Deal years—widening the ambit of what constitute acceptable ideas. "The New Deal was not 'socialist,'" wrote the political scientist Mason Williams. "But to end the story there is to miss the role of socialists in crafting the intellectual world within which the New Deal unfolded. Look not at what socialism was, but at what socialists did, and one sees that the New Deal's progressive achievements do bear a significant historical relationship to reform socialism." (Williams also quoted the cheeky observation of New Deal lawyer Jerome Frank: "We socialists are trying to save capitalism, and the damned capitalists won't let us.")

Williams's conclusion about the relationship of this history to our time is instructive:

> As in the Progressive era, today's socialists have no monopoly on policy ideas like Medicare for All. But they are on the ascent because their systematic critique of today's market society allows them to frame visible, easy-to-understand policies that speak in a direct and powerful way to the lived experiences of contemporary American life, particularly for young people: stagnant wages, insecurity, exploitation, precarity, runaway inequality, indebtedness, the soaring cost of essentials like housing and health care. . . . The example of the New Deal might serve as a reminder of the value that liberalism can draw from schools of social and political thought that cast a more critical eye on American capitalism and the political practices bound up with it.[21]

Republicans will certainly use the socialist menace to try to rally swing voters (and to hold on to conservatives disillusioned by Trumpism by making it a lesser evil). But it's unlikely that the red or pink specter will tear Democrats apart. "That trick has been tried so many times that I think it is losing all meaning," said South Bend mayor Pete Buttigieg, the phenom of the early 2020 Democratic presidential race.[22]

Buttigieg summed up the state of the debate in one short sentence. "The reason we're having this argument over socialism and capitalism," he said in a CNN interview, "is that capitalism has let a lot of people down."[23]

You don't have to be a democratic socialist to believe this. Many middle-of-the-roaders who recoil at the word "socialist" are far less bullish on capitalism than they were in the 1980s and 1990s.

Democratic socialism's new popularity is thus just one element of a larger swing in public opinion against the core claims of Reaganism—and, among Democrats, against the Third Way accommodations by Bill Clinton and Britain's Tony Blair to the supremacy of market ideas. In his widely praised speech announcing his presidential candidacy, the 37-year-old Buttigieg pointedly noted that throughout his lifetime, "Reagan supply-side conservatism . . . created the terms for how Democrats as well as Republicans made policy." He added: "That era . . . is now over."[24]

He's right. The "common sense" of politics, as we saw earlier, was redefined in the Reagan era as a belief in the supremacy of markets and the futility of government action. Now, our common sense, while still skeptical of government's competence (after the Trump years, who could not be?), is deeply troubled by economic concentration, the power of corporations, the growth of monopoly power, and the unfairness of the distribution of wealth and income. And mistrust of government now stems at least as much from a belief that it has been captured by powerful economic interests as from the fears of conservatives—expressed long ago by the economist and libertarian hero Friedrich Hayek—that a strong welfare and regulatory state would put us on "the road to serfdom."[25]

Decades of rising inequality and the shock of the 2008 crash have led Americans in large numbers—whether they think of themselves as socialists, social democrats, or capitalists—to call the fundamentals of our system into question. The resurgence of socialism is a warning sign for those who want to preserve capitalism and an opportunity for those who would reform it. As has happened before, those who want to save capitalism may have to turn to the reformers to get the job done. Public action to rectify capitalism's shortcomings has returned to the political agenda. This is shifting the entire conversation in a more progressive direction.

Many who have been and remain staunch defenders of capitalism have moved to much sharper criticisms of the system as it has developed since the Reagan years. In his 2018 book *Can American Capitalism Survive?*, the Pulitzer Prize–winning economics writer Steven Pearlstein defended efforts in the 1980s to make the American economy more competitive. But he argued that even after these corrections had succeeded, "free market ideologues and those with vested economic interests continued to push these ideas to extremes never envisioned by those who first proposed them. . . . What began as a useful corrective has, 25 years later, become a morally corrupting and self-defeating economic dogma that threatens the future of American capitalism."

He is especially critical of the shift in the 1970s and 1980s in the ideology of the modern corporation. Where once corporations saw themselves as "proud stewards of the American system" with responsibilities to a broad range of stakeholders, they now hold only one obligation sacrosanct: to maximize value for their shareholders. This new disposition ignored Adam Smith's moral lessons, which, as Pearlstein wrote, insisted that "the wealth of nations depends on the vigorous pursuit of self-interest by individuals whose natural and productive selfishness *is tempered by moral sentiments such as compassion, generosity and a sense of fair play.*"

Pearlstein's conclusion: "An economic system that regularly ignores these sentiments forfeits its moral legitimacy. And, in time, it will forfeit its prosperity as well."[26]

In a series of speeches, Representative Joseph Kennedy of Massachusetts sought to define what "moral capitalism" would look like. It was, he said, a system that would be "judged not by how much it produces, but how broadly it empowers, backed by a government unafraid to set the conditions for fair and just markets." Comparing Kennedy's vision with Franklin Roosevelt's "cleareyed, buoyant determination to build a decent society," the historian Michael Kazin concluded of Democrats: "Without moral capitalism or a powerful equivalent, they risk getting stuck in internecine fights while their arrogant adversary rekindles his vow to return America to a 'greatness' he can neither define nor deliver."[27]

It's striking that contemporary critics of capitalism repeatedly invoke the word "moral" to describe the system's shortcomings. Recall how hard George Gilder worked to solidify Reagan-style capitalism's moral underpinnings. Widening inequality and the 2008 crash are undoing the work he and his conservative intellectual allies undertook. Consider, too, that as recently as the 2004 election, pollsters found that voters who said they cast their ballots on the basis of "moral values" were overwhelmingly social and religious conservatives who favored George W. Bush. Talk about "moral values" was presumed to relate to personal morality and issues such as abortion and gay rights. It's certainly true that the religious right's embrace of Trump despite his own behavior has undercut its claims in this sphere. More importantly, we are witnessing a return to an American tradition of subjecting social and economic institutions to moral scrutiny, a commitment that was central to nineteenth-century populism, the early trade union movement, and the Social Gospel. The workings of economic markets are seen not as neutral but as subject to judgments about the values that undergird them and the social and personal outcomes they produce.[28]

Here is the common ground among moderate and progressive capitalists, social democrats and democratic socialists. All are appalled by the extremes to which economic policy has been pushed by a radical, deregulatory, anti-tax right. All worry about the growing disconnection between the economic system and morality—and the dangers unregulated global capitalism poses to democracy itself.

This last point is important in confronting an ethno-nationalist right whose doctrines are as appalling to liberal-minded moderate capitalists as they are to the left. Robert Kuttner, the left-of-center economics writer, asked the question directly in the title of his 2018 book *Can Democracy Survive Global Capitalism?* Because of globalization, he argued, democratic capitalism was becoming "a contradiction in terms." It was undercutting the socially conscious forms of the market system recommended by Pearlstein and the ability of democratic governments to set rules for (or even tax) concentrated wealth. As a result, Kuttner concluded, "predatory capitalism has strengthened populist ultranationalism and further weakened liberal democracy" while also increasing the number of "crony-capitalist" societies that lack both the competitive virtues of genuine capitalism and the democratic virtues of open societies.[29]

Those who see themselves as democratic socialists certainly include in their ranks those who oppose the capitalist system root and branch. Sunkara's socialist manifesto imagines a genuinely democratic socialist commonwealth (a dream that is, by the way, deeply American, reflected in one of the great utopian books in American literature, Edward Bellamy's *Looking Backward*).[30]

But most Americans who answer to the socialist label are closer to being social democrats who share with restive supporters of capitalism a belief that our current system is out of whack and needs a new equilibrium. They seek a better balance between social concerns and enterprise, between the individual and the community, between employees and shareholders, between government and the market. Their opponents on the right reject the need for rebalancing altogether. This is why, for the foreseeable future, moderates and progressives will find themselves as allies. Their political friendship will certainly have moments of contention. They will argue over what a new balance should look like—and, at times, over the word "socialist" and the ideas behind it. If progressives will stress capitalism's shortcomings and the distributional problems it leaves in its wake (of power as well as wealth), moderates will emphasize capitalism's inventiveness and its capacity to produce economic growth (that they agree should be more justly shared). What both sides know is that neither a healthy market system nor a genuinely democratic society will thrive without thoroughgoing reform.

Getting to the right arguments, however, requires settling some of the old ones. The legacy of the Clinton and Obama years is a source of major tension across both the Democratic Party and the larger coalition for change. Moving forward requires acknowledging the areas where these presidents were successful, the constraints under which both operated, and their failures to resolve deep social and economic problems that helped lay the groundwork for Trump.

FIVE

THE CLINTON AND OBAMA LEGACIES

*The Unfinished Work and Blind Spots of
Two Successful Presidencies*

IT HAS BEEN A LONG TIME SINCE DEMOCRATS WERE WILLING
to revel unreservedly in the success of one of their presidents.
Only Franklin Roosevelt stands as a Democratic icon in the
manner that Ronald Reagan still serves as a Republican idol.
And even FDR has come under sharp scrutiny from liberals and
the left in recent decades for largely turning a blind eye to racial
injustice in the South for fear of disturbing his party's alliance
with segregationists. Harry Truman is seen far more fondly by
most Democrats than he was in his own day, although some on
the party's left still refight old battles over his Cold War policies.[1]

Since Truman, Lyndon Johnson, Jimmy Carter, and, more
recently, Bill Clinton and Barack Obama have all been cast as
failing the progressive cause in important ways. There has been
revisionism about John F. Kennedy, too, although the martyred
young president faces less criticism than he might because his
promise was cut short, and because he will always embody a
youthful energy to which Americans, in every generation, aspire.[2]

Thus, the very title of this chapter might be cause for controversy. Calling the Clinton and Obama presidencies "successful"

flies in the face of much sentiment on the left side of a party frustrated with the degree to which both men continued to operate within the Reagan consensus, failed to create durable electoral legacies beyond their own times in office, and left behind deep economic inequalities that Democrats ought to be in the business of reversing.[3]

I don't propose here to offer a sweeping historical assessment of their two presidencies, but I do want to lay out briefly what might be seen as the terms of a settlement, a view of their times in office that would allow progressives, moderates, and reformers of all stripes to move forward. Affection for Obama still runs deep in his party, reflected in "I miss Obama" bumper stickers that are not just about how much more thoughtful, ethical, responsible, eloquent, and competent he was in comparison with Trump. After a round of debates in July 2019, Democratic presidential candidates—Joe Biden was the exception—came under criticism from many quarters for spending more time criticizing Obama's legacy than standing up for it. They engaged in a strategic correction in a September debate, competing over who could praise Obama more lavishly. As for Bill Clinton, there were reasons he received such a rapturous reception at the 2012 Democratic National Convention. He was, after all, the man who ended 12 years of Reagan-era Republican rule, and the 1990s were a period of exceptional economic growth and peace.[4]

The positive assessments reflect the fact that both Clinton and Obama solved the serious immediate problems they inherited—an economic downturn accompanied by rising deficits in Clinton's case, a wholesale economic catastrophe in Obama's. Both left behind thriving economies. Both pushed against rising inequality, in contrast to Republican administrations since Reagan that aggravated the inequities in our economy with large tax cuts tilted heavily toward the wealthy. (The first President Bush is a partial exception to this pattern.) Moreover, both Clinton and Obama were sharply constrained during six of their eight years in office by Republican Congresses that resisted reforms that went beyond those the two men were able to enact in their first two years.[5]

At the same time—except, importantly, in their willingness to raise taxes on the rich—neither tried to overturn the broad assumptions that had governed American economic policy since the 1980s. In Clinton's case, he pushed these assumptions further along with a broad deregulatory program for the banks and the financial industry, an end to the entitlement for welfare, and an enthusiastic embrace of free trade.

Obama inherited an economic disaster created by the irresponsibility of Wall Street and the world of finance as a whole. In cooperation with other national leaders, he righted a global economy in free fall (an achievement for which he still gets too little credit). But he repaired the system without challenging the institutions and structures that led to the disaster in the first place. At the end of the Obama presidency, the overall economy was humming again, but the damage of the 2008 crash was still being felt in many parts of the country—and many of those places produced substantial electoral swings from Obama to Trump in 2016.

Was the country better off because of what both Clinton and Obama did? Yes. Did they leave behind serious social and economic imbalances they should have done more to right? Also yes. That is why their presidencies present such conundrums to progressives.

Let's start with the obvious: Clinton's relationship with a White House intern that led to his impeachment came under renewed and even harsher scrutiny after the rise of the Me Too movement. This has affected overall assessments of his presidency. And politically, his legacy would be received differently if his time in office had been followed by a successful Al Gore presidency. (For one thing, there very likely would not have been a war in Iraq.) As we have already seen, Gore's 2000 campaign was a promise to push in more populist and egalitarian directions. Had he lived up to his pledges, he might have been seen as completing the transformation in politics that Clinton promised. As it was, George W. Bush's policies further aggravated inequalities, and the economic crash on his watch was a disaster for the already vulnerable.[6]

Clinton and his advisers also had reason to argue that the social bargain they struck with the financial world—eliminating the deficit and letting both Wall Street and the tech economy rip—was a reasonable deal for everybody else. Economic growth in the late 1990s was exceptional, disadvantaged groups enjoyed strong income gains, and government (through programs such as a broadly expanded Earned Income Tax Credit) sought to redistribute some of the largesse the economy was producing. The country's strong fiscal position left room for further redistribution efforts. It's also important to remember that Clinton won reelection in part because of his success in resisting Republican cuts to "Medicare, Medicaid, education, and the environment," his M2E2 battle cry that stopped Newt Gingrich's "revolution" in its tracks.[7]

On the other hand, beyond the fact that financial deregulation helped open the way for the calamities of 2008, Clinton's trade policies—not only the North American Free Trade Agreement but, perhaps more importantly, China's accession to the World Trade Organization, pushed by Clinton and formally realized under Bush—sped along deindustrialization that had begun in the 1980s. The brunt of these policies hit hardest in the old industrial states that moved to Trump in 2016. Trade was by no means the only driver here. Automation and technological change were as important, although technological advances in turn contributed to globalization. But promises of relief for those hurt by foreign trade and the other transformations never materialized in a substantial way. And confidence that an economically expansive China would move toward democracy proved misplaced.[8]

With these problems came the death of an idea, summarized

well by *New York* magazine writer Ed Kilgore (who acknowl-edged that he had long been "a loyal foot soldier" in the New Democratic movement). The Clinton-era belief was that "the best way to achieve progressive policy goals was by harnessing and redirecting the wealth that a less-regulated and more-innovative private sector alone could generate." What Kilgore called the "create-then-redistribute model for Democratic economic pol-icy" effectively passed away after 2008 and generated a powerful backlash that hurt Hillary Clinton in 2016.[9]

As for Obama, his legacy, like Clinton's, would look very dif-ferent had he governed for a few more years with a Democratic Congress—and also if Hillary Clinton had prevailed in 2016.

It shouldn't be hard to understand that Obama was so fearful of a comprehensive economic collapse during his first months in office that he resisted putting pressure on the financial sector. Still, he could have done more to hold it accountable once the emergency passed. The Dodd-Frank financial reform was cer-tainly a step forward—important enough that the Trump admin-istration set to work dismantling large parts of it—but it was less far-reaching than it could have been.[10]

The irony is that the most enduring and politically helpful Obama policies were those that most risked accusations of rad-icalism. The most "socialist" and, at the time, most controver-sial of all of Obama's policies—the bailout of the auto industry involving massive government subsidy and large-scale federal intervention—was one of his most successful ventures, substan-tively and politically. The auto industry came back strong, and none of the fears of the program's critics were realized. And there is little doubt that Obama's support for rescuing the industry and Mitt Romney's opposition to it were key to Obama's 2012 victo-ries in both Michigan and Ohio.[11]

Similarly, Obama's resistance during his first months in office to austerity policies—they were very popular among conservatives in Europe as well as the United States—was undoubtedly the right call. His stimulus program was, as we've seen, far smaller than the emergency required, but it was substantial and it did work.[12]

His signature achievement, the Affordable Care Act, reflected what might be seen as the classic Obama synthesis. It took ideas from conservatives (the health care exchanges, insurance subsidies, the mandate to buy insurance) to produce far-reaching social change. But there is, again, the paradox of centrism: The plan might have been even more popular—and Obama's party might have been saved from its current divisive health care debate—if the proposal had included a public option alongside private insurance. It was killed in part because of opposition from moderate Senate Democrats.[13]

Obama's fundamental caution also kicked in as Washington elite consensus—egged on by Republicans in Congress and the rising Tea Party—pushed him to a rhetorical embrace of budget balancing far more quickly than the economic circumstances justified. This made a second, much-needed stimulus package even more difficult politically. As the economics writer Noam Scheiber noted shrewdly in his book *The Escape Artists*, Obama "spent much of his first term more taken with the case against deficits than with the case for jobs." It was, in the oldest sense of the term, a conservative preoccupation.[14]

His caution brought him criticism from both right and left. Many among the wealthy condemned him as a socialist who did not appreciate the heroism of entrepreneurs. Progressives (including actual socialists) saw his administration as far more interested in nursing Wall Street to health than in curtailing its excesses. The financial sector emerged as powerful as ever and, in the Trump years, began the process of dismantling reforms Obama had signed into law and regulations he had put in place. Obama was caught in the middle of all this—"middle" being the appropriate word in many respects.[15]

New York Times columnist David Leonhardt offered a fair and straightforward verdict on Clinton and Obama. Both had records in which they could take pride, yet "for all that both men accomplished, neither changed the fundamental direction of the American economy."[16]

Which meant that the 16 years of Democratic rule under both Clinton and Obama bottled up enormous pressure on the left. It was bound, eventually, to explode. In 2016, it did, in the form of Bernie Sanders's campaign and the backlash on the left against Hillary Clinton.

Even outside the ranks of the Sanders supporters, the reality of the new economy was changing minds and revising assessments of the Clinton and Obama years.

Jake Sullivan, Hillary Clinton's 2016 policy adviser and a defender of her husband's record, argues that wherever one stands on the legacy of the New Democrats, "the economy looks different today than it did in the 1990s." He cites the developing views of Bill Clinton's treasury secretary Larry Summers to argue that "even apolitical economists looking at the 'widening inequality, financial crisis, zero interest rates, rising gaps in life expectancy and opportunity' over the past two decades would move to the left, because their analysis would inevitably lead them there."[17]

You might say that reality itself has moved left since 2008, not to mention 1993.

This was brought home to me when I traveled to Charleston, South Carolina, for a June 2019 meeting organized by Third Way, a group, as its name suggests, that is devoted to moderate Democratic policies. To put matters gently, Bernie Sanders doesn't like the Third Wayers much, and they are not wild about him. Yet the group's president, Jonathan Cowan, was emphatic in insisting that it was not offering "a warmed-over 1990s centrism." Cowan's critique of what were, after all, the years of Bill Clinton's presidency was not hedged: "Back then," he said, "we placed too much trust in the market's ability to provide a reliable and realistic path to prosperity for most Americans. In the last 30 years, we have seen the impact of globalization and automation on our workers. And it is clear that a rising tide will not lift all boats."[18]

Later, Matt Bennett, Third Way's executive vice president, said flatly: "We have to own some of the mistakes of the New Democrats." Among them, he said, was underestimating the effect of trade liberalization on a significant number of blue-collar workers and "the speed and ferocity with which technology would decimate certain sectors of the American workforce." A particularly negative effect of this was the "concentration of opportunity" in certain regions as large parts of the country were left behind. "We need to be working to tame capitalism at this moment, because it is not functioning well," Bennett told me. "We need to do in this century what the progressives and New Dealers did in the last century."[19]

This is what the new moderation looks like. The political center cannot be defined as a halfway point between Democrats and a Republican Party that has veered far to the right. *The New York Times'* Leonhardt described the new terrain well:

> Most voters don't share the centrist preferences of Washington's comfortable pundit class. Most voters want to raise taxes on the rich and corporations. They favor generous Medicare and Social Security, expanded Medicaid, more financial aid for college, a higher minimum wage and a bigger government role in job creation. Remember, Trump won the *Republican* nomination as a populist. A clear majority of Americans wants the government to respond aggressively to our economic problems.[20]

This is consistent with the work of political scientists Jacob Hacker and Paul Pierson. Their research shows that the views of Americans on a range of policy issues have "certainly not shifted sharply to the right," but that those of Republican activists and political leaders most certainly *have*. It was the Republican shift, not changes in public opinion as a whole, that created the impression that the center had veered right when, if anything, it had moved the other way.[21]

Which means that the next decade provides a dramatic opportunity for reform. At such a moment, moderates should welcome, not fear, the left's boldness. As Mason Williams's observation about the New Deal cited earlier suggests, a vibrant left has always been a central component of any successful era of social reform. By offering plans and proposals on what the late socialist writer Michael Harrington called "the left wing of the possible," socialists, social democrats, and left-liberals have redefined the political playing field.[22]

Consider that when Senator Elizabeth Warren proposed a wealth tax on fortunes of $50 million or more, moderate voices responded by saying her idea was too radical or unworkable—and then urged an increase in the capital gains tax or other approaches to taxing large fortunes instead. As the progressive writer Robert Borosage noted in *The Nation*, her proposal underscored a fundamental unfairness in the American system: that while the "primary source of wealth for most middle-class families—their homes—is taxed each year in the property tax," the "primary source of wealth of the very rich—their investments—is only taxed when sold or transferred, if then." This was a conversation few were having before Warren put forward her initiative. And she would use the proceeds from the tax—she estimates it would raise $2.75 trillion over a decade—to finance ambitious social initiatives. This was a policy twofer. Warren simultaneously underscored just how much money is sitting at the top of the economy and then showed how much could be done to lift up those at its lower rungs without resorting to broadly based tax increases. There were legitimate questions raised about how her wealth tax would work and whether it could be effective in a world in which capital can be moved around so easily. She certainly generated a backlash among billionaires, and former New York City mayor Michael Bloomberg's late interest in seeking the Democratic presidential nomination was a response both to Warren's rise in the polls and Biden's perceived weaknesses. But Warren had by then already altered the discussions of how government should raise money in the future.[23]

It took conservative policy innovation and even policy radicalism in the 1970s and early 1980s to push the political debate to the right. The innovations on the left that are now part of the mainstream conversation are similarly transformative. They are part of an effort to restore the idea that only public action— represented in the past by bold programs such as the Homestead and Land-Grant College acts, Social Security, the GI Bill, and the Eisenhower-era student loan program—can solve persistent problems that have torn at our social fabric for a generation. Moderates who think of themselves as problem solvers should welcome the left's initiatives as part of a process of legitimizing the very act of public problem solving. Only when this happens can a real contest begin over how fast and how far we can move at any given moment.[24]

One telltale sign that a political debate is moving in a new direction is the adoption of ideas from the rising side by its adversaries. As we saw earlier, Democrats and liberals in the Atari period ratified the new Reagan disposition by beginning to speak its language and offering policies consistent with its objectives. That both Clinton and, to only a lesser degree, Obama operated within this consensus is why their legacies are complicated.

For the most part, Republicans have resisted moving decisively in a new direction. Only a decisive defeat will open the space needed for a larger GOP reformation. But quietly, leading conservatives and libertarians are acknowledging contemporary capitalism's problems and adopting critiques that originated on the left. Thus did Florida senator Marco Rubio issue a remarkable report arguing that business was underinvesting because of a shift in corporate behavior toward valuing the interests of shareholders over all other stakeholders. "This theory," Rubio argued, "tilts business decision-making towards returning money quickly and predictably to investors rather than building long-term corporate capabilities, reduces investment in research and innovation, and undervalues American workers' contribution to production."[25]

As we have seen, reproaching the idea of shareholder primacy is central to both progressive and center-left critiques of contemporary capitalism, and in the summer of 2019, business leaders themselves weighed in. In a new statement on the purpose of the corporation widely interpreted as a direct response to growing discontent with capitalism, the Business Roundtable explicitly broke with this limited view of the modern corporation's obligations, emphasizing that they extended to other "stakeholders." Proper corporate goals, the CEOs declared, included "investing in our employees," "supporting the communities in which we work," and promoting "a healthy environment." *The New York Times* rightly described the statement as "breaking with decades of long-held corporate orthodoxy."[26]

In the meantime, the most provocative new Washington think tank on the center-right is the Niskanen Center, a haven for onetime libertarians who have had enough of hard-right ideology and are championing a new moderation in politics. The work of two of its leading figures, Jerry Taylor and Samuel Hammond, aroused great interest because it faced up to what has long been true—and explicitly rejected what had long been conservative dogma: Many "big government" countries (in Scandinavia, for example) are also among the freest nations on Earth. It is time, Hammond argues, to blow up the "ideological axis" that runs from "'small government' libertarian" to "'big government' progressive."[27] This, of course, means blowing up the axis that conservative politics built.

128 • Code Red

    It makes little sense, either substantively or politically, for
progressives and moderates to disown the legacies of Clinton
and Obama. They both chipped away at the Reagan consensus even as they lived within it. In particular, they put the lie to
supply-side economics by raising taxes on the wealthy and then
fostering a period of exceptional growth. In Obama's case, the
Affordable Care Act and the rescue of the auto industry are large
achievements and monuments to the good that creative government can do. Moreover, Obama's eloquent arguments for racial
justice and interracial peace—his 2015 speech on the fiftieth an-
niversary of "Bloody Sunday" in Selma, Alabama, will long stand
as the definitive argument for America's capacity to change—are
an antidote to the divisiveness of the Trump era.[28]

    But neither does it make sense to be hamstrung by the as-
sumptions they lived with or the compromises they felt forced
to make. FDR honored the tradition of the Progressive Era tradition but moved beyond it. It is time for another historic leap.

SIX

GETTING FROM HERE TO THERE

Visionary Gradualism and the
Economics of Dignity

IN A BOOK WRITTEN NEAR THE END OF HIS LIFE, MICHAEL Harrington described his commitment to a politics of "visionary gradualism." While Harrington always harbored the hope that his work might one day lead to the triumph of democratic socialism, his prescription motivated many progressives who did not share his aspirations about capitalism's ultimate demise but nonetheless longed for more justice and more equality.[1]

Harrington's formulation is powerful because it recognizes that enduring changes in a democracy are often undertaken a step at a time. The lessons of "visionary gradualism" can be summarized this way: Modest reforms unhinged from larger purposes are usually inadequate and typically ephemeral. But a bold vision disconnected from first steps and early successes can shrivel up and die. The former is an essential progressive argument. The latter is a useful warning from moderates. How can the insights of both sides be put to work?

Donald Trump's 2016 victory was so traumatic for the left, center-left, and moderates alike that it obscured from our view both the collapse of the Reagan consensus—which Trump's own critiques of free trade and the disappearance of manufacturing jobs underscored—and the renewed intellectual vitality among progressives. So much analytical energy was devoted to claims that Hillary Clinton had come up with too many policy ideas and not enough broad brushstroke themes that little attention was paid to how deep her policy trove was—and how it developed further in response to Bernie Sanders's initiatives. This was no accident. Their programs grew out of a decade of practical and scholarly energy as both the left and center-left moved beyond the Third Way policies of the 1990s toward a more aggressive attack on inequality and its social consequences.[2]

What has often been called "the ideas primary" in the 2020 Democratic presidential contest makes clear that intellectual liveliness on the left is now a fact of life in American politics. Policy creativity is no guarantee of electoral victory, but it is a sign of which side is most vibrant, which is most devoted to addressing new problems, and which is most prepared to govern. K. Sabeel Rahman, president of the think tank Demos, pointed to two lessons from the flood of new proposals. They reflect "an increasing move away from micro-scale policies that might poll well but do little toward transformative, structural reforms that reshape the background rules of our economy, our government and our society." And the policy shift has been "accompanied by an urgent moral shift, a deeper questioning of what democracy and equal citizenship actually require."[3]

This is the promise of our moment, but it is also a political challenge. New ideas are most likely to take hold in a democracy when they respond to needs that are deeply felt. The most effective ideas are rooted in long-standing demands that earn popular support over time. Agitation for change often grows in response to proposals that seem (or actually are) radical when they are first put forward. In proposing Social Security, for example, Franklin Roosevelt was responding to mass mobilizing around Dr. Francis Townsend's old-age pension plan and Huey Long's "Share Our Wealth" scheme to provide every family with a $5,000 income. Roosevelt's policy was more measured but still far-reaching.[4]

Policy specifics must be accompanied, as Rahman suggests, by a moral story that speaks simultaneously to public unhappiness over perceived injustices or lost opportunities and to realistic hopes that the proposals in question offer achievable remedies. The criticisms of Hillary Clinton missed the substantive value of many of her policies, but they had a point in that her plans failed to convey a larger vision of where Americans would find themselves in four years or a decade if her platform was enacted.

Progressives and moderates alike must approach the policy debates of the coming years bearing in mind both recent experience and the history of social and political change. Moderates should not regard big ideas as inherently dangerous or automatically radical—and radicalism itself may not be a liability when the problems being addressed are deep and long-standing. Today's radicalism often becomes tomorrow's conventional wisdom. Progressives, in turn, should not dismiss efforts by moderates to adjust progressive ideas to make them more popular or more feasible as signs of timidity. There is much to be done—and deep divisions among those seeking change are the surest way to guarantee that much-needed reforms never happen. Again, both of the words in Harrington's call for "visionary gradualism" are important.[5]

It's also worth bearing in mind that the "bigness" of an idea is not necessarily a test of its seriousness. In praising many of Senator Elizabeth Warren's proposals—he specifically singled out her universal child care plan—*New York Times* columnist and economist Paul Krugman stressed the importance of what he called "medium-size, medium-priced proposals that could deliver major benefits without requiring a political miracle. . . . Visions and values are great, but Democrats also need to be ready to hit the ground running with plans that might actually turn into legislation." Yes, they do.[6]

To bring these general principles to bear on ongoing debates, I turn next to two ideas Bernie Sanders has pushed to the forefront, single-payer health care, eventually endorsed by Warren, and free college, and then to the Green New Deal. All three have placed urgent problems at the center of public discussion, widened the parameters of what's possible, and moved the political center in a more progressive direction. They have also called forth criticisms that can be put to constructive use. To underscore the central point: The challenge—in both campaigning and governing—is to use these ideas as a prod to achieving enduring reforms that can be built on over time.

Later, I will outline a moral case for dignity as a core purpose for progressive politics and policy. The demand for the honor and respect that are at the heart of the definition of dignity cuts across nearly every line of division in our nation's life. The battle for equal dignity is a fight for an America that would see democracy as a way of life and the rock on which national unity can be rebuilt.

When *The Washington Post* asked House Speaker Nancy Pelosi in April 2019 about her view of Medicare for All proposals that would replace the United States' complicated system of private and public insurance with a comprehensive government plan, she pronounced herself "agnostic" and challenged its supporters. "Show me how you think you can get there," Pelosi said.[7]

For good measure, she questioned whether many voters understood the plan in all its details—especially how it would largely abolish private insurance. "When most people say they're for Medicare-for-all, I think they mean health care for all," she said, alluding to polls that show wide support for single-payer health care until it is explained in more detail. "A lot of people love having their employer-based insurance and the Affordable Care Act gave them better benefits." Pelosi was the central figure in pushing Obamacare through Congress, and she was not about to give up on it. Democrats, she suggested, would do better to build on what they had already achieved and leave a radical restructuring of the health care system for another day. Is it any wonder that Democrats' 2018 campaigns prudently focused on safeguarding Obamacare and the health insurance of those with preexisting conditions?[8]

Despite the regular attacks on political litmus tests, they play an entirely legitimate role in defining commitments that individual voters will always look for—and points of view they will always oppose. In the wake of the successful fight for Obamacare, there is a new and legitimate litmus test in Democratic politics: Every one of the party's candidates is and should be expected to endorse a path to decent, affordable health insurance coverage for every American.[9]

But litmus tests should be about goals, not particular plans. There is reason to welcome the attention Medicare for All has received because it has created room for debate that did not exist during the Obamacare struggle. Medicare for All really is "socialized medicine." Obamacare is not, and never was, no matter how often its conservative critics claimed otherwise. Single-payer's supporters should, in turn, recognize that it is just one of many plausible paths to universal coverage, which *is* the legitimate litmus test.[10]

Moreover, as Pelosi hinted, even supporters of Medicare for All should accept that such a sweeping change is unlikely ever to be enacted all at once. The roughly 180 million Americans with private insurance will not be easily persuaded to give up what they have for the promises of what, in the United States, would be a novel system. And millions who work inside the health care system—many of them, by the way, Democrats—will think very carefully before upending the source of their livelihood. Thus did a late September 2019 NBC News/*Wall Street Journal* poll find that while 67 percent of Americans supported "the option to buy their health coverage through the Medicare program," only 41 percent supported "Medicare for All" when it was described as eliminating private insurance.[11]

134 • Code Red

Nonetheless, dialogue between moderates and progressives, between the center-left and the left, has already been fruitful in unleashing a wave of policy innovation on health care. To answer worries about forcing Americans off existing insurance plans against their will, Representatives Rosa DeLauro and Jan Schakowsky introduced a plan they called Medicare for America. DeLauro and Schakowsky would preserve employer-based insurance, provided the plans in question met rigorous federal standards, while gradually moving those on various other public plans into an expanded Medicare system. As *Vox*'s Dylan Scott noted, the proposal's supporters hope that "moving people into Medicare more gradually, rather than transitioning everyone in just a few years, would weaken any Republican arguments intended to scare seniors into believing that the Medicare they currently rely on is at risk." It would also reassure Americans who are now satisfied with their private insurance that they would not be forced out of their plans abruptly.[12]

A variety of other proposals, supported by Senator Amy Klobuchar and Pete Buttigieg, among others, would add a robust public option to Obamacare—Americans could buy insurance from a public system if they wished, creating what Buttigieg, offering his own detailed plan, called "Medicare for All Who Want It"—while expanding Obamacare's subsidies for the purchase of insurance, private or public, to get coverage to those still left out. If Americans moved in large numbers toward the public system, the country would move gradually but decisively toward a form of Medicare for All through voluntary choice.[13]

It must also be said that all these alternatives were more comprehensive than the Affordable Care Act, and the surest sign that single-payer advocates had moved the debate in a far more progressive direction was the release of former vice president Joe Biden's health care plan in mid-July 2019. Biden specifically cast himself as an opponent of Medicare for All—because "it means getting rid of Obamacare"—and thus a staunch defender of the Affordable Care Act. But his actual proposal was far more adventurous than the original. It not only created a public option but would also use it to cover low-income people in states where Republicans had refused to expand Medicaid. He also expanded ACA subsidies and proposed forcing drug companies to negotiate drug prices with Medicare. As *Washington Post* blogger Paul Waldman observed, "In 2009 when the ACA was being debated, a plan like this one would have been considered radically leftist." Not anymore.[14]

The bottom line: Single-payer advocates are not impractical fools. They are right that the American health care system is far more expensive than single-payer and other more socialized approaches, and their efforts have made moderates less fearful of moving aggressively toward universal coverage. But those who seek measured alternatives are not spineless sellouts. As *Vox*'s Ezra Klein pointed out, "Canada and the UK dominate the American single-payer debate, but many health care experts prefer the German, French, Singaporean or Australian systems, which also guarantee coverage to everyone. Why should our debate be focused so narrowly on two alternatives among many?"[15]

The closest analog to the battle for universal health insurance coverage is the fight for Social Security. It fell short of being comprehensive in its initial version but proved so popular that it quickly entrenched itself as part of our national life. Through the years, Congress expanded the ranks of those who were covered and improved its benefits, creating the more generous system we have today. It is one of the best examples, as Princeton sociologist Paul Starr explained in his excellent book *Entrenchment,* of how a progressive policy can be constructed in ways that allow it to endure even when the political winds change. "Americans counted on it not only for themselves but also to avoid having to support their aging parents," Starr wrote. "A government that sought to end Social Security would be seen as violating an implicit contract that people relied on in planning their lives." The same is gradually happening with health coverage.[16]

Consider another idea Sanders popularized: free college. It is by no means as radical as it sounds. Attendance at public colleges and universities was, not that long ago, free or close to it. Lilia Vega, a student journalist at the *Daily Californian* at Berkeley, made this point by studying tuition rates at the University of California since 1868. As recently as 1968, she noted, students paid a registration fee of $300 a year—and that was it for California residents. Their tuition was *free*. Nonresident tuition was $1,200 per year. By the 2012–13 academic year, in-state tuition had risen to $14,460, and nonresident UC undergrads faced a bill of $37,338.

The key to this increase in California, as in so many other states, is a steady reduction in the investment by state governments in public education, shifting the burden from public spending to tuition. As Vega noted, the UC Board of Regents increased tuition by an astonishing 32 percent in 2009. And California was not alone. A 2018 study by the Center on Budget and Policy Priorities found that "overall state funding for public two- and four-year colleges in the school year ending in 2018 was more than $7 billion below its 2008 level, after adjusting for inflation." The resulting tuition increases left students "either saddled with onerous debt or unable to afford college altogether." Since the Great Recession, tuitions were up by more than 20 percent in 40 states, by more than 40 percent in 20 states, and by more than 60 percent in seven states.[17]

The growing popularity of free tuition is a response to these new obstacles to college access at a time when postsecondary education is more important than ever in securing well-paying work. In 2015, President Obama responded by proposing free tuition for two years of community college, a program he advocated, unsuccessfully, for the rest of his presidency. Obama (do we need to say it again?) was no radical. And states with very different political leanings—Tennessee, Georgia, California, Maryland, and

New York among them—have either moved toward free college or substantially expanded scholarship programs, or both.[18]

The demand for free college, like the call for single-payer health care, has forced attention to a genuine problem and called forth alternatives. They include Hillary Clinton's 2016 campaign plan for debt-free college and a variety of proposals to create American versions of apprenticeship programs that have been very successful in Europe.[19]

Critics of free college, among them Pete Buttigieg, have argued that it would simply be a large subsidy for the best-off Americans, since children of the well-to-do are far more likely to go to college than those from families of lesser means. Better, they say, to direct more public money to students most in need—and to finance other programs more directly linked to obtaining well-paying jobs, whether they require college degrees or not.

This points to a related debate over the need for high school and postsecondary training focused less on pushing all young people toward four-year degrees and more on financing programs that help students find well-paying, satisfying work. This is the impetus behind the community college proposals, expansions of vocational training in high schools, and the turn toward apprenticeship. Isabel Sawhill, an economist at the Brookings Institution, has proposed bringing together a number of these ideas as a GI Bill for America's Workers. It would be "geared to skills that are in demand and the jobs that are available" and "encourage work-based learning." She suggests it could be financed through a reimagined unemployment insurance system that would respond to more than cyclical downturns in the economy.[20]

This debate is at times difficult because many supporters of broad college access see the new push for vocational programs as a return to elitism and tracking that would stigmatize poor and minority children. What is needed is a new debate that resolutely avoids elitism but meets the needs and desires of students where they are. It would also involve a cultural change that gives the work done by blue-collar and service workers the respect it deserves. Edward Luce, the *Financial Times* columnist and author of *The Retreat of Western Liberalism*, has noted that Germany and the Scandinavian countries have valued those who perform technical and service jobs in a way the United States and Britain have not. As a result, these societies pursue more egalitarian policies, inspired by a more egalitarian ethos. Democrat Richard Cordray was unsuccessful in his 2018 gubernatorial campaign in Ohio, but he coined a slogan that should be on the lips of every progressive and moderate politician in the country: "You shouldn't need a college degree to be part of the middle class." It holds the potential to transform job training from a technocratic issue and, to some working-class ears, condescending life advice into a populist battle cry.[21]

The demand for free college is a singularly good example of how a clear, simple, and seemingly radical demand can provoke both action (now, mostly at the state level) and policy creativity. It can be usefully compared to the push for access to high school in the Progressive Era. This led to a tenfold increase in the number of high school students between 1890 and 1920—a leap from 7 percent to 32 percent of Americans between the ages of 14 and 17. We are at a comparable turning point. Americans recognize that high school education is no longer enough. It's time for another leap. It would entail expanding access both to four-year institutions and to far more robust post-high-school training.[22]

With few other issues is there a more dramatic gap between conservatives and everyone else than on climate change. This was not always the case. Before Barack Obama's election, conservative Republicans, including the late John McCain and former senator Bob Corker, acknowledged the human role in global warming and offered market-oriented remedies. Now, denial is the dominant position within a GOP whose environmental policies— witness Trump's appointments in the energy and environmental areas—are largely shaped by oil, gas, and coal interests.

And this at a time when denial is more dangerous than ever. The UN Intergovernmental Panel on Climate Change concluded in October 2018 that the world had just 12 years to ensure that global warming will not exceed 1.5 degrees Celsius. Going above that level, it concluded, would substantially increase "the risks of drought, floods, extreme heat and poverty for hundreds of millions of people." In May 2019, sensors at the Mauna Loa Observatory in Hawaii found that the concentration of carbon dioxide in the Earth's atmosphere had climbed to a level last seen 3 million years ago.[23]

The Obama years saw progress on climate, highlighted by the Paris Agreement. A shift away from coal led to a 40 percent decline in power generation by coal-fired plants, which accounted for three-quarters of the drop in CO_2 emissions between 2005 and 2017. But Trump pulled the United States out of the Paris Agreement and led a rhetorical war in favor of coal—even if older coal-fired power plants were destined to be pulled out of service over time.[24]

On climate, as on so many other issues, Republicans are the outliers. A 2018 Gallup survey found that 89 percent of Democrats and 62 percent of Independents said they believe climate change is caused by human activities—compared to only 35 percent of Republicans. Similarly, 67 percent of Democrats and 45 percent of Independents said global warming would pose a serious threat in their lifetimes, but only 18 percent of Republicans thought so. Americans noticed how out of step Republicans were, both with public opinion and with the findings of science. A February 2019 NBC News/*Wall Street Journal* poll found that only 29 percent saw the Republican Party as in the mainstream on climate change; 63 percent saw the GOP as outside it.[25]

The depth of the Democratic consensus was reflected in the substantial blowback when a Biden insider said in May 2019 that the former vice president was seeking a "middle ground" on the issue, implying he would be less aggressive on climate than other

Democrats. Biden quickly disowned the adviser's comments and devoted a significant part of the Philadelphia speech that kicked off his campaign to the urgency of climate action. He followed up by making a strong climate plan one of the first policy rollouts of his campaign.[26]

Ambition was the point of the Green New Deal, introduced by Representative Alexandria Ocasio-Cortez and Senator Ed Markey of Massachusetts. Because it was presented as a resolution, not a bill, it was often described as "aspirational." But those aspirations were high. It pledged to move the country to meet "100 percent of [its] power demand . . . through clean, renewable, and zero-emission energy sources." It proposed to reduce transportation emissions "as much as is technically feasible" through, for example, the expansion of high-speed rail and more rapid production of zero-emission vehicles. It suggested "working collaboratively with farmers and ranchers in the United States to remove pollution and greenhouse gas emissions from the agricultural sector as much as is technologically feasible." This was linked to an ambitious economic agenda to "create millions of good, high-wage jobs and ensure prosperity and economic security for all people of the United States" and to guarantee "a job with a family-sustaining wage, adequate family and medical leave, paid vacations, and retirement security to all people of the United States."[27]

The proposal was quickly mocked by Republicans, partly because of an inaccurate summary released by Ocasio-Cortez's office, but mostly because of the GOP's willingness to do whatever it took to discredit it. They falsely said it would mean a ban on, among other things, cars and air travel—and even livestock. "Say goodbye to dairy, to beef, to family farms, to ranches," said Wyoming's Senator John Barrasso. "American favorites like cheeseburgers and milkshakes will become a thing of the past." (I have relied here on an excellent overview of the controversy by FactCheck.org.)[28]

Needless to say, the Green New Deal's sponsors denied they were against cars, cows, airplanes, milkshakes, or hamburgers.

But the sweeping nature of the outline certainly invited dissent, and the fact that it was a resolution, not a carefully formulated piece of legislation, made caricature easy.

Senate Majority Leader Mitch McConnell proudly prevented new initiatives passed by House Democrats from even coming up for debate in his chamber. "Think of me as the Grim Reaper," McConnell told his constituents in Kentucky. "None of that stuff is going to pass." The habit of blocking bills supported by Democrats would come back to haunt McConnell in the summer of 2019 when his refusal to allow votes on legislation to combat foreign interference in our elections turned "#MoscowMitch" into a Twitter sensation.

Yet he was so eager to highlight Democratic divisions when it came to the Green New Deal that he put the Markey/Ocasio-Cortez resolution to a vote in March 2019. Among Senate Democrats, 43 abstained in protest to what they saw as a political stunt. Every Republican and four Democratic senators voted no. It failed 57 to 0.[29]

The paradox is that the Green New Deal's seeming radicalism was a response to criticism from, among others, political moderates of earlier efforts to deal with climate. The most straightforward approach to the problem, a stiff tax on carbon, invites opposition because, like gas and sales taxes, it hits lower-income and working-class voters hardest. It's especially burdensome for people in rural areas who make heavy use of cars and trucks. The demonstrations of the "yellow vests" against French president Emmanuel Macron were initially spurred by opposition, particularly in the countryside, to his proposed carbon taxes. Ultimately, a carbon tax will almost certainly be necessary as part of any comprehensive climate solution. But it will have to be accompanied by rebates to undo its regressive effects on those at the bottom end of the economy.[30]

In the meantime, the provisions in the Green New Deal to confront employment and income issues were a direct response to long-standing arguments—again, they often came from the political center—about the need to accompany aggressive climate steps with measures to ensure shared economic growth and job creation.

Here again, *The New York Times*' Krugman was shrewd about the underlying politics. "A carbon tax would hurt significant groups of people—and not just fossil-fuel billionaires like the Koch brothers," he wrote. "As a result, a carbon tax on its own is the kind of eat-your-spinach policy that technocrats love but many ordinary citizens hate." The Green New Deal, on the other hand, is an effort "to bundle measures to reduce emissions with a lot of other stuff people want, like big public investment even in areas with only weak direct relationships to climate change." This could be labeled "economic transformation," Krugman wrote, but it could also be seen as an old-fashioned legislative "Christmas tree." This was perfectly acceptable, he said, because "climate action probably won't happen *unless* it's a Christmas tree." The paradox, Krugman concluded, is that the Green New Dealers are "pragmatists despite their big ambitions."[31]

Krugman's analysis is especially helpful because it calls into question our tendency to confuse labels with reality. The Green New Deal is certainly far-reaching, and even sympathizers saw the initial draft as lacking the care and rigor that would be required in developing a more concrete plan. But it cannot be written off just because some call it "radical," and its structure is as pragmatic as Krugman suggests it is. The idea of combining social and environmental reform would certainly not be foreign to the Republican conservationists of Theodore Roosevelt's day. John Cassidy, *The New Yorker*'s economics writer, offered precisely the right verdict. "The rollout of the Green New Deal may have been troubled," Cassidy wrote, "but it has started something." And on climate, it's past time that we "started something."[32]

Even Republican critics of the proposal acknowledged that its ambition had begun nudging their party away from denial. Representative Bill Flores, a Texas Republican who had long counted himself among the climate skeptics, told James Osborne of the *Houston Chronicle:* "The good news about the Green New Deal is it's a wake-up call for Americans to look at different ways to deal with climate change." It often takes big ideas to unblock a stalemate.[33]

History, once again, has lessons. Administrations of both parties were right when they defied those claiming that environmental protection would endanger economic growth. From TR forward, the United States was a world leader in protecting nature's endowments—and an economic leader as well. Being a laggard on climate change is entirely outside our traditions.

None of this means that the climate issue is without risk or that the red flags raised in the first skirmishes over the Green New Deal should be ignored. The progressive writer Harold Meyerson warned that if the environmental movement and the labor movement failed to make peace over how to approach climate change, the issue could turn into a replay of 1960s-style culture wars. He reported on a letter sent by the AFL-CIO's Energy Committee (made up of the presidents of the Mine Workers, the Steelworkers, and a number of construction unions) to Markey and Ocasio-Cortez complaining that their resolution was "far too short on specific solutions that speak to the jobs of our members and the critical sectors of our economy. . . . We will not accept proposals that could cause immediate harm to millions of our members and their families." It was imperative, Meyerson argued, to create "decarbonization plans that link the Green New Deal with the creation of high-wage blue-collar jobs." This approach might well resemble Krugman's legislative "Christmas tree," a commitment, simultaneously, to social justice and coalition building.[34]

The three headline ideas on health care, higher education, and climate were important markers of the Democratic Party's move from Third Way incrementalism to an embrace of large-scale change. They were part of a rebellion against the country's flight from public action that began under Reagan and reached a crescendo with the rise of the Tea Party and the Republican takeover of the House in 2010. In all but four of Clinton and Obama's combined 16 years in office (and then under Trump), conservatives had effective veto power over new initiatives either to invest in public goods or to push against inequality. Progressives could count a few legislative victories after 2010, but they were mostly defensive, the most important being their success in 2017 in blocking repeal of the Affordable Care Act. Still, they could not stop 14 conservative states from preventing the Medicaid expansion and thus limiting the law's capacity to expand health insurance access. The states were empowered by the 2012 Supreme Court decision that declared Obamacare constitutional but struck down the law's requirement that states expand Medicaid or risk losing federal funding. As a result, some 2.5 million Americans, 92 percent of them in the South, lacked health coverage they would have enjoyed if those states had joined the program.[35] The nearly two-decades-long blockade against public problem solving made gradual approaches to change impossible. This fed the hunger of moderates as well as progressives for bolder initiatives to push back against the "private opulence and public squalor" that the liberal economist John Kenneth Galbraith had first described in the 1950s.[36]

The desire for change was not confined to policy wonks. Trump's success pushed the country rightward, but the popular response to his rhetorical rejection of the Reagan economic playbook and to Bernie Sanders's populist brand of socialism pointed to how widespread the demand for something new had become. After years of rising inequality culminating in the economic catastrophe of 2008, Americans were seeking both security and innovation. They sought to restore some of the virtues of the old economy—rising wages and benefits and opportunities for social mobility—in new circumstances involving fiercer international competition and rapid technological transformation. Americans—in inner cities *and* in the smaller towns and rural areas outside the large metropolitan regions—asked why the wonders of the new economy were passing them by, hollowing out communities, and, in many cases, forcing their children to seek opportunity elsewhere.

In the meantime, many who did enjoy prosperity worried about the concentration of economic power, the rise of new forms of monopoly, the potential flight of even highly skilled jobs overseas, the effects of automation, and the short-term orientation of the modern corporation. Even relatively affluent young people (and their parents) suspected that the next generation would not enjoy the same chances for advancement that were available for decades after the end of World War II.

In offering a catalog of new problems that needed to be addressed, former Hillary Clinton adviser Jake Sullivan pointed to how unevenly shared affluence, even in a time of growth, created new policy imperatives. He urged action to address novel problems created by the gig economy, by the outsourcing of jobs as a way of reducing employee benefits, and "the new concentration of wealth and monopoly power." Sullivan also underscored the imperative of addressing "the geography of opportunity so that all regions experience a middle-class revival."[37]

Trump thus created new problems for democracy itself while aggravating the economic injustices he had, rhetorically, promised to confront.

It was obvious to all but the members of his own political base that Trump represented a threat to democratic norms with his embrace of authoritarian regimes and ideas, and a politics of racial and ethnic animosity. He made claims of presidential power to prevent further inquiry into his 2016 campaign's cooperation with Russia that, in any other time, would have outraged members of his own party. Rage over his abuses of office boiled over in September 2019, and Speaker Pelosi announced a formal impeachment inquiry. A move she had deemed un-wise earlier now seemed the only appropriate response.

At the same time, despite his populist language in 2016, Trump embraced his party's opposition to measures (such as Obamacare) aimed at creating a greater degree of social justice. He also used executive action to push back against earlier reforms on behalf of the environment, financial consumer protection, and other forms of regulation. He represented simultaneously a stunning new threat in certain spheres and a doubling down in others on the old threats of a radicalized conservatism.

This is why it is a mistake for those who would roll back Trumpism to cast the strategic alternatives in 2020 and beyond as involving a choice between restoration and transformation.

These two poles certainly exist. Former vice president Joe Biden appealed to the restorationist sentiment in significant parts of the Democratic Party and the anti-Trump movement by arguing that real progress depended first and foremost on Trump's defeat. Preventing Trump from entrenching his approach to governance, Biden argued, was the country's first, essential task. "I believe history will look back on four years of this president and all he embraces as an aberrant moment in time," he said in the video announcing his candidacy in April 2019. "But if we give Donald Trump eight years in the White House, he will forever and fundamentally alter the character of this nation—who we are—and I cannot stand by and watch that happen." More than any specific issue, policy, or plan, this claim appealed to a deep gut feeling in Biden's party, and also to a broader desire for a spell of glorious tranquility after the always-in-your-face chaos of the Trump presidency.[38]

Biden's rivals have appealed to another gut feeling, not as strong as the revulsion against Trump, perhaps, but powerful nonetheless: that the Republican Party and the conservative movement and not just Trump himself are the problem, and that the country cannot afford another four years in which problem solving is stymied. Such paralysis would leave in place the conditions that helped elect Trump and open the way for a comeback of Trumpism if not Trump himself.

Pete Buttigieg spoke to this sentiment when he said: "You don't even get a presidency like this unless something's wrong. A promise to return to normal ignores that normal hasn't been working for a lot of people." Or, as Elizabeth Warren told California Democrats in June 2019: "Some say if we just calm down, the Republicans will come to their senses. But our country is in crisis. The time for small ideas is over." Biden also came under criticism for romanticizing the past, bathing it, wrote Peter Beinart in *The Atlantic*, "in a warm glow without defending it substantively." As a result, "he offers a deeply unconvincing historical narrative in which Trump lands upon the American political scene from outer space."[39]

In fact, voters in most elections are seeking a combination of restoration and transformation. They are concerned about bringing back something they believe has been lost, but hope to do so as a necessary prelude to moving forward. This is because all political movements operate within histories and traditions, one reason I have focused on what progressivism has offered our country in the past and what it means now. After the radical departure Trump represents, the appeal for restoration is especially powerful.

Trump's "Make America Great Again" mantra is, as its critics have pointed out, backward looking to some of the most disreputable aspects of our country's past. House Speaker Nancy Pelosi was explicit in July 2019 about what many had long suggested about Trump's catchphrase. The slogan, she tweeted, has "always been about making America white again."[40]

For some share of his voters, however, there was a less troubling side to Trump's "again." It was a promise to return to a world in which blue-collar work was plentiful and well paid. And in truth, every party and movement—including those promising progressive change—has its own form of "again," an appeal linking past achievements to future triumphs. Consider John F. Kennedy's core argument in the 1960 campaign:

> We are a great country. But I believe we can be a greater country. We are a powerful country. But I believe we can be a more powerful country. The Democratic Party in its past years has served the people—social security, care for the aged, housing, human rights. All these have been products of the liberal tradition in our great party. Now, in 1960, in these dangerous, difficult and challenging times, I believe the Democratic Party can lead again. *I believe we can get this country moving again.*[41]

The italicized line was Kennedy's signature slogan. The word "again" is crucial. It is a commitment to *restoring progress.* That is the task in the years after Trump.

Among the 2020 Democratic presidential candidates, no one was more intent on meeting the demand for new policy breakthroughs than Elizabeth Warren. It seemed, at times, that she was offering a plan a day—on everything from child care to farm policy to college loan debt forgiveness to affordable housing to improving the lives of Native Americans. The candidate responded so often to voters' questions with the words "I have a plan for that" that her campaign printed T-shirts bearing this unlikely slogan. That she rose steadily in the polls during the pre-primary period pointed to the hunger for new initiatives that would reorganize American capitalism while offering specific forms of relief to rebuild a middle class that she saw as dying.[42]

Warren's bywords were "sweeping structural changes"—both adjectives mattered—and her proposals were not a disconnected pile of white papers. They were focused, as Robert Borosage noted in *The Nation*, on "four major areas for fundamental reform: corruption, democracy, economy and social justice." Indeed, her democracy and economy proposals were linked in her proposed changes to corporate governance that would give workers 40 percent of the seats on the boards of major corporations while prohibiting a company from making political contributions unless it obtained approval from 75 percent of its board. New antitrust actions and an attack on concentrated economic power figured in her policies to diversify the digital economy and defend family farming.[43]

She also proposed a comprehensive anti-corruption law going well beyond post-Watergate reforms, and her critique of the nation's capital was more pointed than a general condemnation of its swampiness. "Washington works great for the wealthy and well-connected," she said again and again, "but it doesn't work for anyone else." Her ideas had much in common with the comprehensive reform bill passed by House Democrats in early 2019 as HR 1. The focus on structural reforms by both Warren and the House—they included a restored Voting Rights Act, curbs on gerrymandering, full access to the ballot, and sweeping changes in the rules for financing campaigns—reflected the lessons of the New Deal on the importance of democratizing political power. Warren's plan for universal child care and her linking of free college to extensive debt relief were aimed at rebuilding the middle class and its capacity to move from debt to savings. Other candidates, notably Senator Kirsten Gillibrand, before she dropped out of the race, and former Housing and Urban Development secretary Julián Castro, also focused on packages of ideas oriented to families and children, including expanded child care and pre-K programs as well as more generous family leave policies.[44]

And Warren's wealth tax, as we saw in the last chapter, underscored that public action could be financed by reallocating resources now concentrated at the very top of the economy.[45]

Warren made clear that you don't have to be a socialist to advocate far-reaching reform of capitalism. As she put it in a CNBC interview:

> I am a capitalist. . . . I believe in markets. What I don't believe in is theft, what I don't believe in is cheating. That's where the difference is. I love what markets can do, I love what functioning economies can do. They are what make us rich, they are what create opportunity. But only fair markets, markets with rules.[46]

Yet if Warren's policy inventory was especially rich, she was far from alone among her fellow candidates in offering large-scale ideas. Indeed, the *Post*'s Waldman suggested that Warren helped set off "a kind of policy arms race." Senator Kamala Harris approached the issue of distribution from the opposite direction, providing a tax *cut* in the form of a refundable tax credit to families earning less than $100,000 annually. The credit would be worth $6,000 for married couples earning up to $60,000 a year, and $3,000 both for single filers earning up to $30,000 and single parents earning up to $80,000; it would gradually phase out at higher income levels. Under her proposal, taxpayers could receive the benefit on a monthly basis, making it a trimmed-down version of Universal Basic Income. Harris would also give a tax credit to renters, an attempt to bring some balance to a tax system that has historically tilted toward homeowners.[47]

Combined with her support for repealing the Trump tax cuts, Harris's plan underscored how tax policy can either aggravate inequality—as the 2017 bill and the Reagan- and Bush-era tax cuts did—or reduce it, the effect of her proposal. Moving in a similar direction, Senators Michael Bennet and Sherrod Brown introduced the American Family Act to provide $300 a month per child to families with children under the age of six, and $250 a month per child for kids aged six to 18. Their plan would be especially beneficial for families earning between $40,000 and $100,000 annually and would cut child poverty in half. Another Harris initiative would close what she called the "teacher pay gap"—the widening difference between what teachers are paid in the United States and in other well-off developed countries.[48]

Operating closer to the political center, Senator Amy Klobuchar made her first major policy proposal a $1 trillion infrastructure plan that included funding for not only roads, bridges, and transit but also school construction, water systems, and guaranteed internet access, which would especially benefit rural areas. The Minnesota senator was not going to be outdone on specifics: She put out a list of 137 things she would accomplish in her first 100 days. As we've seen, Biden, too, stepped up his policy output—on health care, climate, and education. Biden was determined to fight the idea that he would be a mere "restorationist."[49]

The proposals and plans from all wings of the anti-Trump movement pointed to the shared eagerness of moderates and progressives to respond to the end of the Reagan dispensation. It's not surprising that progressives want to break free, but moderates have also made clear that they are not interested in cramped incrementalism, or thinking small. The mood the historian Arthur Schlesinger Jr. detected at the beginning of the 1960s closely matches the temper of our time. "At periodic moments in our history," Schlesinger wrote, "our country has paused on the threshold of a new epoch in our national life, unable for a moment to open the door, but aware that it must advance if it is to preserve its national vitality and identity. One feels that we are approaching such a moment now."[50]

Policies are essential to realizing the promise of such an era. But they are not sufficient. Here is where we can learn from Hillary

Clinton's defeat. Smart plans will not connect with the country unless they are linked to a larger purpose.

For our time, the galvanizing idea should be *dignity*—in our public life and politics, but also in the lives of our citizens and in the way we treat each other. Listen carefully, and you will hear the word invoked regularly by progressives like Alexandria Ocasio-Cortez, moderates like Joe Biden, and labor liberals like Sherrod Brown. Gene Sperling, a top economic adviser to both Bill Clinton and Barack Obama, argues that dignity "should be the singular end goal for economic policy" and the key value guiding policy priorities.[51]

For Sperling, economic dignity rests on three pillars: "the capacity to care for family and experience its joys"; the "pursuit of potential and purpose"; and "economic participation without domination or humiliation."

The first points to why family-friendly policies surrounding work are so important, but also to the roots of the frustration of many lower-income Americans, including those who have been displaced from good jobs. The inability to provide for one's family is a source of anger, despondency, and often shame. In many communities, men who were once accustomed to decent incomes found their old provider roles undercut—not because they were hurt by demands for gender equity but because their incomes collapsed. Most families now have a powerful interest in fair and equal pay because they are so dependent on at least two incomes. But in so many low- and middle-income households, the lost earning power of men has not been offset by increased earning power for women.

A politics of dignity means that talk of "family values" would no longer be about denying rights to LGBTQ people but about strengthening the ability of Americans across every divide to find satisfaction and fulfillment in their family responsibilities.

Similarly, Sperling argues that for millions of Americans, "the American promise of limitless potential and second chances feels distant." While these losses—including "deaths of despair" from suicide and addiction—are often discussed as if they involve "two completely different segments of America," Sperling writes, "what sadly links the laid-off white Rust Belt worker in his 50s to the low-income minority youth from a dysfunctional school and economically disadvantaged community is the dignity hit of feeling denied a real chance to pursue his or her full potential and purpose." Finally, Sperling notes the costs of the decline of the trade union movement and the drift away from the New Deal traditions of lifting up workers. The result is a rise in "humiliation, dominance, harassment and discrimination" in the workplace.[52]

A politics of dignity also means fighting against a leadership that has built its power by dividing Americans from each other and encouraging some groups of Americans to look down upon others—whether the native-born against immigrants, whites against blacks, or elites against those with less schooling. Mistrust has grown between metropolitan and small-town America and between the secular and the religious. We need to edit Trump's signature slogan. We need to make America empathetic again. And we need economic policies with empathy at their heart.

How do we do this? In our book *One Nation After Trump*, my colleagues Norm Ornstein and Tom Mann and I laid out a series of policies that we organized around the themes of a New Economy, a New Patriotism, a New Civil Society, and a New Democracy. There is no need to repeat them here, but I would underscore three themes from our account. First, a more democratic political structure—meaning one in which the power of money and the influence of the connected are reduced—is essential to moving the country toward fairer economic policies. Second, our nation needs to worry not only about the material costs of economic turmoil but also about the fraying of community and family bonds. Rebuilding community, strengthening the institutions of civil society, and shoring up families should be a priority—and it ought to unite left and right. Third, our nation needs to experiment with more ambitious regional and place-based policies. A vibrant nation that is both socially and geographically mobile will always experience unequal development; many places have undergone declines and revivals. But the extreme regional (and, within cities, neighborhood) inequalities we are experiencing are dangerous to our social and political health. We need to address them more forcefully.

To accomplish anything at all, progressives and moderates must both defend government and, by reforming it, persuade Americans that it can accomplish the things progressives promise. The long Reagan era cast government as inevitably clumsy, inefficient, and uncreative—when it was not being oppressive, meddlesome, and coercive. The most unvarnished expression of this view came from Representative Dick Armey, the Republican majority leader in the Gingrich years: "The market is rational and the government is dumb."[53]

This is, quite simply, wrong. The market and government alike are capable of irrationality, even as both can accomplish exceptional things. Government has been and can still be a source of innovation (from the internet to medical research), of opportunity (from the Morrill Act to the GI Bill), of rights (from the Wagner Act to civil rights laws), and, yes, of beauty. Consider our national parks (pioneered by Republicans) and our extraordinary public universities. Reforms in how government works, how it hires people, and how it interacts with citizens have often been a middle-of-the-road cause, but they should engage all who propose to use government for progressive purposes

As Ganesh Sitaraman and Anne Alstott reminded us in their 2019 book, *The Public Option*, some of the most useful and beloved institutions in American life, from the local public library to our parks (both local and national) and even our often-derided but exceptional postal service, are public. The public sphere can "expand freedom, increase opportunity and promote equality" by providing alternatives to the options offered by the market. Government can thus play a role that is at once entrepreneurial and egalitarian. Sitaraman and Alstott argue persuasively that well-conceived public options can spur innovation no less than the private sector can. Their emphasis on freedom is particularly important: The availability of goods and services outside the marketplace—health coverage is the obvious example—materially expands the freedom of those with limited financial resources. To paraphrase my *Washington Post* colleague Elizabeth Bruenig, there is an obligation to challenge a system that guarantees citizens only the freedom their money can buy.[54]

The value of debate between progressives and moderates in refining and improving policy was underscored by the premier plan-maker of the campaign, Elizabeth Warren. Her experience with the health care issue brought home both the practical and the political challenges of matching aspirations with plausible paths toward achieving them.

Sensing a need to protect her left political flank from Bernie Sanders, Warren endorsed Medicare-for-All at a Democratic debate in June 2019, after first suggesting she would pursue a more gradual approach to reform. Under further pressure, she put forward a detailed accounting of how she would finance the plan in early November.

Despite her specificity, she confronted a barrage of skeptical questions from the policy world and sharp criticisms from her rivals. Rapidly shifting virtually all health costs to the federal government is complicated and rife with the potential for unintended consequences.

So in mid-November, Warren made a midcourse correction. If elected, she said, she would postpone pressing for a single-payer system until later in her term of office. In the interim, she would build on Obamacare with public options and regulatory changes to expand coverage and hold down prescription drug costs. In the process, she moved closer to proposals that Biden and Buttigieg had put forward.[55]

Warren's evolution was one more sign (if any more were needed) of the political perils of far-reaching health care reform and the merits of step-by-step approaches. But it also showed that, in principle at least, it is possible to accompany a long-term vision with practical, immediate measures to achieve an urgent objective—in this case, getting health insurance to more Americans. It is the premier issue on which the politics of more, the politics of visionary gradualism, and the politics of dignity must meet.

A politics of dignity can bring progressives and moderates together and also begin to close the deep social divides that have distorted our politics and torn our country asunder. Opening the way to a new spirit of solidarity requires something else as well: An honest reckoning with the urgency of overcoming the injuries of race and gender but also with those of class.

SEVEN

OUT OF MANY . . . WHAT, EXACTLY?

*The Politics of Recognition and
the Politics of Class*

WE CAN DEBATE ALL WE WANT ABOUT THE MERITS OF "IDENTITY politics." But the Trump era made identity politics inescapable because the president of the United States chose to make the vilest forms of racism and nativism central to seeking and maintaining power. This was obvious on the very first day of his presidential candidacy when he called Mexican immigrants to the United States "rapists," and also long before, when he made birtherism's false claims about Barack Obama's origins his calling card.[1]

Resistance to calling out Trump's racism largely crumbled—except in his own party, of course—on July 14, 2019, when he tweeted an attack on Alexandria Ocasio-Cortez, Ilhan Omar, Ayanna Pressley, and Rashida Tlaib, all of them nonwhite, all of them progressive, and two of them Muslim. He suggested that the young congresswomen who had assailed his immigration policies "go back and help fix the totally broken and crime infested places from which they came," combining a variety of racial slurs in 16 words. "Go back to where you came from" is the language of the street bigot, and nativists have long ascribed criminality to non–Anglo Saxon immigrants. Never mind that three of the four women were born in the United States.

Two days later, Democrats in the House of Representatives passed a resolution explicitly condemning Trump's racism, chock-full of quotations from Ronald Reagan. But all the Gipper citations in the world couldn't break Republican solidarity with Trump. Only four Republicans joined the Democrats to condemn the president's ugly outburst. Unsurprisingly, many Republicans defended him by saying he was only attacking members of "the Squad" for their "socialist" views.[2]

It says a lot about this moment in politics that within hours of the House vote, journalists were turning to the idea that Trump was immensely *happy* with the whole episode. He saw playing identity politics as his best route to reelection. As *The New York Times* put it, "2020 will be a racially divisive reprise of the strategy that helped Trump narrowly capture the White House in 2016."[3]

Let's start by acknowledging that the very phrase "identity politics" is controversial. It can be used neutrally, but it is often seen by members of minority groups as an implicit rebuke to their efforts to defend themselves against discrimination. Calls for an end to identity politics are reasonably interpreted by African Americans, Latinos, women, and LGBTQ people as not-so-veiled attempts to make politics primarily about straight white men (again). Many who rail against identity politics ignore the fact that the identities in question arose in large part as a response to oppression.

But there is another strong, if fluid, identity at play in politics and social life: class. Many critics of identity politics within the Democratic Party fear that replacing a politics of class with a politics of race, gender, and sexual orientation dilutes a robust focus on the interests of working-class men and women of all races. They worry that this shift deprives liberals of a rhetoric that can appeal across our divides and leads them to downplay one of the premier social problems of our time: the rise of extraordinary disparities of wealth and income.

Identity is highly combustible. "Identities are not just things we have, they define who we are," wrote Yale University political theorist Steven B. Smith in a reflection on the work of the philosopher Isaiah Berlin. "We can compromise and balance interests," Smith added. "We cannot so easily adjudicate our identities."[4]

Smith is broadly right, but the purpose of this chapter is to insist nonetheless that there can be a productive give and take around a politics of identity. Doing so requires acknowledging multiple forms of injustice and the need for overlapping strategies of social inclusion and democratic change. In proposing a way forward, I will draw on the work of the political scientist Nancy Fraser, who argues that social justice requires both a "politics of redistribution," to combat the injuries related to class, and a "politics of recognition," to combat the injuries related to gender, race, religion, and sexual orientation. Class matters, she argues, but so does status.[5]

To claim an absolute divide between class politics and identity politics—between social democracy and multiculturalism—is to create a false choice. Class, after all, is a form of identity, too, and a phrase like "white working class" is no less about identity politics than references to African Americans, Latinos, Asians, or Muslims. As we have already seen, the New Deal focused on the injustices of class while largely ignoring those related to race. It's true that the New Deal improved the material circumstances of many African Americans, but far from ending the injuries of Jim Crow, it often reinforced them. Inequalities of gender have always crisscrossed class lines, and class politics had little to say about the often vicious exclusion of LGBTQ people. Justice requires attention to both identity and class. "Practically," Fraser writes, "the task is to devise a programmatic political orientation that can integrate the best of the politics of redistribution with the best of the politics of recognition." Of course, this is easier said than done, as Fraser knows. But it is the only option available to supporters of a more inclusive society, progressives and moderates alike.[6]

Arguments over class and status, identity and economics do not fall neatly along moderate/progressive or center/left lines. Some on the left continue to insist on the priority of class politics. Some who hold middle-of-the road views on economics are strong advocates of equality in the spheres of gender, race, and sexual orientation. There are also legitimate objections to drawing excessively sharp lines between class and status politics; these obviously interact in complicated ways. Staunch advocates of greater equality would insist that equality is indivisible—that there is a natural link connecting advocacy for greater equality of wealth and income with support for gender, race, and marriage equality. Movements on behalf of all of these causes are typically allied.

Nonetheless, particularly in the wake of the 2016 election, arguments over identity politics have been fierce and often divisive, pitting potential allies against each other. Finding a path through this contention is essential. Building a broad alliance of progressives and moderates to defend democratic values requires a solidarity built around our willingness to uphold each other's rights—partly to protect our own rights but also to fashion a more just social order. In grappling with the tensions entailed in identity politics, we might recall Rabbi Hillel's celebrated observation: "If I am not for myself, who will be for me? If I am only for myself, what am I?" Hillel was not a political consultant, but his balanced approach remains sound, strategically as well as morally.[7]

How can we realize his vision? Before turning to the substantive debates over identity politics, let's look at the political roots of the arguments within the broad anti-Trump coalition.

Attitudes toward identity politics are very much shaped by views of how his success is explained.

The temptation on one side of this debate is to argue that Trump's victory resulted primarily from the legitimate anger of a white working class that felt increasingly marginalized economically and ignored or patronized by liberal elites. In the pure version of this perspective, focusing on the racism, sexism, or nativism of Trump supporters is merely an attempt to sweep aside the concerns of a large group of Americans who feel forgotten.

The temptation on the other side is to see the Trump constituency as inspired almost entirely by racism, sexism, and nativism. Trumpism, in this view, successfully mobilized the resentment bred by those who felt they were losing ground in an increasingly multicultural nation. Those who make this case see a focus on class as a different kind of evasion, a denial of how deeply corrosive racism, nativism, and sexism had become.

The first diagnosis led to an aggressive argument for pushing identity politics aside and bringing white working-class voters back into the Democratic coalition. "The paradox of identity liberalism is that it paralyzes the capacity to think and act in a way that would actually accomplish the things it professes to want," wrote the political theorist Mark Lilla in *The Once and Future Liberal: After Identity Politics*, one of the earliest and most biting of the post-2016 critiques of identity politics. "Identity is not the future of the left. It is not a force hostile to neoliberalism. Identity is Reaganism for lefties."[8]

The second analysis pointed to the futility of winning over defectors to Trump and argued for a focus on the "coalition of the ascendant" that included racial minorities, the young, and liberal-minded whites in metropolitan areas.[9]

Because of the "centrality of identity" to our politics, John Sides, Michael Tesler, and Lynn Vavreck argued in *Identity Crisis: The 2016 Presidential Campaign and the Battle for the Meaning of America*, Democrats might do better to advocate for and rally minority voters than to try to reclaim (white) Trump-supporting Obama voters. "In the 2020 election," they wrote, "Democrats may find it easier to mobilize or win back Obama supporters who did not vote in 2016 or voted for a third party candidate."[10]

On the matter of raw electoral strategy, the first approach focuses on winning back Michigan, Pennsylvania, and Wisconsin. The second points to winning Florida, Georgia, North Carolina, Arizona, and Texas, states where substantial African American and Latino populations could be marshalled into a new majority. At this stage, the electoral math will lead both sides to agree on the urgency of contesting both rapidly changing Arizona and very swingy Florida while taking steps to recoup ground in the Midwest and Pennsylvania. Similarly, for the longer run, Georgia, North Carolina, and Texas are promising for progressives who can point to the political transformation of Virginia as a model for what can happen elsewhere. Nonetheless, as the *Washington Post's* veteran political reporter Dan Balz argued on the basis of a mountain of data, "[j]ust four states are likely to determine the outcome in 2020," Pennsylvania, Michigan, Wisconsin, and Florida.[11]

Those who explain the 2016 outcome as reflecting a backlash around race, culture, and immigration certainly have much evidence to muster. Studies after the election found that a sizable share of voters who shifted their allegiance from Obama to Trump were motivated in significant part by backlash around race. Virtually every study pointed to the importance of the immigration issue to Trump voters. Culturally conservative whites, particularly in the South, were drawn to Trump as a protector of both their status and their traditionalist attitudes in a country whose values were changing rapidly. Racial backlash was definitely part of this story.[12]

One of the best academic studies of the election, *Identity Crisis*, concluded that identity trumped or, perhaps more accurately, inflected economic attitudes. "Instead of a pure economic anxiety," Sides, Tesler, and Vavreck wrote, "what mattered was racialized economics." Race, they argued, "shaped the way voters understood economic outcomes." They defined "racialized economics" as "the belief that undeserving groups are getting ahead while your group is left behind" and they found that "racialized perceptions of economic deservingness were . . . strongly related to support for Donald Trump." They added: "Voters' attitudes on racial issues accounted for the 'diploma divide' between less and better educated whites."[13]

To pretend that race and identity were not central to the 2016 result is a form of denial. Sides, Tesler, and Vavreck were shrewd in pointing to how Trump redefined class politics (for whites) as white nationalist politics around race, culture, and immigration. And, following a long-standing conservative strategy, he redirected anti-elite anger away from the wealthy and toward cultural and educational institutions and, especially, the media.

Yet it's important to remember the other aspect of the "again" in Trump's greatness slogan: an attack on decades of free trade agreements, globalization, and the flight of American manufacturing jobs to China after it joined the World Trade Organization. Anti-globalization politics can easily be assimilated to nationalist and anti-immigrant politics, but they are not the same thing. Ross Perot drew substantial support in his 1992 and 1996 presidential campaigns for his opposition to free trade (he spoke of the "giant sucking sound" of American jobs moving abroad) without making any appeals around race or immigration.[14]

It's true that the 2016 exit poll found that voters who said immigration was most important to their vote backed Trump 64 percent to 33 percent. But it's also true that voters who said trade with other countries took away American jobs backed him by almost exactly the same margin, 64 to 32 percent. Both sets of views, of course, reflected a brand of nationalism, but the second brand was far more directly linked to economics.

Moreover, it needs to be stressed that the core of Trump's vote came not from blue-collar switchers from Obama but from *traditional conservative Republicans*. Recall that Trump carried nearly 90 percent of self-described Republicans and 80 percent of self-described conservatives. For all the talk of an education gap, 59 percent of college-educated white men voted for Trump. Many of them, no doubt, supported his promises of tax cuts. Among Trump's noncollege voters, large numbers, especially in the South, shifted their loyalties to the GOP long ago. Much is made of the fact that Trump defeated Clinton by 66 percent to 29 percent among white voters without a college degree. It's forgotten that in 2012, Mitt Romney carried this group overwhelmingly, too, by 61 percent to 36 percent.[15]

Two points are clear: First, the flight of noncollege whites to the Republicans, especially in the South, began long before Trump, so it can't be said that Trump invented a new backlash constituency. He built on trends that long predated his candidacy. Second, the impact of that swing was magnified in key states. Noncollege whites in Wisconsin, for example, gave Obama 45 percent of their ballots in 2012 but Clinton only 34 percent of their votes in 2016. The pattern was similar in Pennsylvania, Michigan, and Ohio. The lesson, as we saw in chapter 1, is that given the existence of the Electoral College, the Obama coalition (the "coalition of the ascendant") cannot succeed in the near term without a more significant share of the noncollege white vote than Clinton managed in the key industrial states.[16]

It's true that Clinton was also hurt by a drop in African American turnout in Philadelphia, Milwaukee, and Detroit—although some decline was inevitable after two elections won by the first African American president in American history. The Milwaukee drop-off, moreover, was aggravated by Republican-sponsored laws restricting access to the ballot. A careful analysis by Rob Griffin, Ruy Teixeira, and John Halpin of the Center for American Progress found that if African American turnout had held to 2012 levels, Clinton would have overturned Trump's small margins in Michigan and Wisconsin. But even with 2012 black turnout levels, she would still have lost Pennsylvania, and also North Carolina and Florida—and, with them, the presidency. Moreover, the CAP analysts found that Clinton's losses in Michigan and Pennsylvania could also be attributed to turnout *increases* among noncollege whites excited by Trump.[17]

A strategy based on mobilizing nonwhites, the young, and more liberal white metropolitan voters can certainly create a national popular vote majority. Clinton, after all, got 2.9 million more votes than Trump did. Generational change in the electorate means that this approach could indeed create a progressive and Democratic Electoral College majority within a decade or so, since Trump and his party are strongest among the oldest voters and weakest among the youngest. But if Democrats are to prevail in 2020 and 2024, they need to win back a share of Trump's white working-class voters in the key states. A large swing is not required. Getting back just one in ten non-college white voters would be more than sufficient to reverse Trump's 2016 margins.

Here is where it is important to understand the economic context that allowed Trump to prevail where he had to. Studies of the election that focused on public opinion surveys did indeed emphasize the role of race, culture, and immigration, as well as partisanship and ideology. Investigations that focused on *geography* put heavier stress on economics. One of the single most important facts about the election was this one: Clinton carried only 16 percent of the nation's roughly 3,100 counties, but they represented 64 percent of the nation's GDP. The 84 percent of counties that voted for Trump represented just 36 percent of GDP. Something economic was going on here.[18]

The role of economics in the election is often dismissed because places with higher unemployment rates were no more likely to vote for Trump than other areas. But unemployment is not the only measure of economic distress. Ben Casselman, the chief economics writer for *FiveThirtyEight,* found that "the slower a county's job growth had been since 2007, the more it shifted toward Trump." He went on to offer a litany of other economic indicators: "More subprime loans? More Trump support. More residents receiving disability payments? More Trump support. Lower earning among full-time workers? More Trump support." Casselman cited his colleague Andrew Flowers's observation that Trump Country "isn't the part of America where people are in the worst financial shape; it's the part of America where their economic prospects are on the steepest decline."[19]

There is no escaping the triple bottom line of 2016: Longstanding Republican and conservative loyalties mattered most of all. Race and culture mattered enormously. But the election's economic context mattered, too.

For much of the twentieth century, progressives spoke for those confronting economic injustice and won a majority of their ballots. In 2016, Trump channeled this anger among white voters in an ethno-nationalist direction. What accounts for this? Was the left's version of identity politics to blame?[20]

Mark Lilla certainly thought so. So did another prominent intellectual, Francis Fukuyama, whose *Identity: The Demand for Dignity and the Politics of Resentment* reflects a strain of liberal thinking genuinely alarmed by the rise of right-wing nationalism but fearful that identity politics on the left is stirring the very backlash that progressives are trying to contain.

Lilla's polemic grew out of a *New York Times* piece shortly after the 2016 election, "The End of Identity Liberalism." His view is rooted in his commitment to "civic liberalism," and his thinking on this subject has developed over many years. Writing in 1985 about the New Deal, Lilla noted that it had won acceptance "in no small part because Franklin Delano Roosevelt spoke *to* citizens, *about* citizens," and because it "promised to be a great act of civic inclusion."[21]

And this, in Lilla's 2017 view, pointed to precisely what was wrong with identity politics:

> Identity liberalism banished the word *we* to the outer reaches of respectable political discourse. Yet there is no long-term future for liberalism without it. Historically, liberals have called on *us* to ensure equal rights, they want *us* to feel a sense of solidarity with the unfortunate and help them. *We* is where everything begins. . . . But by abandoning the word [we], identity liberals have landed themselves in a strategic contradiction. When speaking about themselves, they want to assert their difference and react testily to any hint that their particular experience or needs are being erased. But when they call for political action to assist their group *X*, they demand it from people they have defined as *not-X* and whose experiences cannot, they say, be compared with their own.[22]

There is an anti-democratic underside to identity politics, Lilla insisted. "[By] getting so focused on themselves and the groups they felt they belonged to, identity liberals acquired additional disdain for ordinary democratic politics because it means engaging with and persuading people unlike themselves. Instead they began delivering sermons to the unwashed from a raised pulpit." Lilla sees both 1980s conservatism and identity liberalism as arising from the same spirit of radical individualism—thus his view of identity politics as "Reaganism for lefties."

"Citizenship dropped out of the picture," he wrote. As "people began to speak instead of their personal identities . . . JFK's challenge, 'What can I do for my country?'—which had inspired the early sixties generation—became unintelligible. The only meaningful question became a personal one: what does my country owe me by virtue of my identity?"

And Lilla made a point in his *New York Times* piece that we will come back to: "If you're going to mention groups in America," he wrote, "you'd better mention all of them."[23]

If Lilla's book was short, pungent, and aimed straight at the American political debate, Fukuyama offered a broad argument about the crisis of democracy around the world.[24]

Identity politics, Fukuyama argued, "has become a master concept that explains much of what is going on in global affairs" and "leaves modern liberal democracies facing an important challenge." His gloomy prognosis:

> Globalization has brought rapid economic and social change and made these societies far more diverse, creating demands for recognition on the part of groups that were once invisible to mainstream society. These demands have led to a backlash among other groups, which are feeling a loss of status and a sense of displacement. Democratic societies are fracturing into segments based on ever-narrower identities, threatening the possibility of deliberation and collective action by society as a whole. This is a road that leads only to state breakdown and, ultimately, failure. Unless such liberal democracies can work their way back to more universal understandings of human dignity, they will doom themselves—and the world—to continuing conflict.

Both Lilla and Fukuyama fear what happens when a politics built around class is replaced by a politics of racial, ethnic, gender, and sexual identity. In a *Foreign Affairs* symposium around his book, Fukuyama wrote:

> For the most part, twentieth-century politics was defined by economic issues. . . . Now, in many democracies, the left focuses less on creating broad economic equality and more on promoting the interests of a wide variety of marginalized

groups, such as ethnic minorities, immigrants and refugees, women, and LGBT people. The right, meanwhile, has redefined its core mission as the patriotic protection of traditional national identity, which is often explicitly connected to race, ethnicity, or religion.

Fukuyama is careful to acknowledge that the politics of identity "has brought about welcome changes in cultural norms and has produced concrete public policies that have helped many people." Thus, "the left's embrace of identity politics was both understandable and necessary." Understandable and necessary, perhaps, but still a problem in his view, since "the tendency of identity politics to focus on cultural issues has diverted energy and attention away from serious thinking on the part of progressives about how to reverse the 30-year trend in most liberal democracies toward greater socioeconomic inequality."

He largely blames the left for the rise of white identity politics. "The worst thing about identity politics as currently practiced by the left is that it has stimulated the rise of identity politics on the right," he argued. "This is due in no small part to the left's embrace of political correctness, a social norm that prohibits people from publicly expressing their beliefs or opinions without fearing moral opprobrium."

Like Lilla, Fukuyama mourns the impact of identity on the operation of democracy itself. "Societies need to protect marginalized and excluded groups, but they also need to achieve common goals through deliberation and consensus," he wrote. "The shift in the agendas of both the left and the right toward the protection of narrow group identities ultimately threatens that process."

But does it? More specifically, have the agendas shifted as much as Lilla and Fukuyama suggest? Is what has happened on the left equivalent to what's occurred on the right? Put another way: Are all forms of identity politics created equal?

Unsurprisingly, both writers came in for tough and often angry criticism. Lilla's account gave little ground to his opponents, and he could not resist taking shot after shot at his intellectual adversaries. They responded in kind. The Yale historian Beverly Gage challenged Lilla's understanding of the quietly revolutionary slogan "the personal is political," which she interprets as meaning "that we are all social and political beings even in the most intimate settings."

"Lilla rejects what most feminists would say about that venerable phrase: that it opened up new areas of life to political analysis and civic action," Gage wrote. "To the contrary, he sees it as a disastrous turn inward, a rejection of tough-minded electoral warfare in favor of 'aimless self-expression.'" Lilla, said Gage, "urges fellow liberals to focus on 'the hard and unglamorous task of persuading people very different from themselves to join a common effort,' then proceeds to insult his own audience."[25]

Gage also challenged Lilla's separation of movement politics from electoral politics. "Lilla acts as if there are easy answers to these questions," she wrote, citing his observation: "We need no more marchers. We need more mayors." She asked, archly but fairly, "But isn't it possible that we need both?"

Despite her sharp response, Gage acknowledged that Lilla raised questions that are vital to the future of the left, including, "How should the Democratic Party balance diversity with a common vision of citizenship?" This is indeed the heart of the matter.[26]

Similarly, Arlie Russell Hochschild, the author of *Strangers in Their Own Land*, an empathetic look at the white working class, credited Lilla for offering "an important, passionate and highly critical wake-up call to liberals" but argued that his account refused to acknowledge that many Americans came to electoral politics *through* movement politics—including movements related to identity. She cited her own story as a case in point. "When I was in high school, politics seemed very much a male realm," she wrote. "It was through feminism that I learned that I, too, had a voice, could join the conversation, advocate, petition, vote. Again, it was as a civil rights worker in the South that I got a frightening look at the link between race and electoral politics."[27]

One of the most powerful ripostes to Fukuyama's perspective came from Stacey Abrams, who, as we saw in chapter 1, lost the 2018 governor's race in Georgia by just 54,000 votes (and may well have been kept out of office by voter suppression directed against African Americans). In the *Foreign Affairs* symposium, she made the essential point about identity politics: that "minorities and the marginalized have little choice but to fight against the particular methods of discrimination employed against them. *The marginalized did not create identity politics: their identities have been forced on them by dominant groups, and politics is the most effective method of revolt*" (emphasis added).[28]

"When the groups most affected by these issues insist on acknowledgment of their intrinsic difference," she continued, "it should not be viewed as divisive. Embracing the distinct histories and identities of groups in a democracy enhances the complexity and capacity of the whole."

Abrams specifically challenged the preference for class politics over other forms of political action. "Fukuyama and other critics of identity politics contend that broad categories such as economic class contain multitudes and that all attention should focus on wide constructs rather than the substrates of inequality," she wrote. "But such arguments fail to acknowledge that some members of any particular economic class have advantages not enjoyed by others in their cohort. U.S. history abounds with examples of members of dominant groups abandoning class solidarity after concluding that opportunity is a zero-sum game."

Fukuyama was seen by other critics as having placed too much of the blame on the left for both the rise of identity politics and the collapse of consensual problem solving. The sociologist Alan Wolfe scorned Fukuyama for claiming "against all evidence, that our present stalemate over immigration is caused by those who oppose any form of 'amnesty' and those 'opposed to stricter enforcement of existing rules,' when in fact it is on the right, and the right only, where intransigence and unyielding intolerance reigns."[29]

Sides, Tesler, and Vavreck noted that Fukuyama's "favored political agenda closely resembles that of Democratic voters and the Democratic Party" and that the "most forceful opposition to such ideas has come from the Trump administration and its Republican allies and supporters." Yet they pointed out how Fukuyama put the burden on the Democrats to choose between "the mobilization of . . . identity groups" or efforts "to win back some of the white working-class voters . . . who have defected" to the GOP. In fact, they insisted, "if Fukuyama wants federal action on his policy agenda in an era of divided government and narrow congressional majorities, the real onus is on Republicans to support his ideas."[30]

Fukuyama's reply: "I agree that the burden is on Republican politicians to stop defending Trump, but they will do so only when they realize that their own voters are turning against him."[31]

Which, unfortunately, let Republican politicians off the hook by denying that they had any responsibility to lead "their own voters" away from their overwhelming and often passionate loyalty to Trump.[32]

So where, finally, does "the onus" in the identity politics debate lie?

Lilla and Fukuyama are right about a very important goal, but their proposed path—a comprehensive and straightforward rejection of identity politics—will not achieve it.

Lilla and Fukuyama are at their most persuasive when they insist that republican democracies require a sense of "we," a commitment to the obligations of a shared citizenship, and a willingness to embed immediate individual interests in a sense of the common good. Constitutional democracy cannot be sustained if politics is reduced *only* to a zero-sum game in which groups struggle with each other for power and economic advantage. Solidarity across our lines of division is an irreducible requirement of democracy, and empathy toward those unlike us is an essential virtue for those who would sustain a system of self-rule. The political philosopher Michael Sandel defined the core aspiration of a successful democratic system as faith in the proposition that common endeavor is both ennobling and enriching. "When politics goes well," he wrote, "we can know a good in common that we cannot know alone."[33]

What Lilla, Fukuyama, and those who share their perspective miss is the messiness of the process that gets us from here to there. The "clash of interests" critics of identity politics celebrate when discussing how they were dealt with by, say, Madison, Hamilton, and Jefferson—or, for that matter, Lincoln and Roosevelt—has always involved brands of identity politics. The Scots-Irish tended to oppose a centralizing Constitution, while Yankees advocated Federalism. Baptists led the fights against established churches. It is no accident that Lincoln purchased a German-language newspaper to further his political career. He understood that multiculturalism—a term not yet invented—

was a fact of American life and that the new Republican Party's large German immigrant constituency needed to be addressed on its own terms. The entire Reconstruction project after the Civil War acknowledged the need to dismantle a system of power built on racial oppression—and it was the resurgence of racism that brought Reconstruction to an end in the 1870s. Franklin Roosevelt was not shy about speaking out on behalf of the vast immigrant populations that filled the big cities and became the base for his New Deal coalition. It should be remembered that dominant native-born groups regularly racialized new immigrants—first from Ireland and later from Eastern and Southern Europe—in order to assert their alleged unfitness for democratic citizenship.[34]

Today's critics of identity politics romanticize our past, sometimes suggesting that class politics regularly predominated over status, race, and ethnicity, while at other times yearning for a degree of selfless devotion to the commonweal that was never as pure or complete as our imaginations have it. John F. Kennedy did indeed ask us to focus on what we could do for our country—but he was elected in part because nearly 80 percent of American Catholics voted to break the barrier that had blocked members of their faith from leading the nation. Was this not a form of identity politics? Was its exercise not both understandable and salutary?[35]

Contemporary struggles for racial justice are far more similar in spirit to the civil rights movement of the 1950s and 1960s than a sanitized view of our past would suggest. It's true that Martin Luther King Jr. spoke of a multiracial "beloved community" and appealed regularly to the nation's founding documents and scripture to make the case for racial justice. But the same Martin Luther King Jr. also issued his searing "Letter from Birmingham Jail." He spoke with real anger about the middle-of-the-roaders of his times, confessing that he was nearing "the regrettable conclusion that the Negro's great stumbling block in his stride toward freedom is not the White Citizen's Counciler or the Ku Klux Klanner, but the white moderate, who is more devoted to 'order' than to justice . . . who paternalistically believes he can set the timetable for another man's freedom . . . who constantly advises the Negro to wait for a 'more convenient season.'" Black Lives Matter and voting rights activists are lodging similar complaints today, reminding us that many of the specific issues of our time are unresolved questions from the King era.[36]

Stacey Abrams and her allies are struggling to preserve voting rights against today's methods of voter suppression that are simply the old literacy tests and poll taxes in a new guise. The Rev. William Barber has consciously rekindled the Poor People's Campaign that defined King's work at the end of his life. The mistreatment of African Americans by the police was as live an issue in 1966 as in 2020.[37]

Of course battles by and on behalf of marginalized groups for inclusion and recognition can be inconvenient to the political establishments in every era and highly disruptive to long-standing political arrangements. This, you might say, is precisely their point. Thus did the intensification of the battle against slavery in the 1840s and 1850s destroy a Whig Party that tried and failed to push the issue aside. The struggle for women's rights, going back to the suffragist movement, and the more recent demands of the LGBTQ movement, were disruptive, too.[38]

But what of Lilla's observation, "If you're going to mention groups in America, you'd better mention all of them"?[39]

Behind his statement is an insistence that class politics still matters. And it does. It has always lived side by side with, and sometimes overlapped, the politics of race, ethnicity, and gender. Lilla and Fukuyama are right to insist that progressive politics makes no sense if it ignores economic inequalities, even if it's wrong to argue that the left has walked away from these concerns. Inequalities of wealth and income affect African Americans and Latinos disproportionately, but they have hit the white working class hard as well. This means that progressives and their moderate allies must do what they have, at their best, always done, and address inequalities of class and status at the same time.[40]

Here is where Nancy Fraser's insights are so important. She insists that social justice requires both "redistribution" and "recognition." "Neither alone is sufficient," she writes. A politics of social justice must "accommodate both defensible claims for social equality and defensible claims of recognition of difference."[41]

Redistribution can mean government action to move income directly from one group to another (progressive taxes to support food stamps or access to affordable health insurance, for example). It can also involve strengthening the bargaining power of those at the middle or bottom of the class structure so they can improve their market incomes (through, for example, a revival of unions and other forms of working-class organization). The political scientist Jacob Hacker has called the latter concern "pre-distribution."[42]

In effect, the politics Fraser describes allows, in Lilla's terms, the naming of "all" groups who have a claim to relief from unfair outcomes. By addressing concerns about both class and status— the particular burdens facing African Americans, women, LGBTQ people, Latinos, and immigrants—her approach allows for a politics that is both more honest and more inclusive.[43]

The "exploitation," "economic marginalization," and "deprivation" caused by class inequality are real, she writes, but so are the costs of "misrecognition" along lines of culture and status: They include "cultural domination," "nonrecognition," and "disrespect."[44]

It is wrong to say that a white blue-collar man who has seen his job disappear or his earnings slashed has no cause for complaint. But it is also wrong to say that this white man has *exactly the same claim* as his African American workmate who simultaneously faces economic distress *and* racial discrimination. It is a terrible mistake to divide the white and black worker from each other in their common struggle for economic justice by focusing only on what differentiates them. But while both have a shared distributional claim, the African American worker faces burdens—fears over how his teenage son will be treated by the police, for one—that the white worker does not. A progressive politics that denies legitimacy to the white worker's economic claims will fail. A progressive politics that denies the legitimacy of the black worker's additional concerns—related not to class but to racial status—will also fail.

Fraser's approach acknowledges that class claims can interact with status claims, and that a democratic society must grapple with them simultaneously. Here is where Fukuyama's argument that identity claims are always binary—"either you recognize me, or you don't"—needs to be challenged. Fraser argues that "theorists of justice should reject the idea of an either/or choice between the distributive paradigm and the recognition paradigm; instead, they should adopt a two-dimensional conception of justice premised on the norm of participatory parity." Justice requires seeking "social arrangements that permit all (adult) members of society to interact with one another as peers." Put simply: We are all created equal and have equal rights to equal treatment. It is wrong to deny those rights through an unfair economy *or* through discriminatory social practices.

Working out these various claims, Fraser writes, requires "democratic deliberation." This presumes something other than zero-sum games. It demands rejecting political leadership that encourages divisiveness rather than honest negotiation. It calls for empathy and mutual respect.

In politics, all this is easier said than done. A coherent intellectual framework is not the same as a workable approach to everyday challenges. Struggle is part of the process. Negotiations can often be bitter. Wedge issues will always arise.

But absent a coherent framework, we are doomed to engage in the same fruitless arguments, over and over. We cannot reject identity politics because it addresses genuine injustices. We cannot ignore other social wounds and leave them unhealed.

Fraser's emphasis on "democratic deliberation" reminds us of the void left by the loss of institutions that have historically encouraged bargaining, honest conversation, and coalition building around race and class. The collapse of the trade union movement, particularly in the private sector, deprives us of a force that not only provided the working class with bargaining power but also created interracial coalitions for justice.[45]

This is still true, despite the weakening of unions, as the political scientists Paul Frymer and Jacob Grumbach found in an important 2019 study. They concluded that "union membership is associated with moderate to substantial reductions in racial resentment among whites" and also that "these white union members are consistently more supportive of affirmative action and other policies designed to benefit African Americans."

"Taken together," they wrote, "the results suggest that unions play a considerable role in increasing the racial liberalism of their white members." Interestingly, their data also suggested that union membership increases identification with the Democratic Party, which "may increase the racial liberalism of white workers." The right wing's ongoing war on unions thus has a double, interactive effect: It weakens a force that encourages racial liberalism even as it also undermines the Democratic Party, which is itself a conduit for more inclusive views on race.[46]

The decline of the churches and of the role of religion within the progressive movement is also a problem for an interracial politics of social justice. While there is some evidence that

Trumpism is stronger among nonreligious conservatives than among the more religious, white evangelicals, particularly in the South, have long had conservative racial attitudes, and Trump encouraged the rise of an even harsher Christian nationalism. The rise of opposition to abortion as the sine qua non issue among conservative Protestants and Catholics further diminishes the witness of a large share of the religious community on behalf of racial justice.[47]

All of which makes the strengthening of alliances between African American churches and progressive Christian, Jewish, and Muslim groups especially important. The Reclaiming Jesus movement, led by the progressive Christian activist and writer Jim Wallis and Episcopal bishop Michael Curry, is an important pushback against Christian nationalism and a powerful witness on behalf of racial equality. In his 2019 book *Christ in Crisis*, Wallis argued that a proper theological understanding of Christ's teachings fosters solidarity rather than division and a commitment to the least among us across all our current lines of conflict. Democratic presidential candidates Pete Buttigieg, Cory Booker, Elizabeth Warren, and Joe Biden have all been particularly outspoken on behalf of a Christian vision that is at once progressive and unifying.[48]

The unions and the churches were central to the civil rights movement, and they will be important now to turning conflict into cooperation around the issues of identity and class. We have forgotten that the United Auto Workers was a major force behind the 1963 March on Washington where Dr. King defined his dream. We also forget that its full name was the March on Washington for Jobs and Freedom. The top billing given to jobs was an acknowledgment that the ability to enjoy liberty and equality depends upon having the economic wherewithal to exercise our rights.[49]

The architects of our greatest advances toward racial equality never forgot that social and economic justice are intertwined. We shouldn't, either. An overtly racist president should remind us of the urgency of the quest for a beloved community and a defense of our common—and equal—citizenship.

EIGHT

"TAKE BACK CONTROL"

Nationalism, Patriotism, and Solidarity

THERE IS MUCH TO FEAR ABOUT RIGHT-WING NATIONALISM. IT
has led to fascism, war, the persecution and slaughter of minorities, and the undermining of democracy in the name of national
unity. With their regular denunciations of the give and take of
party politics as a force dividing and corrupting "the people," nationalists can open the path to rule by ruthless, cynical autocrats.
In our time, they already have.[1]

But those who would save liberal democracy, including all
who advance a progressive political outlook, need to be honest
with themselves and less arrogant toward those who currently
find nationalism attractive. A gulf has opened between affluent
metropolitan areas and smaller cities, towns, and rural regions
far removed from tech booms and the world of finance. This divide is a neuralgic factor in politics not only in the United States
but also across the affluent world.

Globalization married to rapid technological change has,
as we've seen, been very good for the well educated in the big
cities and their suburban areas. It has been a catastrophe for
many citizens outside of them—and also for the poor of the

great metropolitan regions themselves. It took the economic and policy elites too long to recognize what was happening.

The dispossessed often turn to nationalism for relief against their own sense of powerlessness. The Brexit slogan "Take Back Control" captured these feelings with surgical precision (even if the advocates of Brexit were purposely vague about how their grand plan would work out in practice). As the British political scientist Tim Haughton noted: "'Take back control' effectively combined not just a sense of a positive future albeit never defined or elaborated, but also suggested a sense of rightful ownership. Moreover, it helped to mobilize the anti-establishment support of voters who felt let down by their politicians. . . . Frustrated by the sense that the political class had failed them, many ordinary citizens took the opportunity to vent their fury." Much the same could be said of many of Trump's voters, and, to some degree, of 2016 Sanders Democratic primary supporters as well.[2]

Worries about the decay of national sovereignty are not the automatic marks of a reactionary. Love of one's country is not the same as an exclusionary chauvinism. Patriotism—the sentiment I prefer to nationalism, partly because it carries less nasty histori-cal baggage—can inspire solidarity and sacrifice for the common good. And in the United States, a nation where citizenship is de-fined not by blood but by commitments to liberty, equality, and self-rule, patriotism and the defense of constitutional democracy are one and the same.

Progressives and moderates alike should embrace the polit-ical thinker Yascha Mounk's endorsement of an "inclusive pa-triotism," which—pointing to the ways in which patriotism and nationalism can elide—is similar to the political philosopher William Galston's call for a "decent, responsible nationalism." A patriotism of this sort, Mounk argues, does not "privilege the nation to such an extent that it either oppresses minorities within the country or promotes conflict with other countries." Nor does it ignore the instances in which we've failed to uphold the values we proclaim. But it does "build on the tradition of multi-ethnic democracy to show that the ties that bind us go well beyond ethnicity and religion." At an intellectual level, it involves, as Galston argues, a deep respect for pluralism, in stark contrast to ethno-nationalism.[3]

Those bonds carry obligations. Service cannot simply be something for which citizens thank others. Moving beyond the Trump era will require a reengagement with the idea of national service, civilian as well as military. Service is a concrete expression of love for country. It backs up words with deeds. Common endeavor could also begin to break down barriers dividing us along every imaginable line—particularly, in our day, the barricades built from partisanship and ideology.

Just as the broad center-left cannot leave it to the right to define "freedom," so must they not cede the meaning of "patriotism" or "nation." As the historian Jill Lepore wrote, "To confuse nationalism with patriotism is to mistake contempt for love and fear for valor." But she added:

> The hard work isn't condemning nationalism; it's making the case for the liberal nation-state. This is an argument of political necessity and moral urgency. So far, Democrats haven't made it. Instead, in much the same way that they gave up the word "liberalism" in the 1980s, they've gotten skittish about the word "nation," as if fearing that to use it means descending into nationalism. . . . In a world made up of nations, there is no more powerful way to fight prejudice, intolerance and injustice than by a devotion to citizenship and equal rights under a nation of laws.[4]

When House Democrats condemned Trump's racism in July 2019, *Washington Post* blogger Greg Sargent noted that their resolution was in keeping with Lepore's "civic patriotism." It told the story of a nation "founded on universal ideals of liberty and equality, and the act of belonging to this nation is defined mostly through a commitment to these ideals."[5]

This view lies at the heart of opposition to Trump's hideous policies toward immigrants and refugees. Reversing Trump's actions—from family separation and fostering religious discrimination against Muslim migrants to the ungodly treatment of young children—is a moral imperative.

The challenge for advocates of humane immigration policies is to move the debate away from Trump's cruelty, falsehoods, and angry abstractions about "open borders" toward a practical engagement with basic questions: What level of immigration is optimal for the nation as a whole at any given time? What will it take to reach a consensus on creating a path to citizenship for undocumented immigrants? How do we build a stronger civic culture that acknowledges the rights and duties of the native-born and immigrants alike?

Progress on immigration will require bringing together the politics of compromise that moderates yearn for with the politics of justice that progressives champion. This, in turn, means distinguishing between the nationalist xenophobes and the larger group of Americans struggling to balance their generous instincts with their worries about security. Those at Trump rallies who shouted "Send her back!" at the mention of the name of Representative Ilhan Omar—who became a citizen after coming to the United States as a refugee from Somalia—will never be satisfied with balanced solutions on the subject that ignites their passions. Many of them, after all, are unhappy with the number of immigrants already here. (That was true of immigration opponents who backed Brexit, too.)[6]

Poll after poll, however, has shown that a large majority of Americans favor policies that combine competing goods: a broadly welcoming attitude toward immigrants with reasonable and sustainable limitations on the number admitted each year; humane treatment of those who arrive, especially refugees fleeing violence, combined with border security; a quick path to citizenship for the Dreamers brought here as children; and a gradual path for the millions who have lived and worked in the U.S. for years, in many cases decades. A new politics must enable the majority that supports such an approach to govern.[7]

There is nothing new or indecent about citizens saying that nations have a right to control their borders and to decide on what levels of immigration they want to accept at any given time. Virtually all who criticized Trump believed this. Proposals for immigration reform that advanced through Congress consistently linked relief for undocumented immigrants to border security and limitations of various kinds on future immigration flows. This was the model of the 2013 immigration bill that passed the Senate with support from all 52 Democrats, both Independents, and 14 Republicans.[8]

Finding agreement will be harder now that Trump has moved so much of his party away from the decent pragmatism that once inspired broad bipartisan cooperation. Yet as George W. Bush and Karl Rove understood, a GOP hoping for a future beyond Trumpism will not thrive in the long run as a nativist party in an increasingly diverse nation.

Progressives and moderates alike might plausibly argue that a resurgent right-wing nationalism is an effort by opportunistic politicians to distract from their failure to resolve other problems. They see it as a demagogic way to consolidate power by dividing and demonizing their opponents. Why take it seriously? They might assert as well that opposition to immigration is certainly nothing new, in the United States or elsewhere. The extreme nativism Trump represented, in this view, will gradually subside, allowing a return to more traditional politics around the issue. Advocates of reasonable immigration policies should just go about their business. Finally, they would insist that they need no lectures about patriotism, since their love of country should be obvious—and that the greatest love for a nation is often shown by those who criticize it in the name of its highest ideals.

In normal times, these might be reasonable assertions. We are not in normal times. The threat to liberal democracy, the collapse of consensual politics, new flows of immigrants and refugees accompanied by the growing fervor of anti-immigrant feeling—these are new realities that cannot be swept aside. Nationalism and anti-immigrant sentiment both reflect a sense of powerlessness felt by older, native-born citizens that, if allowed to fester, will continue to endanger the democratic project.

Arguments about nationalism, like arguments about identity politics, do not cut cleanly across the progressive/moderate divide. Many on the progressive side who are especially critical of nationalism as a general proposition, for example, share aspects of the nationalist critique of free trade. Some who are progressive and moderate would favor significantly higher levels of immigration; others, again on both sides, would not. What they share in common is a desire to defend democracy and free institutions, to oppose bigotry and cruelty, and to restore the brand of civic patriotism Lepore advances. To do so, they must come to terms with nationalism and the rise of anti-immigrant feeling.

This is why I turn next to the thinking of John Judis, whose analysis of both populism and nationalism serves as a useful challenge to currents of thought on both the center and the left.

Populism and nationalism are not the same thing, even though they are often spoken of in the same breath. Populism comes in many varieties. Some nationalist movements are populist, but others—those rooted in monarchism, traditional elitism, or military rule—are not. Yet because of the rise of movements in the United States and Europe that are both populist and nationalist, the two words have, for many, become interchangeable.

This is a mistake. It ignores both the strongly progressive and democratic aspects of the original populist movement in the United States and the existence of left-wing populist parties in Europe.

Judis, an American journalist and an often dissident thinker on the left, has devoted his recent work to drawing distinctions of this sort. While my main focus here is on his writing about nationalism, his 2016 book *The Populist Explosion* made an important contribution by pushing against scholars who argued that populism must necessarily be authoritarian and exclusionary. Judis saw populism more expansively, with both democratic and autocratic possibilities.

"It is not an ideology, but a political logic—a way of thinking about politics," he writes. Judis cites the historian Michael Kazin's definition of populism as part of what he has in mind—"a language whose speakers conceive of ordinary people as a noble assemblage not bounded narrowly by class; view their elite opponents as self-serving and undemocratic; and seek to mobilize the former against the latter."[9]

Populists, Judis argues, wave warning flags that establishments are foolish to ignore. "They signal that the prevailing political ideology isn't working and needs repair, and the standard worldview is breaking down." That both the Sanders and Trump campaigns could be fairly called populist drove home Judis's central argument that populism existed on the left and the right (and, in the case of Ross Perot's presidential candidacies in the 1990s, in the center, too). In Europe, France's far right National Front was populist, but so were Syriza in Greece and Podemos in Spain, both of them parties of the left.

Nationalism is the harder challenge, intellectually, politically, and morally. In his 2018 book *The Nationalist Revival: Trade, Immigration and the Revolt Against Globalization*, Judis continues to insist on conceptual nuance. Nationalism "can be the basis of

188 • Code Red

social generosity or of bigoted exclusion." It can be "an essential ingredient of political democracies" or "the basis for fascist and authoritarian regimes."[10]

Unlike many others on the left, Judis has a long history of sympathy for nationalism. Along with his earlier coauthor Michael Lind, he had pointed to the important role it played in the thinking of American leaders including Alexander Hamilton, John Quincy Adams, Abraham Lincoln, and Theodore Roosevelt. TR's 1912 Progressive Party program was proudly known as "the New Nationalism."[11]

For Judis, you can't have a more egalitarian economy if you don't defend the nation-state, and you can't have democracy either, since democracy works through national governments (the European Union being a partial exception). The institutions necessary for greater economic justice, he argues, are under attack by globalization. "The emergence of globalization in the 1970s has undermined the labor union and the locally owned factory and business and the community they sustained," he writes. "Finding themselves at the mercy of currency flows, footloose multinational corporations, and migrant flows, and afflicted by anomie and a sense of powerlessness—the individual has little recourse except the nation."[12]

Judis points toward the prophetic and critical work of the economist Dani Rodrik on the paradoxes and costs of globalization. Had more attention been paid to Rodrik's warnings in the 1990s about the political and social disruptions globalization was unleashing, the nationalist backlash of our era might have been avoided or, at the least, mitigated. Nor should friends of democracy have ignored a significant body of research, summarized by the political scientist Fletcher Cox: "Inequality undermines democratic resilience. Inequality increases political polarization, disrupts social cohesion and undermines trust in and support for democracy."[13]

One of Judis's conceptual contributions is to draw a sharp

line between globalism, which he opposes, and internationalism, which he supports. Globalism, he says, "subordinates nations and national governments to market forces or to the priorities of multinational corporations." Internationalism, on the other hand, refers to the decision of nations to "cede part of their sovereignty to international and regional bodies to address problems they could not adequately address on their own."[14]

It should be noted that attacks on globalism have a dark history on parts of the right and have often been deployed against the very internationalist policies Judis supports. Nonetheless, the distinction he offers is useful and helps explain arguments within the British left about the European Union. Most left-wing opponents of the EU in Britain have always seen it as serving international capitalism. In Judis's terms, they saw it as globalism's agent. A majority of the British left has come to see it instead as a classic case of internationalism, an effort to pool sovereignty—in a democratic way, if imperfectly so—for the purpose of empowering its members within the global system. This became clear when large numbers of traditional Labour voters defected to pro-Europe parties, particularly the Liberal Democrats and the Greens, in the May 2019 European elections to support this benign reading of the EU's role.

Judis's critique of globalism, his discussion of the impact of trade on manufacturing jobs, and his argument that national sovereignty has been essential in advancing broadly social democratic policies should appeal to progressives and moderates who acknowledge that unfettered globalization left many behind. And he's right that national feeling has been central to the social solidarity that generous welfare states require.

Nationalism will always be problematic for those who argue that the proper location of solidarity is global, and a strong case can be made from both religious and secular perspectives that more attention should be paid in our day-to-day politics to the poorest people in the poorest countries on earth. Egalitarianism begins at home, though, and economic justice within nations is a precondition to a sustainable politics of economic justice that stretches across borders. As I'll argue later, earning support for forms of international engagement that advance human rights and democracy requires the makers of foreign policy to acknowledge their obligations to the well-being of their own citizens, particularly those whose living standards are most threatened by new global arrangements.

In trying to vindicate democratic forms of nationalism, Judis is pushing uphill for many on the left and in the center. After World War II, he writes, "the leaders of the victorious powers tried to prevent the revival of the toxic, aggressive nationalism that had arisen in Germany, Italy and Japan." The result? "In Europe and to some extent in the United States, the very term 'nationalism' and its cognates acquired a pejorative connotation. To call someone a 'nationalist' insinuated some underlying sympathy for Nazis or fascists."

Well, yes. For many of us, it's hard to divorce nationalism from its murderous downside in the 1930s and 1940s. It's why we prefer the idea of patriotism, following the advice of George Orwell. He saw patriotism as stemming from "devotion to a particular place and a particular way of life" while insisting that "nationalism . . . is inseparable from the desire for power." The fascist experience still matters. As Isaiah Berlin noted in the early 1970s, those who foresaw more benign forms of nationalism in the nineteenth century never contemplated "the pathological developments of nationalism in our own times. . . . No one, as far as I know," Berlin continued, "had ever prophesied the rise of modern national narcissism: the self-adoration of peoples, of their conviction of their own immeasurable superiority to others and consequent right to domination over them." Former secretary of state Madeleine Albright is a sober thinker not given to alarmism or fevered rhetoric. Yet in 2018, she offered a book called *Fascism: A Warning* precisely because she sees eerie parallels between today's ethno-nationalism and fascist movements of the 1920s and 1930s.[15]

It is not mere sentiment to challenge the idea that we can now safely ignore the toxicity that attached itself to nationalism in the decades after World War I. The Trump movement and the far right parties in Europe often echo ethno-nationalist slogans and ideas from the 1930s that culminated in the rise of fascism. If this makes many on the liberal left nervous, well, it should.

On immigration, the picture is more complicated. Judis is right to point out that there has been a sharp change in the ethnic composition of the pool of immigrants since the 1965 Immigration Act, and the proportion of our population that is foreign-born has risen dramatically, from 4.7 percent in 1970 to 13.7 percent today. Suggesting that it is not surprising these factors have produced a reaction is not the same as justifying either racism or nativism. Nor, as we've seen already, is Judis wrong to argue that winning support for generous immigration policies will require difficult compromises. It should, however, be stressed that opposition to immigration, while high in areas where immigration is a new phenomenon, is often highest in areas where there are few, if any, immigrants. The fear is often of an abstract "other" or of a perceived loss by the native-born of national dominance, not necessarily a response to immediate changes in a given local community.[16]

Judis is sometimes too quick to rationalize the fears of the anti-immigration movement. He seems more morally offended by the obtuseness of the privileged, footloose cosmopolitans whom the British author David Goodhart labeled "Anywheres" than by the rage of Goodhart's "Somewheres," those deeply attached to their localities who are quite capable of their own old-fashioned prejudices. Nonetheless, those who live in prosperous precincts should ask themselves what role their indifference to the costs of the last three decades of economic change played in creating the mess we're in. And you do not have to be a Trumpist to argue that trade policies, particularly China's accession to the World Trade Organization in 2001, had a far more immediate and devastating impact in sending industrial jobs overseas than promoters of freer trade anticipated.[17]

What's important about Judis's argument is that it forces supporters of liberal democracy, progressive and moderate alike, to grapple with the paradoxes of their own position. Those who defend democracy need to understand the ways in which globalization can—and frequently has—undercut democracy itself. Those who support greater economic equality need to see how the open global economy, in many ways a substantial achievement, has challenged living standards, particularly among the least advantaged in the wealthiest countries. Trump is a uniquely odious figure, but Trumpism is not a one-off. Dealing with the discontents bred by globalization is the task of a generation.

The rise of nationalism also forces its critics to grapple with the questions of solidarity, social cohesion, and the obligations and rewards of a shared citizenship. The American republic does not work unless it honors not only its respect for individualism but also the quest for community that is equally embedded in our national character.[18]

Trumpian nationalism is the product of many forces, but Pete Buttigieg put his finger on one of them when he spoke of "a kind of disorientation and loss of community and identity." Similarly, the conservative writer Timothy Carney's 2019 book, *Alienated America*, spoke of Trump's core supporters as the "unattached, unconnected, dispossessed" and argued that while economic decline played a role in Trump's victory, the collapse of social capital in many communities left "a scar far deeper than an unemployment rate." Buttigieg turned this argument on its head by noting that the "very basic human desire for belonging" had historically "often been supplied by the workplace . . . based on the presumption of a lifelong relationship with a single employer." The decline of secure and durable employment ties—and, one might add, of the unions often associated with them—leads to broken human bonds and the very sense of dispossession Carney described. The interaction among broken local economies, broken civic ties, and broken workplace relationships can be deadly for individuals and for once-lively communities.[19]

Belonging and connectedness are not often spoken of as political issues, yet they provide the fiber for a healthy democratic polity that can resist demagoguery and exclusionary forms of nationalism. They are also antibodies against drug addiction and hopelessness—and against the violence and extremism that social isolation can breed.

A broadly liberal outlook stressing individual autonomy is always vulnerable to attack for failing to provide a civic glue that holds a society together, a strong basis for local community that offers individuals membership and meaning, and a historical narrative that binds the generations together.

A critique of this sort is emerging on a new "postliberal" right that rejects not only today's liberal left but the longer liberal tradition going back to the Enlightenment.[20] This postliberalism is a decidedly minority creed, embraced by a relatively small band of religious traditionalists. But like Trumpism (from which it differs in many important ways), it is a symptom of the breakdown of community-building institutions that tempered the liberal individualism that was dominant in the West after World War II.

Churches and unions are far weaker than they once were. Local economies are more influenced than ever by the decisions of national and global corporations (one reason for the rise of "buy local" movements). Local media have lost influence to national media and are often simply subsidiaries of larger conglomerates.

New technologies complicate this picture. They can simultaneously encourage a self-involved individualism and provide new ways for individuals to band together in new forms of community. Some of these communities are local and neighborhood-based, but many of them are national or transnational, and the technologies allow those who hold views once seen as marginal to find each other and organize. This development is also a mixed blessing. It allows oppressed minorities to find a voice and creative, dissenting ideas to gain traction. But it can also broaden the reach of extremist views. The global rise of ethno-nationalism is partly a product of this transformation as forms of backward-looking prejudice mobilize the most advanced techniques to sow division and animosity. Sometimes these efforts are encouraged and supported by national actors, as Vladimir Putin's Russia has shown in the United States and Europe.

We must, of course, fight foreign interference in our democracy and face up to how our deep divisions make us vulnerable to such manipulation. For the longer run, we should not pretend that there are easy, short-term solutions to challenges that have been gestating for decades. Still, there is no getting around the urgency of reducing alienation and anomie.

This effort, as I suggested in the last chapter, must also happen inside our religious traditions. Some liberals are tempted to write off religion as hopelessly compromised by the deep entanglement of Christian conservatives in Trumpian nationalism. But to abandon Christianity to the far right is to walk away from the central role it has played in American history in movements for reform, renewal, and justice. The moment calls not only for criticizing the rise of Christian Nationalism but also for embracing the capacity of Christianity and other faith traditions to renew communities rooted in empathy and solidarity.

The large majority that has risen up against Trumpian nationalism and in support of a broadly open outlook must make reweaving community bonds and strengthening civil society high priorities. These concerns should influence the design of new programs, the rhetoric of moderate and progressive politicians, and the thinking of intellectuals working to defend liberal democracy against the new threats it now faces.

Challenging ethno-nationalism with a renewed and inclusive patriotism requires keeping two ideas in balance. It is urgent that we see ourselves as citizens of the world who take seriously our stewardship obligations toward a warming planet and our responsibilities toward fellow human beings far removed from our own situations. But this should not diminish the immediate obligations we feel as citizens of our own country any more than the deep and particular love we have for our own families allows (and even enables) us to forge strong bonds of affection and loyalty toward those outside of them.

To love your own country means not going it alone in the world but seeking friends and allies who share your nation's values, commitments, and priorities. It certainly does *not* mean acting as Trump did in Syria in the fall of 2019: Abandoning the Kurds, the United States' long-time partners against ISIS, by greenlighting an invasion by Turkey in a conversation with Turkish President Erdogan that caught our country's diplomats and military entirely by surprise. Trump embarked on a "policy" that was nothing more than a whim based on his bizarrely inflated sense of his own rapport with other world leaders, preferably of the authoritarian sort. What followed was a pell-mell withdrawal of American troops, enhancing Russian and Iranian power and strengthening the brutal regime of Bashar Assad. It was a betrayal that took a jackhammer to American credibility. "Who can trust Trump's America?" asked *The Economist*. The answer was pretty much no one. "Is there anything left to the 'America First' agenda?" asked *Washington Post* foreign affairs columnist Jackson Diehl. His answer: "Not really."[21] Trump's approach was not even nationalism. It was recklessness married to weakness.

For once, even Republicans felt obliged to speak up. In the

House, 129 Republicans voted with the Democrats to condemn Trump's debacle, leaving the president with only 60 GOP loyalists.

The disaster in Syria was an extreme example of how Trump's approach has united progressives and moderates (and, in this instance, many conservatives as well). Across the center and left, there is revulsion over his unilateral and incoherent approach and his embrace of strongmen who loathe democracy, liberty, and free expression. Whatever their differences, moderates and progressives want to move in a new direction.

But what does this look like in practice? What would a post-Trump foreign policy look like?

NINE

WHO IN THE WORLD ARE WE?

A Foreign Policy for Democracy—
and Main Street

IN INTERNATIONAL RELATIONS AS IN SO MANY OTHER AREAS, Donald Trump helped Americans in large numbers discover (or remember) what they believe by reminding them of what they are against. He has shown us that the values we embrace at home can be as important to our standing in the world as any foreign policy choice or military decision.

He has also forced the traditional stewards of our country's power to come to terms with how deeply alienated so many of our fellow citizens are from the ways in which elites think about international relations.

Understanding both sides of this story is essential to repairing the damage he has done to our country's position in the international community and to moving our country's commitment to democratic values and human rights to stronger ground.

The catalog of horrors is obvious enough. Trump coddled autocrats and dictators, attacked democratic allies, and pursued a disjointedly transactional approach to the world. He dismissed a United Nations request for the FBI to investigate the murder of the dissident journalist Jamal Khashoggi because, he said, it could endanger American weapons sales to Saudi Arabia. It was impossible to forget that Trump was elected with help from the Russian regime of Vladimir Putin and that Special Counsel Robert Mueller detailed the many ways in which the president tried to block inquiries into what Russia did and how much Trump himself was involved. He said he was committed to "America First," but it might best be understood as "Trump First."[1] Nowhere was this clearer than in his willingness to use American aid as a lever to push the Ukrainian government to launch an investigation of Joe Biden. It was the charge that finally forced an impeachment inquiry. And then came the Syrian fiasco.

Trump's repudiation of so much we took for granted had an effect. Trump reminded tens of millions of Americans holding very diverse views that they still regard democracy as a lodestar for the United States' role in the world, believe in alliances with like-minded nations, and see the advancement of human rights—despite our country's sometimes glaring inconsistencies in defending them—as linked with America's long-term interests.[2]

Trump's ethno-nationalism itself undercut American influence in the world, an aspect of his recklessness that has received too little attention. "It's easy to forget how our country's tradition of immigration and openness has enhanced American power in indirect but essential ways," said Heather Hurlburt, a former Clinton administration official who directs the New Models of Policy Change project at the think tank New America. "We absorbed both sides of other people's wars—and prospered. This was one of the things the rest of the world admired about the US. The loss of this view of us may be one of the worst casualties of the Trump era."[3]

Indeed, Trump's explicit racism endangered the very project the United States had advanced around the world, if imperfectly, since the 1960s. "If multiracial democracy cannot be defended in America, it will not be defended elsewhere," wrote *The Atlantic*'s Adam Serwer. "What Americans do now, in the face of this, will define us forever." And it will.[4]

This book is premised on the idea that moderates and progressives have much to teach each other, and nowhere is this more true than in how we should think about our role in the world.

The broad center and left have long been divided between those who cast themselves as "internationalists" and support robust American engagement and those wary of American power and the ways it has been used. The war in Iraq stengthened the hand of the anti-interventionists. The country's dominant view is to be skeptical of new adventures. Trump himself (characteristically lying about the matter) boosted his chances for the Republican presidential nomination by claiming he had opposed the Iraq War. That Republican primary voters effectively turned their backs on their own party's initiative speaks volumes about the depth of public disenchantment with foreign intervention.[5]

Yet the Trump effect is paradoxical. If George W. Bush's theory that democracy could be successfully imposed by force created doubt among progressives about the United States' democratic mission to the world—Bush turned many onetime supporters of humanitarian intervention into cold-eyed realists deeply skeptical of foreign adventurism—Trump reminded them of the moral and practical perils of abandoning the country's democratic commitments altogether.

The power of Trump's "America First" slogan and his attacks on free trade should sound an alarm for traditional internationalists by making clear how out of touch with public sentiment they have become. Americans—in large numbers and on both sides of the ideological divide—are doubtful that foreign policy elites spend a lot of time thinking about how their decisions affect life on Main Street or on the shop floor.[6]

This didn't mean that Americans liked what Trump was doing. Approval of his slapdash foreign policy was low. His warm encomiums to the brutal dictator Kim Jong Un seemed just plain weird, not to mention repugnant. His arbitrary and high-handed use of tariffs divided the country, even if many on both sides of politics agreed that China deserved a comeuppance. But it's clear that foreign policy cannot simply return to the old status quo once Trump is gone. The old elites need to absorb this.

It is a sign of how inward-looking Americans have become and how frustrated they are with foreign engagement that foreign policy played only a bit part in early debates among 2020 Democratic presidential candidates. Absent a major crisis, it is likely to remain on the Democratic back burner until the party has a president required to make choices.

There were certainly obvious pillars of a shared worldview among Democrats, as *Vox*'s Alex Ward pointed out: the urgency of confronting climate change; the need to promote democracy and challenge corruption; the importance of strengthening alliances; and the need to rebuild the United States itself (an echo of foreign policy realist Richard Haass's 2013 book, *Foreign Policy Begins at Home*). These commitments were hardly the stuff of a new grand strategy—but beneath the surface lay an important dialogue that could provide a stronger foundation for American engagement with the world in the years ahead.[7]

In the early stages of the campaign, Joe Biden and Pete Buttigieg in particular issued strong defenses of traditional liberal internationalism.

"As president, I will ensure that democracy is once more the watchword of U.S. foreign policy—not to launch some moral crusade, but because it is in our enlightened self-interest," Biden declared. "We must restore our ability to rally the Free World—so we can once more make our stand upon new fields of action and together face new challenges."[8]

Buttigieg spoke along similar lines: "The world needs an America ready to reverse the rise of authoritarianism while revitalizing democracy at home and advancing it among our allies."[9]

Kamala Harris, who was less outspoken about foreign policy

at the outset of her campaign, took a similar view, specifically calling for the restoration of relationships with critical allies. Their past records and public statements suggested that Senators Amy Klobuchar and Michael Bennet shared a similar view. [10]

Elizabeth Warren and Bernie Sanders, by contrast, expressed a deep suspicion about the foreign policy of the past.

"While the authoritarian axis is committed to tearing down a post–World War II global order that they see as limiting their access to power and wealth, it is not enough for us to simply defend that order as it exists," Sanders insisted. "We must look honestly at how that order has failed to deliver on many of its promises, and how authoritarians have adeptly exploited those failures in order to build support for their agenda." He went on to champion "a vision of shared prosperity, security and dignity for all people . . . that addresses the massive global inequality that exists, not only in wealth but in political power."[11]

Similarly, Warren spoke of "a story Americans like to tell ourselves about how we built a liberal international order—one based on democratic principles, committed to civil and human rights, accountable to citizens, bound by the rule of law, and focused on economic prosperity for all. It's a good story, with deep roots," she wrote in *Foreign Affairs*. "But in recent decades, Washington's focus has shifted from policies that benefit everyone to policies that benefit a handful of elites."

Warren noted how wrong policymakers had been in the 1990s and 2000s when they assumed that "open markets would lead to open societies." On the contrary, she wrote, Russia "became belligerent and resurgent" while China "weaponized its economy without ever loosening its domestic political constraints." In the meantime, the terms of various trade deals were tilted by "multinational corporations" in ways that "favored their own bottom lines." She linked her reformist program at home with her approach overseas by invoking Franklin Roosevelt. "This will of the American people," FDR had said in 1941, "will not be frustrated, either by threats from powerful enemies abroad or by small, selfish groups or individuals at home."[12]

This is at the heart of the Warren-Sanders critique: It focuses on battling kleptocratic dictators and crony capitalists and putting the interests of the American worker at the center of thinking about international relations. The way back from Trump certainly involves a reengagement with traditional allies, a turn away from the world's dictators, and a renewed commitment to democracy as a guiding value in our dealings with other nations. But it must also mean rediscovering what Franklin Roosevelt and Harry Truman understood: that an American foreign policy disconnected from the economic interests of working Americans will never rally popular support for the role the United States must play in a dangerous world.

If foreign policy ever does become a flashpoint among Democrats, it's in the nature of campaigns that those on opposite sides of this divide will highlight their differences. In fact, these seemingly contrasting worldviews need to be seen as two sides of a new foreign policy.

Liberal internationalists like Biden are right that American power must play an important role in the coming years because the vacuum created by much-diminished American influence would be filled by powers hostile to democracy and our nation's values. A warning issued in the 1990s by John Judis and Michael Lind remains relevant: The United States, they said, needed to avoid both "indiscriminate retrenchment and indiscriminate commitment." Defining what that means in practice has been the stuff of foreign policy arguments for decades; it is the right starting point now.[13]

Americans will remain skeptical of *any* foreign policy they see as entirely disconnected from their everyday lives and their economic interests. As Vanderbilt law professor and longtime Warren adviser Ganesh Sitaraman noted, the new progressive approach places "far greater emphasis on how foreign policy impacts the

United States at home—and particularly on how foreign policy (including international economic policy) has impacted the domestic economy. . . . Progressive foreign policy places this at the center of its analysis rather than seeing it as peripheral."[14]

Marrying this progressive worldview to liberal internationalism is a necessary response to Trump's rise. It is the only way to begin rebuilding a consensus open to the United States' obligations to defend liberal democracy in a world where it is imperiled. It is also a requirement for creating a just nation in a more just world.

A May 2019 poll by the Center for American Progress drove the point home: A foreign policy that fails to take full account of domestic economic concerns is no longer viable.

When Americans look at the world, the CAP study found, they think primarily about how their government can keep them safe and how it can bolster their economic opportunities: "At the most basic level, voters want U.S. foreign policy and national security policies to focus on two concrete goals: protecting the U.S. homeland and its people from external threats—particularly terrorist attacks—and protecting jobs for American workers. American voters want the United States to be 'strong at home' first and foremost to help it compete in the world."

Americans, the polling showed, "express a clear desire for more investment in U.S. infrastructure, health care, and education—and less of an exclusive focus on military and defense spending—as part of a revamped foreign policy approach that gets America ready to compete with other countries." Again: Foreign policy begins at home.[15]

John Halpin, the lead author of the study, pointed to a paradox: Most Americans said they disliked Trump's approach to foreign affairs, disapproving of his handling of foreign policy by a margin of 57 percent to 40 percent. And 62 percent agreed with the statement that "under President Trump, America is losing respect around the world and alienating historic allies."

Nonetheless, Trump's distance from the old foreign policy establishment proved to be a political asset. "The language and policies of the foreign policy expert community simply don't work with many voters," Halpin said. "People are confused by abstract calls to defend the liberal international order or fight authoritarianism. The lack of clarity about goals and visions on the center-left opens the door for Trump-like nationalism to take hold, even though the president himself is unpopular."[16]

How much trouble is the middle-of-the-road foreign policy establishment in? The CAP poll used 20 questions to capture and map voters' priorities and values. About a fifth of those surveyed were so disengaged from foreign policy issues that their views could not be classified. The largest group, at 33 percent, were described by the researchers as "Trump Nationalists." They prioritized military spending, fighting terrorism, focusing on concerns at home, and opposing the United States' role as the world's policeman. Close behind—and at the opposite end of opinion—were the "Global Activists" at 28 percent. They emphasized working with allies on climate change, disease, poverty, and equal rights and stressed the importance of international institutions.

The *smallest* group reflected the attitudes of those who have dominated mainstream foreign policy debates for decades. "Traditional Internationalists," at 18 percent (represented in roughly equal proportions among Republicans and Democrats), focused on the United States' duty to engage in world affairs, the benefits of trade and alliances, the importance of defending democratic values, and the obligation to use force in response to threats.

As a practical matter, the first task of those who would create a majority against Trump Nationalism is to find common ground between the Global Activists and the Traditional Internationalists. Together, they outnumber supporters of his worldview. But that is not enough. They must also persuade at least some of the nationalists and many among the disengaged that it is possible to build a new U.S. approach to the world that places their legitimate interests at the center of policymaking. This is where the insights of the new progressive foreign policy are crucial for traditional internationalists. They must relearn the lessons taught by the architects of the post–World War II order: An internationalism that does not produce widely shared prosperity at home and proclaim it as a central goal is doomed to failure.

Linking domestic and international concerns is very much in keeping with an older tradition of American foreign policy, a tradition we have largely forgotten. The international institution building that the United States led after World War II, and the postwar economic arrangements on currency and trade that grew out of the New Deal, certainly strengthened global capitalism, but they were also based on the New Deal's social democratic bargain. Combined with egalitarian domestic policies, they succeeded in creating a broad middle class in both the United States and Western Europe and ushered in a three-decade-long period of unprecedented growth.[17]

The framers of the postwar system were also acutely aware that trade wars and beggar-thy-neighbor tariffs contributed to both World War I and World War II. They saw stable, open economic policies—again, within the framework of generous welfare states and adequate regulation—as being good for working people. The world is very different now, and a trade regime designed in a period of American economic dominance is in need of radical revision. But that, in a sense, is the point. The world needs, yes, a new deal that fosters democracy by promoting shared prosperity.[18]

The notion that liberal internationalists might learn from the new progressive foreign policy is not fanciful. When Joe Biden offered his foreign policy views in a detailed speech in July 2019, he devoted a large part of it to economics. He went out of his way to describe his approach as "a foreign policy for the middle class" and insisted that "economic security is national security." Perhaps the times are changing.

The Sanders-Warren approach needs development and correction, too. The critiques of their ideas from more traditional internationalists focused on how their concerns were almost entirely economic. Warren and Sanders spoke little about the role of American power, particularly American military power, except skeptically. In this, they were reflecting the view of many of their supporters on the left who, in calling for a retrenchment of American power, regularly pointed to the United States' support during the Cold War for repressive anti-Communist regimes and for military coups against left-wing governments in, among other places, Iran, Guatemala, and Chile.[19]

The left is right to call out our nation's past hypocrisies. Facing up to them is essential to moving forward. But even after they are acknowledged, there remains a strong case for engagement by the United States. Would democracy, human rights, environmental responsibility, and the battle against terrorism in all its varieties be well served by a radical reduction in American influence? Given the alternatives, the answer is no. The powers challenging the United States—China and Russia in particular—are not friends of progressive, liberal, or democratic values. The case for engagement was put well by Hurlburt:

The US does face real threats, from peer competitors such as Russia and China and more broadly from undemocratic powers who want not only to oppress their own people but to weaken democracy, openness, and human rights worldwide; from regimes that seek to acquire nuclear weapons to blackmail us and others; and from global warming, which simply cannot be managed without strong international coordination. Whether we're talking about the oxygen of rights and freedoms or the actual oxygen our planet needs, the US needs a healthy international system to flourish.[20]

Barack Obama, nobody's idea of a global adventurist, counseled against American retreat in his 2017 Farewell Address. He highlighted the values the United States can lift up in the world. "We cannot withdraw from big global fights—to expand democracy, and human rights, and women's rights, and LGBT rights," he declared. "No matter how imperfect our efforts, no matter how expedient ignoring such values may seem, that's part of defending America. . . . If the scope of freedom and respect for the rule of law shrinks around the world, the likelihood of war within and between nations increases, and our own freedoms will eventually be threatened."[21]

At the same time, few Americans want a repeat of the unilateral interventionism of the first decade of the twenty-first century. And yes, our foreign policy must address the ways in which kleptocracy and corruption undermine democracy, rebuild a consensus around climate, and never again make the economic interests of Americans a second thought (or not a thought at all) in our nation's global engagement.

The answer lies in what might be called Progressive Realism. It's a term first used by the writer Robert Wright that I endow with my own meaning here, although some of our views coincide. Progressive Realism would highlight democratic and social justice concerns but also take seriously the challenges we face from China and Russia—and from regional autocracies such as North Korea and Iran seeking, respectively, to use and develop nuclear weapons to propel themselves onto the world stage. Michael Mandelbaum, the veteran foreign policy scholar, has argued for a policy of "containment" that would echo our containment policy toward the Soviet Union, although in very different circumstances. Focusing on China, Russia, and Iran, he sees a containment policy in cooperation with like-minded nations as a logical way forward because it "exploits Washington's greatest strength: its ability to attract allies and create powerful coalitions against isolated opponents."[22]

Containment accepts that the United States has ongoing military obligations but sets limits on adventurism. Using it "as a strategic frame," Mandelbaum went on, "would also help restrain Washington's occasional impulses to do more (try to transform other societies) or less (retreat from global engagement altogether)." Containment would require a continued U.S. military presence in Europe and "a robust U.S. naval presence to fend off China's campaign to dominate the western Pacific." It would not, however, require a new large-scale commitment of American troops to the Middle East. And it would be entirely consistent with Obama's efforts to negotiate constraints on Iran's nuclear program. Recall that the Soviet containment policy was accompanied by agreements limiting nuclear arsenals.

A policy along Mandelbaum's lines would mean energetic efforts by the United States to rebuild its "soft power" by working with developing nations to check China's aggressive moves in this field, exemplified by its "Belt and Road" initiative. This would require renovating a hollowed-out State Department and the U.S. Agency for International Development. It would also mean shifting resources and functions away from the Department of Defense. Former defense secretary Robert Gates was no fan of defense cuts, but he has long been a champion of strengthening the State Department and other civilian agencies. "We must focus our energies beyond the guns and steel of the military, beyond just our brave soldiers, sailors, Marines and airmen," Gates said, calling for "a dramatic increase in spending on the civilian instruments of national security—diplomacy, strategic communications, foreign assistance, civic action, and economic reconstruction and development." He said this in 2007. The situation in our civilian agencies has only worsened since.[23]

The Marshall Plan rebuilt Western Europe and helped create the powerhouse American economy of the 1950s and 1960s. In our time, we should be capable of finding policies that simultaneously lift up the world's poor and improve the living standards of the least prosperous Americans. In keeping with this goal, Jennifer Harris, senior fellow for special projects at the Hewlett Foundation, has made the case for "a middle-class minded international economic policy." She argued for a new bargain with corporations that would link benefits, including trade assistance, to their meeting certain conditions—"a sufficiently equitable pay ratio between top executives and other workers, fair treatment of contract workers, neutrality toward unions, profit sharing, or repatriation of profits." Her proposal might be expanded to entail a corporate commitment to sustainable livelihoods on both ends of the supply chain—abroad as well as in the United States.[24]

Containment is only the beginning of a conversation, and, as Mandelbaum notes, containment relative to China, Russia, and Iran would be more conceptually complicated than it was toward the old Soviet Union. The United States' relationship with the Soviet Union had few economic stakes. The economic stakes with China are enormous. China and the U.S. are deeply embedded in each other's economies. If Trump's approach to trade problems with China was flawed, many of the issues he raised about China's practices are legitimate. Yet significant parts of the American economy also profit from the relationship. And the United States and China must, in the end, cooperate in any successful effort to keep the earth habitable in the face of climate change. Competition with the Soviet Union involved influence and military power. Competition with China involves this and much more. At the other end of the spectrum, Russia and Iran do not pose the same threats that the old Soviet Union did—and Iran's threat is at a regional, not a global, level. Nonetheless, Mandelbaum is right that containment as an organizing proposition could calibrate American engagement at broadly the right level, guarding against both retreat from the world and the excessive military interventionism that has characterized the last two decades.

The term "containment" is controversial with respect to China, carrying as it does the implications of a new Cold War that few Americans want. Former Obama administration officials Kurt Campbell and Jake Sullivan argue that the United States needs to learn "Cold War lessons" with respect to China but not apply "Cold War logic" to the relationship. They thus resist "neo-containment" in favor of what they call "sustainable deterrence." Because of all the ways in which China is so different from the old Soviet Union, the United States' relationship will necessarily involve "elements of competition and cooperation." The Cold War analogy, they say, both "exaggerates the existential threat posed by China" (we don't confront the possibility of mutual nuclear annihilation, as we did with the Soviet Union) and "discounts the strengths Beijing brings to long-term competition with the United States" (for example, its status as "the top trading partner for more than two-thirds of the world's nations").

In their dealings with China, the United States and its allies will need to balance imperatives that are in tension: "to confront, compete and cooperate," as *Financial Times* columnist Martin Wolf noted. Whatever the differences between Mandelbaum's pragmatic approach to containment and Campbell and Sullivan's tough-minded take on sustainable deterrence, both views emphasize "seeing alliances as assets to be invested in rather than costs to be cut," as Campbell and Sullivan put it. Both require being aware that "China's rise to superpower status will exert a pull toward autocracy," heightening the imperative of the United States' support for (and embodiment of) democratic values.

And even as it confronts an enhanced economic rivalry with

China, our government has been moving in precisely the wrong direction, turning away, Campbell and Sullivan note, "from precisely the kind of ambitious public investments it made" during the Eisenhower years after the Soviet Union launched its Sputnik satellite.[25]

David Ignatius, *The Washington Post*'s veteran foreign affairs columnist, noticed how the imperatives of "the competition, hopefully peaceful, with a rising China" fit with a broadly progressive agenda at home. "The domestic issues that animate Democratic voters come into better focus when we see them as part of this call to combat China," he wrote. "We need better schools, a fairer economy, and an inclusive, diverse, welcoming society; not just because these values are morally right, but because they help rebuild our democratic political system so that it works again and, yes, can compete with an autocratic and intolerant China."[26]

It is another reason why it's time to get our country moving again.

History has dealt the United States responsibilities from which it cannot walk away, but Americans will only embrace them if they have confidence that the stewards of diplomacy and military power accept their own responsibilities toward the citizens who bear the burdens of their choices. Advocates of even prudent forms of engagement will find no audience as long as foreign policy elites are seen as disconnected from the daily concerns of Americans, indifferent to their economic struggles, and detached from the sacrifices they call on others to make. Roosevelt and Truman both understood this when they fashioned a foreign policy that linked the country's security to social justice and widely shared prosperity. Their tradition summons us again. It was Henry Kissinger, nobody's idea of a populist, who observed: "No foreign policy—no matter how ingenious—has any chance of success if it is born in the minds of a few and carried in the hearts of none."[27]

Trump misled Americans in a great many ways, but one of his most deceptive ploys was his "America First" slogan. The history of the phrase is disturbing enough, given its roots in the movement to keep the United States out of the fight against Hitler before World War II. And despite Trump's showy confrontations over trade and his claims that he stood up for Americans against foreigners who don't spend enough in their own defense, his policies, at home and abroad, left the country weaker. Under Trump, the United States saw its influence and prestige decline and its image as a tolerant, open nation shattered. Our long-standing democratic allies were pushed aside as the president embraced dictators and endorsed political movements that sought to weaken liberal democracy in other nations. His misadventure in Syria was the culmination of all that was wrong in his approach to the world and to the United States' responsibilities.

These impulses inspired alarm and opposition across a very broad spectrum of American opinion, among progressives and moderates but also among conservatives who remain dedicated to a democratic vision of America's purpose.

A commitment to democratic values, an embrace of broadly shared prosperity, a decent respect for the opinions of humankind, an appreciation of what the United States, at its best, stands for: These are the ties that bind opposition to Trump's policies abroad with resistance to his approach at home. Across both spheres, solidarity, empathy, and hope must triumph over hostility, bigotry, and fear.

TEN

WHY CHANGE CAN'T WAIT

*And Why It Takes a Coalition to
Save a Country*

WE ARE AT A POINT IN OUR COUNTRY'S HISTORY WHEN IT seems that the biggest lie a politician can tell is: "I will bring Americans together."

Perhaps there are candidates who truly believe in their capacity to unite a nation torn by race and region, class and culture, age and gender, religion, ideology, and party. But it has not been a good bet since we began to come apart in the 1960s. We sharply polarized across party lines in the 1990s, came together briefly after September 11, 2001, and then divided again over the Iraq War. We have found ourselves in a profoundly surly mood since the economic meltdown of 2008. Americans in metropolitan areas and those in small towns and the countryside regard each other with mistrust. A large swath of white America sees its dominance and its values threatened by immigration and cultural change. Americans of color, immigrants especially, feel under siege.

Donald Trump's rise to power was the culmination of this long distemper, the conflagration set off by unresolved contradictions, built-up racial and generational resentments, the economic fallout from globalization and radical market policies, and the increasing lack of fit between our electoral institutions and a changing country. Trump was the second president in 16 years to take the White House after losing the popular vote. This underscored the growing disconnect between an Electoral College (and also a U.S. Senate) ill suited to representing a population increasingly crowded into metropolitan areas.[1]

He also connected with a global sense of alienation that has created a crisis for liberal democracies around the world. Economic globalization and large flows of immigrants and refugees—pushed to emigrate by war and political crisis in the Middle East and North Africa and by crime and economic crisis in Latin America—have created an ethno-nationalist backlash. Europe is riven by many of the same forces that are pushing Americans apart: great cities against small towns and rural areas, the cosmopolitan against the local, the well-off against those on the economic margins, white against nonwhite, Christian against Muslim. During past crises of democracy, particularly in the 1930s and 1940s, the United States was on the side of the democrats. At this moment, we are not.[2]

For all the lies Trump has told, there is one he has largely avoided: He did not base his claim to leadership on his capacity to bridge the gulfs that divide us. On the contrary, he has built his movement by keeping us outraged and riven. He speaks only to and for a "base" that represents, at most, 4 Americans in 10. It is an approach that has bred a backlash against him that has few precedents. The premise of this book is that the majority that spoke in the elections held on November 6, 2018, can be durable—and can grow—if those who built it understand who came together on that day.

They were Americans fed up with Trump's divisiveness and indecency, his racism and his sexism, his love of strongmen abroad, and his autocratic tendencies at home. They were citizens who wanted a president who took his job seriously, who was not in their face all the time, who was not a narcissist, and who did not put his own personal and economic interests above just about everything else. They wanted an end to the ad hoc chaos of a president who seemed to govern by whim.

They were also tired of a Republican Party and a conservative movement that refused to understand that some problems require public solutions, that our economic system will not work properly or fairly without the countervailing rule-making power of government, that the public sector needs to step in when the market fails—and that its intervention is especially urgent in guaranteeing everyone affordable health insurance that can't be threatened by past or current illness. These Americans think that government ought to be able to do what it always did in the past: build and fix the damn roads, expand our transit systems, educate our children, and bring new technologies and growth to the parts of the country being left behind. They are furious at those who acquiesce to the gun lobby and block every effort to reform our weapons laws, no matter how many people die in mass shootings. They supported a $15-an-hour minimum wage and saw little benefit in enormous tax cuts for corporations and the wealthy. They worried about a Supreme Court packed with conservatives aspiring to bring jurisprudence back to the days before FDR. Although they may have moral differences about abortion, they saw grave dangers in criminalizing it. They were resolutely opposed to discrimination against an LGBTQ community that is made up of their friends, relatives, and co-workers, their sons and their daughters—and their fellow citizens in the armed services risking their lives for our nation.

They were Americans who looked toward a new era of progressive reform that would right capitalism's injustices; prevent our planet's death from climate change; turn minimum wages into living wages; act decisively to contain gun violence; and reform our systems for delivering health care, paying for higher education, and preparing workers for a new economy. They include those who admire capitalism's inventiveness and those who are skeptical of how the system concentrates economic power. Yet across both groups, there is a desire to rein in monopoly, distribute wealth more fairly, create a universal system of child care, give those in the gig economy and irregular service jobs the protections enjoyed by those in traditional employment, and make the responsibilities of work compatible with the responsibilities of parenthood.

They were, in short, moderates and progressives. They were pragmatists and visionaries. They were capitalists, socialists, and social democrats. They came from all races. They were religious and secular. They were poor and working class, middle class and well-off. Some of them had even voted for Donald Trump in 2016 hoping he would shake things up and then came to realize that Trumpian chaos and corruption were antithetical to draining the swamp. Implicitly, they all understood Stacey Abrams's rule about coalition politics: "We do not succeed alone."[3]

This book offers what might be called articles of conciliation, ways in which members of this coalition for dignity, decency, democracy, and fairness might reason together. I have argued that moderates will not find a comfortable home on the right end of our politics because the radicalization of conservatism and the Republican Party has gone too far. Moderates are repelled by both the acrimony embedded in Trumpism and the wholesale rejection of public action that is, against the party's own history, at the heart of the current Republican creed. I have also argued that progressives need moderates, not only because their votes are required to build a majority but also because the virtues moderates embrace—conciliation, balance, pluralism, and an allergy to extremism—are virtues that any successful democracy requires. Moderates, in turn, need progressives for the activism and energy they bring, the moral challenges they pose to the privileged and the comfortable, and the space they have opened up in a political debate that was hemmed in too long by conservative assumptions.

Similarly, I have insisted that the last thing we need across the center and the left is a war over "identity politics." We should acknowledge that identity politics was imposed on subordinate groups by long histories of discrimination and exclusion. Recognizing the injuries of status—linked to race, gender, religion, and sexual orientation—in no way precludes recognizing the related but separate injuries of class. We needed both the Wagner Act and the civil rights bills. We need to address both forms of inequality.

This is one reason why I have laid so much stress on the idea of dignity. The quest for dignity and equal recognition animates struggles around both civil rights and workers' rights. When these two causes link arms, they can push aside racial animosity and transform a nation. This is what the organizers of the Jobs and Freedom march in 1963 understood and what Robert F. Kennedy demonstrated in his tragically short-lived 1968 campaign.

For all who would move forward, there is no other option but to defeat Trumpism and a radicalized conservatism.

But, yes, there will be an ongoing struggle beyond 2020. Barack Obama's hope—I admit I shared it—was that his reelection in 2012 would "break the fever" in Washington. It proved false. It is equally unrealistic to imagine that simply bringing Trump's presidency to a close will write an abrupt and happy ending to this chapter in our history. The changes in the Republican Party and the divisions in the nation run too deep. The power of the right-wing media, which has an interest in stoking bitterness, is too strong. Resistance to serious reforms in our economic system will be well financed and well organized. This is why promises to bring Americans together in the short run should be heard with great skepticism.[4]

What of the long run? Must we remain this divided? Can we thrive as a successful democratic nation if we do?

The easiest answer is that demography will solve our problem. The rising generation is far more tolerant, open, adventurous, and reform-minded than are its elders. It is also more diverse. Seen this way, the Trump movement is the last gasp of an older America about to pass on. This is certainly something the Republican Party must think about as it places its bets on an America that will no longer exist in a generation. A decisive defeat in 2020 might encourage the party to speed its transformation.

The world, however, will continue to move on as we Americans sort through our difficulties. Ayanna Pressley's 2018 campaign slogan, "Change Can't Wait," comes to mind. Thus, the task of the victorious coalition of progressives and moderates I have in mind is not simply to begin righting the injustices in our country that led to Trump's election. It is also to make clear that the United States will take on the task of once again leading the democratic world by example—to show that a racially, ethnically, and religiously diverse society can find common purpose, that the opportunity and mobility our country has always claimed to embody can be made a reality for those who are now sidelined and see themselves as forgotten, that a globalized economy does not have to leave large numbers of our fellow citizens behind. We must show that we are capable of reforming outdated structures that make our country far less democratic than we claim it to be. We must demonstrate that we can meet new challenges in a world where the forces of liberal democracy are weaker than they were two decades ago. We need to build a new model of a thriving, competitive, and fair economy now that the assumptions of the 1980s have collapsed.

We also need to have arguments worthy of a nation that has long seen itself as exceptional in modeling what a democratic republic is supposed to look like. I have strong political views, but I would not want to live in a country where everyone agreed with me. I doubt you would, either. I long for a very different sort of debate, one in which remedy supplants rancor as its driving force and empathy becomes a social and not simply an individual virtue. We need to rediscover the first word of our Constitution. We must learn to say "We" about *all* of our fellow citizens—and mean it.

How, you might fairly ask, does such a plea square with an argument that has been unabashedly critical of one side of our politics, and of the man who became our president in 2017? Aren't those I take to task also part of that "We"?

Of course they are. And they must be defeated precisely because at this point in our history, their approach to politics embodies a denial of the capacious "We" our nation requires. Trump undercut our sense of common citizenship, common obligation, and common humanity on a daily basis. His party not only enabled him but has also put itself on a course to sustain levels of inequality that are incompatible with both successful republican government and our obligations to each other. One can hope that they will abandon this path and reengage with the honorable chapters of their own history. The country would be better for it. But this will not happen without struggle.

Which leaves it up to the progressives and the moderates. A time of crisis never allows for a simple return to where we started. It can end in catastrophe and decline, or lead to recovery and renewal. This generation's task is to restore progress—to get the country moving again by demonstrating anew our nation's capacity for self-correction, social reconstruction, and democratic self-government.

ACKNOWLEDGMENTS

Democracy, the historian Christopher Lasch wrote, may not always be the most efficient form of government, but it ought to be the most educational because it involves ongoing debate and a constant exchange of ideas and views. Our democracy is not living up to Lasch's aspiration, but in writing this book, I have experienced the joys of a democratic education because I have been assisted by so many people—progressives and moderates, but also conservatives and radicals. I can't name them all (although many are mentioned in Acknowledgments to earlier books), but I thank them for enlarging my thinking and instructing me when I have been wrong.

This book went through many rounds of revision, and some of the most important improvements came in response to exceptionally detailed and deeply thoughtful reviews of earlier drafts by Tom Mann and Adam Waters. They devoted far more time, thought, and care to this project than any friend had a right to expect. This brief thank-you does not begin to do justice to their generosity and their insight. Heather Hurlburt was also generous in reading and rereading my chapter on foreign policy and helped make it so much better than it was, in some cases by let-

ting me cite her thoughts in the text. Thanks also to Norm Ornstein for his intellectual and political energy and for inviting me
into a partnership with him and Tom that led to our book *One
Nation After Trump*.

I owe a special thanks to the editors of *Foreign Affairs* who
allowed me to draw extensively from a fascinating symposium
around Francis Fukuyama's book on identity politics, and to
Zachary Hastings Hooper for arranging its inclusion in the book.
Readers will notice that other important pieces in the magazine
influenced my thinking. And thanks to David Eisenhower for
kindly making clear that I could use a long quotation from his
grandfather.

My appreciation also goes to Harold Meyerson, Robert Kuttner, and Paul Starr, my friends at *The American Prospect*, for
inviting me to review John Judis' thoughtful book on nationalism
and permitting me to draw on parts of that essay in chapter 8. I
am also grateful for my long engagement with *Democracy* journal as chair of its editorial committee, and in particular to Michael Tomasky, Andrei Cherny, and Kenneth Baer. I first wrote
about the Politics of More in a brief contribution to a *Democracy*
symposium, and several important essays from a magazine that
is a model for constructive engagement between moderates and
progressives are key to my arguments here.

I am enormously blessed by my long association with *The
Washington Post*. Some of the ideas I was working on for this
book made their way early on into my *Post* column, and some of
my work for the column (particularly during the 2018 midterm
campaign) made its way into these pages. Thanking all the *Post*
colleagues and line editors who would require an extensive mast-
head. For now, I offer my deep thanks to Fred Hiatt, the editorial
page editor who has run my column for many years, and also to
Ruth Marcus, Jackson Diehl, Michael Larrabee, Michael Duffy,
Richard Aldacushion, Sophie Yarborough, Josh Alvarez, and
Karen Green. Thanks also to Dan Balz, the once-in-generation

political writer who miraculously combines tough-mindedness with warm-heartedness. And thank you to my friends and colleagues at NPR and MSNBC.

I write about the importance of the word "we," and I am lucky to be able to use it in relation to colleagues at three institutions devoted to learning that have allowed me to be part of their respective communities.

At the Brookings Institution, I owe particular debts to Darrell West, John Allen, and Bill Galston. Friendship with Bill makes you part of a running high-level seminar on politics and philosophy, and Bill and I have partnered on many projects. These include a very fruitful polling partnership with Robert Jones and PRRI, and an essay on socialism for Brookings' FixGov website that we worked on while I was writing this book. The interaction greatly improved the analysis of socialism offered in these pages.

I have many debts to Georgetown University: My profound gratitude to President Jack DiGioia; Joe Ferrara, his chief of staff; Dean Maria Cancian of the McCourt School of Public Policy; my previous deans, Ed Montgomery and Judy Feder; Shaun Casey of the Berkley Center; and Mo Elleithee of the Institute of Politics and Public Service.

My debts to Harvard University are also great: to former president Drew Faust; deans David Hempton of the Divinity School and Doug Elmendorf of the Kennedy School of Government; Nancy Gibbs and Setti Warren at the Shorenstein Center on Media, Politics and Public Policy; and Nicco Mele, the center's former director; Archon Fung and Miles Rapoport at the Ash Center for Democratic Governance and Innovation; and Mark Gearan and Amy Howell at the John F. Kennedy Institute of Politics. Thanks as well to President Larry Bacow, who shares with Drew Faust and Jack DiGioia a deep devotion to public service.

It is not common to thank editors of earlier books published by other houses, but I must thank Alice Mayhew of Simon and Schuster, Anton Mueller of Bloomsbury, and Peter Dougherty and Fred Appel of Princeton University Press. The thinking and research that went into the books I worked on with them and their guidance are reflected here in many ways. Alice, a legend in the world of books, became my friend before she became my editor. She has been an ongoing source of inspiration, advice, and wisdom—and also of shrewd political analysis and historical perspective. My debt to her is unpayable. Anton, Peter, and Fred have also generously contributed to my understanding, and the opportunity Anton offered my friend Joy-Ann Reid and me to edit a collection of Barack Obama's speeches greatly enhanced my understanding of the man, his times, and his administration.

I'm deeply appreciative to Gail Ross, my agent, who has been there through almost all of these projects. Gail simply makes thing happen, is staggeringly loyal to all her authors, and provides shrewd advice about absolutely everything.

I do not have the space to list all the contributions made by Amber Herrle, my research assistant, a title that doesn't begin to capture the extent of her contributions. From her close attention to the use and misuse of words, her knowledge of politics across the globe, her "Hi, team" notes to all involved to encourage things along, her mastery of tenses (including present perfect), her careful fact-checking and her sense of irony linked to an embrace of hope—this is a partial list of the reasons why I owe her such deep gratitude. I especially appreciate her encouraging me to understand perspectives that might otherwise elude me. Christopher Lasch (whom her dad and I both admire) would, I think, honor this about her, too.

Thanks as well to my brilliant interns, Ketaki Gujar and Zachary Koslowski, who made many substantive contributions and undertook the painstaking work of organizing the notes.

I have often asked myself how I got so lucky as to work with the exceptional people at St. Martin's Press. Tim Bartlett is an editor's editor and a writer's editor all at once. He understands what makes books work, and also knows instinctively how to draw the best from those who try to write them. I'm thankful that he responded immediately and with great enthusiasm to the idea for this book and for smart, perceptive, informed, and timely advice, from beginning to end. Thanks especially for excellent counsel on how to deal with a political environment that was changing rapidly as this book went to press—and for caring so deeply about our country.

The team at St. Martin's is exemplary: welcoming, efficient, smart, and consistently warm. My thanks to Alice Pfeifer, for great advice and for keeping this project moving; India Cooper for excellent copy-editing; Alan Bradshaw, a master of production who combined superb wordsmithing with great flexibility in making changes possible late in the process; and to Martin Quinn and Gabrielle Gantz for caring as much as any author does about getting the word out on a new book. Thanks as well to Jennifer Enderlin, the publisher; Laura Clark, the associate publisher; Sally Richardson, the chairman; Tracey Guest, director of publicity; Andrew Martin, executive publishing director; and Rob Grom, a superb and creative jacket designer.

I am deeply blessed with a warm, thoughtful, opinionated, well-informed, and passionate family. They make joy and laughter part of my life every day. My wife, Mary Boyle, and our children, James, Julia, and Margot, are not responsible for anything I have written here. Yet every chapter reflects their insights, along with cultural and political knowledge about which I would have been entirely ignorant had they not offered me instruction. I feel very fortunate in this difficult time for our country to share bonds of love and solidarity with Mary—as wise a thinker and as generous a soul as I will ever know—and our children. And I have included James, Julia, and Margot in the dedication because all three of them, in their different ways, are engaged in the work of justice and democratic renewal. I am counting on them—and their generation.

NOTES

Introduction

1. Aurelian Craiutu, *Faces of Moderation: The Art of Balance in an Age of Extremes* (Philadelphia: University of Pennsylvania Press, 2017), 229–30, 239, 282.
2. Ezra Klein, "No One's Less Moderate Than Moderates," *Vox*, July 8, 2014, https://www.vox.com/2014/7/8/5878293/lets-stop-using-the-word-moderate.
3. Martin Luther King Jr., "I Have a Dream: Full Text March on Washington Speech," August 28, 1963, NAACP, https://www.naacp.org/i-have-a-dream-speech-full-march-on-washington/.
4. For President Trump claiming Democrats want open borders, see John Bowden, "Trump Knocks Democrats on 'Open Borders,'" *The Hill*, June 26, 2019, https://thehill.com/homenews/administration/450375-trump-knocks-democrats-on-open-borders.
5. Michelle Alexander, *The New Jim Crow: Mass Incarceration in the Age of Colorblindness* (New York: New Press, 2012); Chris Hayes, *A Colony in a Nation* (New York: W. W. Norton, 2017); K. Sabeel Rahman, "The Moral Vision After Neoliberalism," *Democracy Journal*, Summer 2019, https://democracyjournal.org/magazine/53/the-moral-vision-after-neoliberalism/.
6. "2018 House Popular Vote Tracker," *Cook Political Report*, January 10, 2019, https://cookpolitical.com/analysis/house/house-charts/2018-house-popular-vote-tracker.

Chapter I

1. "Nancy Pelosi: I'm Confident Democrats Will Retake the House," AP News, October 16, 2018, https://apnews.com/7417eaae2163475ea289a29373d2de18.
2. For detailed findings on the 2018 election, see Molly Reynolds, "Vital Statistics on Congress," Brookings Institution, March 4, 2019, https://www.brookings.edu/multi-chapter-report/vital-statistics-on-congress/. For AP analysis, see David A. Lieb, "AP: GOP Won More Seats in 2018 Than Suggested by Vote Share," AP News, March 21, 2019, https://apnews.com/9fd72a4c1c5742aead977ee27815d776.
3. Cheryl L. Johnson, "Statistics of the Congressional Election of November 6, 2018," Office of the Clerk, U.S. House of Representatives, February 28, 2019, http://clerk.house.gov/member_info/electionInfo/2018/statistics2018.pdf. For the 2014 election, see Karen Haas, "Statistics of the Congressional Election of November 4, 2014," Office of the Clerk, U.S. House of Representatives, March 9, 2015, https://history.house.gov/Institution/Election-Statistics/.
4. "1836 Presidential Election," 270 to Win, accessed May 21, 2019, https://www.270towin.com/1836_Election/.
5. Michael McDonald, "Voter Turnout Data," United States Elections Project, accessed May 21, 2019, http://www.electproject.org/home/voter-turnout/voter-turnout-data; "Exit Polls: 2018," CNN, accessed May 21, 2019, https://www.cnn.com/election/2018/exit-polls.
6. Lara Putnam and Theda Skocpol, "Middle America Reboots Democracy," *Democracy Journal*, February 20, 2018, https://democracyjournal.org/arguments/middle-america-reboots-democracy/.
7. Jordan Misra, "Behind the 2018 U.S. Midterm Election Turnout," U.S. Census Bureau, accessed July 17, 2019, https://www.census.gov/library/stories/2019/04/behind-2018-united-states-midterm-election-turnout.html.

8. Max Greenwood, "The 31 Trump Districts That Will Determine the Next House Majority," *The Hill*, March 15, 2019, https://thehill.com/homenews/house/434113-the-31-trump-districts-that-will-determine-the-next-house-majority.

9. Michael Tomasky, *If We Can Keep It: How the Republic Collapsed and How It Might Be Saved* (New York: Liveright, 2019), 183; Matt Grossman and David A. Hopkins, *Asymmetric Politics: Ideological Republicans and Group Interest Democrats* (New York: Oxford University Press, 2016), 258–59.

10. Alan Abramowitz, "Moderation in the Pursuit of Reelection May Not Help: Evidence from the 2018 House Elections," *Rasmussen Reports*, December 20, 2018, http://www.rasmussenreports.com/public_content/political_commentary/commentary_by_alan_i_abramowitz/moderation_in_the_pursuit_of_reelection_may_not_help_evidence_from_the_2018_house_elections.

11. Ronald Brownstein, "The Midterms Sent an Unmistakable Message to Republicans," *The Atlantic*, November 15, 2018, https://www.theatlantic.com/politics/archive/2018/11/trumps-cost-gop-midterms/575884/. For labor statistics under Reagan, see "Labor Force Statistics from the Current Population Survey," Bureau of Labor Statistics, accessed May 21, 2019, https://www.bls.gov/opub/mlr/1983/02/art1full.pdf.

12. Gary C. Jacobson, "Extreme Referendum: Donald Trump and the 2018 Midterm Elections," *Political Science Quarterly* 134, no. 1 (2019): 9–38.

13. Stanley B. Greenberg, *R.I.P. G.O.P.* (New York: Thomas Dunne Books, 2019), 167.

14. Greenberg, *R.I.P. G.O.P.*, 167.

15. "Exit Polls, 2018," CNN.

16. Lydia Saad, "U.S. Still Leans Conservative, but Liberals Keep Recent Gains," Gallup, January 8, 2019, https://news.gallup.com/poll/245813/leans-conservative-liberals-keep-recent-gains.aspx.

17. I am grateful to my student Allexa Gardner at Georgetown University's McCourt School of Public Policy for an excellent paper on how reporting about the Affordable Care Act shifted between 2009–10 and 2017.

18. "Exit Polls, 2018," CNN.

19. Mark Muro and Sifan Liu, "Another Clinton-Trump Divide: High-Output America vs Low-Output America," Brookings Institution *The Avenue* blog, November 11, 2016, https://www.brookings.edu/blog/the-avenue/2016/11/29/another-clinton-trump-divide-high-output-america-vs-low-output-america/.

20. "Pivot Counties: The Counties That Voted Obama-Obama-Trump from 2008–2016," Ballotpedia, accessed May 22, 2019, https://ballotpedia.org/Pivot_Counties:_The_counties_that_voted_Obama-Obama-Trump_from_2008-2016.

21. For all references to Frey, see William H. Frey, "A Vast Majority of Counties Showed Increased Democratic Support in 2018 House Election," Brookings Institution, March 1, 2019, https://www.brookings.edu/research/a-vast-majority-of-counties-showed-increased-democratic-support-in-2018-house-election/.

22. Interview with author, October 2018.

23. Interview with author, October 2018.

24. Interview with author, July 2018.

25. "New Jersey Election Results: Third House District," *New York Times*, January 28, 2019, https://www.nytimes.com/elections/results/new-jersey-house-district-3; "Virginia's 7th House District Election Results: Dave Brat vs. Abigail Spanberger," *New York Times*, January 28, 2019, https://www.nytimes.com/elections/results/virginia-house-district-7.

26. "Massachusetts Primary Election Results," *New York Times*, September 28, 2016; Kristin Toussaint, "Ayanna Pressley Is Ready to Make More Political History," *Metro US*, August 29, 2018, https://www.metro.us/news/local-news/boston/ayanna-pressley-q-and-a-primary-election.

27. Jenna Portnoy, "Rep. Abigail Spanberger: A Moderate Democrat Working to Survive in the AOC Era," *Washington Post*, May 28, 2019, https://www.washingtonpost.com/local

/virginia-politics/rep-abigail-spanberger-a-moderate-democrat-working-to-survive
-in-the-aoc-era/2019/05/16/a2ff11e4-700c-11e9-8be0-ca575670e91c_story.html?utm
_term=.55c03f30d2a2.

28. Interview with author, October 2018.
29. Interview with author, July 2018.
30. Interview with author, July 2018.
31. Phone interview with author, May 2018.
32. Gil Cisneros, Jason Crow, Chrissy Houlahan, Elaine Luria, Mikie Sherrill, Elissa Slotkin, and Abigail Spanberger, "Seven Freshman Democrats: These Allegations Are a Threat to All We Have Sworn to Protect," *Washington Post*, September 24, 2019, https://www.washingtonpost.com/opinions/2019/09/24/seven-freshman-democrats-these-allegations-are-threat-all-we-have-sworn-protect/.
33. Interview with author, October 2018.
34. "2018 Official Election Results," Ohio Secretary of State, February 13, 2019, https://www.sos.state.oh.us/elections/election-results-and-data/2018-official-elections-results/.
35. "Kobach: Undocumented Immigrants 'Draining Money out of the State Budget,'" KWCH (Wichita), June 9, 2017, https://www.kwch.com/content/news/Kobach—427543023.html; Mitch Smith, "Laura Kelly, a Kansas Democrat, Tops Kobach in Governor's Race," *New York Times*, November 6, 2018, https://www.nytimes.com/2018/11/06/us/laura-kelly-wins-kansas-governors-race.html.
36. Vilsack quoted in E. J. Dionne, Jr., "How Trump Lost the Midterms," *Washington Post*, November 7, 2018.
37. For more on voter suppression in Georgia, see P. R. Lockhart, "House Democrats Have Launched an Investigation into Voter Suppression in Georgia," *Vox*, March 6, 2019, https://www.vox.com/policy-and-politics/2019/3/6/18253689/voter-suppression-georgia-kemp-investigation-cummings. This and subsequent quotes from Abrams are from interview with author, October 2018.
38. "Georgia Governor Election Results," 2019, *New York Times*, January 28, 2019, https://www.nytimes.com/elections/results/georgia-governor; "Georgia Election Results," 2014, *New York Times*, December 17, 2014, https://www.nytimes.com/elections/2014/georgia-elections.
39. For Abrams's full remarks, see Tara Law, "Stacey Abrams' State of the Union Response: Full Transcript," February 6, 2019, https://time.com/5521939/state-of-the-union-democratic-response-transcript/.
40. For Trump's remarks after the 2018 elections, see "President Trump on 2018 Election Results," C-SPAN video, November 7, 2018, https://www.c-span.org/video/?454223-1/president-trump-calls-2018-midterm-elections-very-close-complete-victory.
41. For 2014 versus 2018 turnout analysis, see Dan Keating and Kate Rabinowitz, "Analysis: Turnout Was High for a Midterm and Even Rivaled a Presidential Election," *Washington Post*, November 8, 2018, https://www.washingtonpost.com/graphics/2018/politics/midterms-voter-enthusiasm/?utm_term=.d1860e968748/.
42. Jamelle Bouie, "Opinion: The Senate Is as Much of a Problem as Trump," *New York Times*, May 10, 2019, https://www.nytimes.com/2019/05/10/opinion/sunday/senate-democrats-trump.html; "Florida Senate Election Results: Bill Nelson vs. Rick Scott," *New York Times*, January 28, 2019, https://www.nytimes.com/elections/results/florida-senate.
43. Philip Bump, "Another Warning for Republicans: Trump Can't Win You your Election," *Washington Post*, November 17, 2019, https://www.washingtonpost.com/politics/2019/11/17/another-warning-republicans-trump-cant-win-you-your-election/.

Chapter 2
1. Heather Cox Richardson, *To Make Men Free: A History of the Republican Party* (New York: Basic Books, 2014).
2. United States Department of Agriculture, "NIFA Land-Grant Colleges and Universities,"

accessed May 22, 2019, https://nifa.usda.gov/sites/default/files/resource/LGU-Map-03 -18-19.pdf.

3. Theodore Roosevelt, "State of the Union Speech," December 2, 1902, http://www.let .rug.nl/usa/presidents/theodore-roosevelt/state-of-the-union-1902.php; Attorney General P. C. Knox quoted in *United States Congressional Serial Set* (Washington, DC: United States Government Printing Office, 1903), 20.

4. Thomas E. Dewey, "Inaugural Address," January 1, 1947, New York, *Scarsdale Inquirer*, January 3, 1947, Historical Newspapers, https://news.hrvh.org/veridian/?a=d&d =scarsdaleinquire19470103.2.78.

5. Richard O. Davies, "'Mr. Republican' Turns 'Socialist': Robert A. Taft and Public Housing," *Ohio History* 73 (Summer 1964): 135.

6. Stephen Ambrose, *Eisenhower: The President* (New York: Touchstone Books, 1985), 116.

7. Dwight Eisenhower, "Letter to Edgar Newton Eisenhower," November 8, 1954, https:// teachingamericanhistory.org/library/document/letter-to-edgar-newton-eisenhower/.

8. "President's 'War on Poverty' Approved," *CQ Almanac*, 1964, https://library.cqpress .com/cqalmanac/document.php?id=cqal64-1304191.

9. Mark Shields, "Our Last Liberal President," *Washington Post*, August 4, 1996, https:// www.washingtonpost.com/archive/opinions/1996/08/04/our-last-liberal-president /cec55416-5f85-4872-9fde-2a93eaa49b88/; Eduardo Porter, "G.O.P. Shift Moves Center Far to Right," *New York Times*, September 4, 2012, https://www.nytimes.com/2012 /09/05/business/the-gops-journey-from-the-liberal-days-of-nixon.html.

10. Ronald Reagan, "News Conference," August 12, 1986, https://www.reaganfoundation .org/ronald-reagan/reagan-quotes-speeches/news-conference-1/.

11. Ronald Reagan, "Remarks at the Presentation Ceremony for the Presidential Medal of Freedom," January 19, 1989, https://www.reaganlibrary.gov/research/speeches /011989b.

12. Ronald Reagan, "Farewell Address to the Nation," January 11, 1989, https://www .reaganlibrary.gov/research/speeches/011189i.

13. Dana Milbank, "George H. W. Bush's Funeral Was a Powerful Renunciation of Trump," *Washington Post*, December 5, 2018, https://www.washingtonpost.com/opinions /george-hw-bushs-funeral-was-a-powerful-renunciation-of-trump/2018/12/05 /e8c2a8a0-f8d2-11e8-8c9a-860ce2a8148f_story.html?utm_term=.90b0ec16244c; Brian Mulroney, remarks at George H. W. Bush's funeral service, December 5, 2018, https://www.washingtonpost.com/video/politics/former-canadian-prime-minister -remembers-george-hw-bush/2018/12/05/51976697-bb47-43d9-b1d6-229296b2cf75 _video.html?utm_term=.a5f9059237b8.

14. My view of Burke is shaped by Greg Weiner, *American Burke: The Uncommon Liberalism of Daniel Patrick Moynihan* (Lawrence: University Press of Kansas, 2015); and Jesse Norman, *Edmund Burke: The First Conservative* (New York: Basic Books, 2013).

15. George W. Bush, "'Islam Is Peace' Says President," remarks at Islamic Center of Washington, DC, September 17, 2001, https://georgewbush-whitehouse.archives.gov/news /releases/2001/09/20010917-11.html.

16. Karl Rove, *The Triumph of William McKinley: Why the Election of 1896 Still Matters* (New York: Simon & Schuster Paperbacks, 2015), 367.

17. "Bush's Speech on Immigration," *New York Times*, May 15, 2006, https://www.nytimes .com/2006/05/15/washington/15text-bush.html.

18. Robert Pear and Carl Hulse, "Immigration Bill Fails to Survive Senate Vote," *New York Times*, June 28, 2007, https://www.nytimes.com/2007/06/28/washington/28cnd -immig.html.

19. Banu Akdenizli, "News Coverage of Immigration 2007: A Political Story, Not an Issue, Covered Episodically," Project for Excellence in Journalism, 2008, https://www.brookings .edu/wp-content/uploads/2016/07/0925_immigration_banu.pdf.

20. Robert Suro, "The Triumph of No: How the Media Influence the Immigration Debate,"

Annenberg School for Communication at the University of Southern California, 2008, https://www.brookings.edu/wp-content/uploads/2016/07/0925_immigration_suro .pdf.

21. Isaac Chotiner, "How a Historian Uncovered Ronald Reagan's Racist Remarks to Richard Nixon," *New Yorker,* August 2, 2019, https://www.newyorker.com/news/q-and-a /how-a-historian-uncovered-ronald-reagans-racist-remarks-to-richard-nixon; Renée Graham, "Why Is Anyone Surprised by Reagan's Racism?," *Boston Globe,* August 2, 2019, https://www.bostonglobe.com/opinion/2019/08/02/why-anyone-surprised -reagan-racism/wVSXLxvnSXV2WlUJ3rbcQL/story.html.

22. Joel Achenbach, Scott Higham, and Sari Horwitz, "How NRA's True Believers Converted a Marksmanship Group into a Mighty Gun Lobby," *Washington Post,* January 12, 2013, https://www.washingtonpost.com/politics/how-nras-true-believers -converted-a-marksmanship-group-into-a-mighty-gun-lobby/2013/01/12/51c62288 -59b9-11e2-88d0-c4cf65c3ad15_story.html?utm_term=.9cae301d9e9d.

23. "Gravely Ill, Atwater Offers Apology," *New York Times,* January 13, 1991, https://www .nytimes.com/1991/01/13/us/gravely-ill-atwater-offers-apology.html.

24. "Exit Polls 2012: How the Vote Has Shifted," *Washington Post,* updated November 8, 2012, http://www.washingtonpost.com/wp-srv/special/politics/2012-exit-polls/table .html.

25. "RNC Report 2013: Growth and Opportunity Project," *Politico,* March 18, 2013, https://www.politico.com/story/2013/03/rnc-report-growth-and-opportunity-88987 .html.

26. Edmund Haislmaier, "The Significance of Massachusetts Health Reform," Heritage Foundation, April 11, 2006, https://www.heritage.org/health-care-reform/report /the-significance-massachusetts-health-reform; Robert E. Moffit, "The Rationale for a Statewide Health Insurance Exchange," Heritage Foundation, October 5, 2006, https://www.heritage.org/health-care-reform/report/the-rationale-statewide-health -insurance-exchange.

27. "President Bush Discusses Iraq with Reporters," September 13, 2002, https:// georgewbush-whitehouse.archives.gov/news/releases/2002/09/20020913.html.

28. Aaron Blake, "The Trump White House Has Turned Questioning Patriotism into a Talking Point," *Washington Post,* April 23, 2018, https://www.washingtonpost.com /news/the-fix/wp/2018/04/23/the-trump-white-house-has-turned-questioning-ones -patriotism-into-a-talking-point/?utm_term=.a4e489cfef30.

29. Roger Cohen and International Herald Tribune, "Globalist: The Republicans' Barb: John Kerry 'Looks French,'" *New York Times,* April 3, 2004, https://www.nytimes .com/2004/04/03/news/globalist-the-republicans-barbjohn-kerry-looks-french .html.

30. Patrick D. Healy, "Rove Criticizes Liberals on 9/11," *New York Times,* June 23, 2005, https://www.nytimes.com/2005/06/23/us/rove-criticizes-liberals-on-911.htm; Brendan Nyhan, "Media Failing to Report Rove's Most Offensive Comments," Brendan Nyhan Blog, June 25, 2005, https://www.brendan-nyhan.com/blog/2005/06/reporters _fail_.html.

31. "President Calls for Constitutional Amendment Protecting Marriage," February 24, 2004, https://georgewbush-whitehouse.archives.gov/news/releases/2004/02/20040224 -2.html.

32. Nate Silver, "'Real' America Looks Different to Palin, Obama," *FiveThirtyEight,* October 18, 2008, https://fivethirtyeight.com/features/real-america-looks-different-to -palin/.

33. For more on congressional obstruction in the Obama years, see Michael Grunwald, "The Victory of 'No,'" *Politico,* December 4, 2016, https://www.politico.com /magazine/story/2016/12/republican-party-obstructionism-victory-trump-214498; Philip Bump, "The Many Investigations into the Administration of Barack Obama," *Washington Post,* February 7, 2019, https://www.washingtonpost.com/politics

/2019/02/07/many-investigations-into-administration-barack-obama/?utm_term=
.9d159481629a.

34. For more on evangelicals and the courts, see Emma Green, "Even Never Trump Evangelicals Might Be Swayed by the Supreme Court," *The Atlantic*, July 15, 2018, https://www.theatlantic.com/politics/archive/2018/07/trump-supreme-court-divided-evangelicals/565004/; John Fea, "Why Do White Evangelicals Still Staunchly Support Donald Trump?," *Washington Post*, April 5, 2019, https://www.washingtonpost.com/outlook/2019/04/05/why-do-white-evangelicals-still-staunchly-support-donald-trump/?utm_term=.4dcbf303efe1.

35. "2016 Election Results: Exit Polls," CNN, updated November 23, 2012, https://www.cnn.com/election/2016/results/exit-polls; "Exit Polls 2012: How the Vote Has Shifted," *Washington Post*, updated November 8, 2012, http://www.washingtonpost.com/wp-srv/special/politics/2012-exit-polls/table.html.

36. "Annotated Transcript: The Aug. 6 GOP Debate," *Washington Post*, August 6, 2015, https://www.washingtonpost.com/news/post-politics/wp/2015/08/06/annotated-transcript-the-aug-6-gop-debate/.

37. The story in question is available online under a slightly different headline: Jonathan Martin and Maggie Haberman, "Trump Relies on Populist Language, but He Mostly Sides with Corporate Interests," *New York Times*, July 23, 2019, https://www.nytimes.com/2019/07/23/us/politics/trump-working-class.html.

38. Ross Douthat, "The Mick Mulvaney Presidency," *New York Times*, March 30, 2019, https://www.nytimes.com/2019/03/30/opinion/trump-obamacare-mulvaney.html.

Chapter 3

1. James T. Kloppenberg, *Uncertain Victory: Social Democracy and Progressivism in European and American Thought, 1870–1920* (New York and Oxford: Oxford University Press, 1986); Daniel T. Rodgers, *Atlantic Crossings: Social Politics in a Progressive Age* (Cambridge: Harvard University Press, 1998); David Motadel, "The Far Right Says There's Nothing Dirtier Than Internationalism—But They Depend on It," *New York Times*, July 3, 2019, https://www.nytimes.com/2019/07/03/opinion/the-surprising-history-of-nationalist-internationalism.html.

2. For liberal claims of conservativism in the 1950s, see Neil Jumonville and Kevin Mattson, eds., *Liberalism for a New Century* (Berkeley: University of California Press, 2007), 58–62; Kent M. Beck, "What Was Liberalism in the 1950s?," *Political Science Quarterly* 102, no. 2 (1987): 240, doi:10.2307/2151351.

3. For more on the terms "liberal" and "progressive," see Sean Wilentz, "Fighting Words," *Democracy Journal*, Spring 2018, https://democracyjournal.org/magazine/48/fighting-words/.

4. Howard Zinn, *LaGuardia in Congress* (Ithaca: Cornell University Press, 1958), 259–60.

5. For more on Franklin Roosevelt and the labor movement, see "Wagner Act," Roosevelt Institute, June 20, 2012, https://rooseveltinstitute.org/wagner-act/; William E. Leuchtenburg, "Franklin D. Roosevelt: The American Franchise," University of Virginia Miller Center, accessed July 10, 2019, https://millercenter.org/president/fdroosevelt/the-american-franchise; Nathan Glick, "FDR'S Left-Hand Man," *Washington Post*, August 18, 1991, https://www.washingtonpost.com/archive/entertainment/books/1991/08/18/fdrs-left-hand-man/2a44c174-069b-429f-a462-d33e7fffd299/?utm_term=.84bd119f8325. For "make me do it," see Peter Dreier, *The 100 Greatest Americans of the 20th Century: A Social Justice Hall of Fame* (New York: Nation Books, 2012), 118.

6. Ira Katznelson, *When Affirmative Action Was White: An Untold History of Racial Inequality in Twentieth-Century America* (New York: W. W. Norton, 2005).

7. Geoffrey Nunberg, "The Liberal Label," *American Prospect*, August 20, 2003, https://prospect.org/article/liberal-label; John F. Kennedy, "Address Accepting the Liberal Party Nomination for President," September 14, 1960, https://www.jfklibrary.org

/archives/other-resources/john-f-kennedy-speeches/liberal-party-nomination-nyc-19600914.

8. G. Calvin Mackenzie and Robert Weisbrot, *The Liberal Hour: Washington and the Politics of Change in the 1960s* (New York: Penguin, 2008), 2; Linda Charlton, "Funeral Being Held at Church That Johnson Attended Often," *New York Times*, January 24, 1973, https://www.nytimes.com/1973/01/24/archives/funeral-being-held-at-church-that-johnson-attended-often-room-for.html.

9. Steve Fraser, "Liberalism Is Under Attack from the Left and the Right," *The Nation*, June 2, 2016, https://www.thenation.com/article/liberalism-is-under-attack-from-the-left-and-the-right/.

10. Students for a Democratic Society, "The Port Huron Statement," 1962, http://web.mit.edu/21h.102/www/Primary%20source%20collections/Civil%20Rights/Port_Huron.htm.

11. Louis Menand, "Lessons from the Election of 1968," *New Yorker*, January 1, 2018, https://www.newyorker.com/magazine/2018/01/08/lessons-from-the-election-of-1968.

12. Todd Gitlin, "This Was the Most Gutting Month for Liberals in Half a Century," *Washington Post*, June 29, 2019, https://www.washingtonpost.com/outlook/this-was-the-most-gutting-month-for-liberals-in-half-a-century/2018/06/29/2f9eb864-7b23-11e8-93cc-6d3beccdd7a3_story.html?utm_term=.d2b7688e473a.

13. Jeffrey Toobin, "The Dirty Trickster," *New Yorker*, May 23, 2008, https://www.newyorker.com/magazine/2008/06/02/the-dirty-trickster.

14. For more on the House of Representatives Class of 1974, see Ken Rudin, "The Watergate Class of 1974: How They Arrived in Congress, How They Left," NPR, June 19, 2012, https://www.npr.org/sections/politicaljunkie/2012/06/19/155063336/the-watergate-class-of-1974-how-they-arrived-in-congress-how-they-left.

15. John Lawrence, *The Class of '74: Congress After Watergate and the Roots of Partisanship* (Baltimore: Johns Hopkins University Press, 2018), 8.

16. William Schneider, "A Primary That May Be Decisive. Or Not," *National Journal*, January 1, 2000, https://www.aei.org/publication/a-primary-that-may-be-decisive-or-not/; R. W. Apple Jr., "Carter and the Poll," *New York Times*, February 13, 1976, https://www.nytimes.com/1976/02/13/archives/carter-and-the-poll-he-is-viewed-as-best-unity-candidate-but-his.html.

17. John Cassidy, "Reagan and Keynes: The Love That Dare Not Speak Its Name," *New Yorker*, April 30, 2014, https://www.newyorker.com/news/john-cassidy/reagan-and-keynes-the-love-that-dare-not-speak-its-name; Roger Cohen, "Globalist: Dirty Word 'Liberal' Boasts a Proud History," *New York Times*, October 27, 2004. https://www.nytimes.com/2004/10/27/news/globalist-dirty-word-liberal-boasts-a-proud-history.html.

18. George Gilder, *Wealth and Poverty* (New York: Basic Books, 1981); quotations are from *Wealth and Poverty: A New Edition for the Twenty-First Century* (Washington, DC: Regnery, 2012), 27, 136, 352, 363.

19. Marcia Landy, *Film, Politics, and Gramsci* (Minneapolis and London: University of Minnesota Press, 1994), 12; Daniel T. Rodgers, *Age of Fracture* (Cambridge: Belknap Press of Harvard University Press, 2011), 5; Margaret Thatcher, "Interview for *Woman's Own*," September 23, 1987, https://www.margaretthatcher.org/document/106689.

20. Randall Rothenberg, *The Neoliberals: Creating the New American Politics* (New York: Simon & Schuster, 1984), 245.

21. Gilder, *Wealth and Poverty*, 114.

22. Richard Cohen, "History Was on Gary Hart's Side, but That Wasn't Enough," *Washington Post*, June 10, 1984, https://www.washingtonpost.com/archive/opinions/1984/06/10/history-was-on-gary-harts-side-but-that-wasnt-enough/5c74923d-67e6-491a-94bf-14ac664bdb60/?utm_term=.d8d5681f6401; James Fallows, "Was Gary Hart Set Up?," *The Atlantic*, November 2018, https://www.theatlantic.com/magazine/archive/2018/11/was-gary-hart-set-up/570802/.

23. Full disclosure requires that I note my own modest role in this strange saga. For a *New York Times Magazine* profile of Hart that was in many ways positive, I had two long interviews with him, and his most memorable declaration came in response to a question about widely circulating rumors about his alleged womanizing. "Follow me around. I don't care," he told me. "I'm serious. If anybody wants to put a tail on me, go ahead. They'd be very bored." The *Miami Herald*'s stakeout began before the article was formally published, but after printed copies of the magazine began circulating. His quotation closed off Hart's best line of defense, which was to ask why in the world reporters were following him around. The episode definitively ended the reportorial habit of declaring the sex lives of politicians off-limits, although there was little consistency about who would and who would not be brought under scrutiny. The 1987 incident might also be seen as the first step down the long road to the #MeToo movement of our time—although both Bill Clinton and, even more egregiously, Donald Trump would survive more scandalous behavior.

24. Lily Geismer, "Atari Democrats," *Jacobin*, February 8, 2016, https://www.jacobinmag .com/2016/02/geismer-democratic-party-atari-tech-silicon-valley-mondale/; David G. Savage, "Strategy Focuses Attention on Liberal Rights Group: Bush Stresses Dukakis' Affiliation with ACLU," *Los Angeles Times*, August 30, 1988, https://www.latimes .com/archives/la-xpm-1988-08-30-mn-1308-story.html.

25. Mathew Cooper, "Who Will Be the Republican Al From?," *The Atlantic*, June 16, 2009, https://www.theatlantic.com/politics/archive/2009/06/who-will-be-the-republican-al -from/19484/.

26. Geismer, "Atari Democrats."

27. Text of Clinton's acceptance speech at the Democratic National Convention, *Washington Post*, July 17, 1992, https://www.washingtonpost.com/archive/politics/1992/07/17 /we-offer-our-people-a-new-choice-based-on-old-values/70505378-1e95-4a2c-a3b0 -5aff5afaa160/?utm_term=.58cc281be0de.

28. Dylan Matthews, "The Clinton Economy, in Charts," *Washington Post*, September 5, 2012, https://www.washingtonpost.com/news/wonk/wp/2012/09/05/the-clinton -economy-in-charts/?utm_term=.11e2d0bd5287; Amy Chozick, "Bill Clinton Defends His Economic Legacy," *New York Times*, April 30, 2014, https://www.nytimes .com/2014/05/01/us/politics/bill-clinton-defends-his-economic-legacy.html; Robert J. Samuelson, "Since the '60s, Imperfect Progress on Race," *Washington Post*, July 13, 2016, https://www.washingtonpost.com/opinions/since-the-60s-imperfect-progress -on-race/2016/07/13/a1674346-490f-11e6-90a8-fb84201e0645_story.html?utm_term =.a77c52f0aaad.

29. Caryn James, "Return of the War Room: Not-So-Extreme Makeover," *Huffpost*, October 12, 2008, https://www.huffpost.com/entry/return-of-the-war-room-no_b_133909.

30. "Party Divisions of the House of Representatives, 1789 to Present," History, Art & Archives: U.S. House, https://history.house.gov/Institution/Party-Divisions/Party -Divisions/; "Party Division," U.S. Senate, https://www.senate.gov/history/partydiv .htm; "United States Gubernatorial Election Results," *Dave Leip's Atlas of U.S. Elections*, https://uselectionatlas.org/RESULTS/index.html; all accessed May 10, 2019.

31. For more on free trade and the labor movement, see Thomas B. Edsall, "Issue Has Aroused the Left," *Washington Post*, November 8, 1993, https://www.washingtonpost .com/archive/politics/1993/11/08/issue-has-aroused-the-left/3787790e-a457-415d-a6e1 -fcc1182040f7/?utm_term=.e59383d306af; Adam Behsudi, "Democrats' Civil War over Free Trade," *Politico*, April 16, 2015, https://www.politico.com/story/2015/04/democrats -free-trade-bill-117066https://www.politico.com/story/2015/04/democrats-free-trade -bill-117066; Associated Press, "Unions Oppose Free Trade Deal 20 Years After Losing Battle to Stop NAFTA," *The Guardian*, January 13, 2015, https://www.theguardian.com /business/2015/jan/13/unions-oppose-free-trade-deal-battle-stop-nafta.

32. Stanley Greenberg, "After the Republican Surge," *American Prospect*, Fall 1995, https:// prospect.org/article/after-republican-surge.

33. Danielle Kurtzleben, "Democrats Won the Suburbs. Now They Have to Hold Them," NPR, November 23, 2018, https://www.npr.org/2018/11/23/670009814/democrats -won-the-suburbs-now-they-have-to-hold-them; Dan Balz, "Clinton Broke Republican Grip on Some Suburban County Strongholds," *Washington Post*, November 10, 1996, https://www.washingtonpost.com/archive/politics/1996/11/10/clinton-broke -republican-grip-on-some-suburban-county-strongholds/b4e7fc98-722c-47cc-930d -115dc542fd41/?utm_term=.8f928886351f.
34. Frank Bruni, "Bush Calls on Gore to Denounce Clinton Affair," *New York Times*, August 12, 2000, https://archive.nytimes.com/www.nytimes.com/library/politics/camp /081200wh-bush.html.
35. "Acceptance Speech of Al Gore, Democratic National Convention," NPR, August 17, 2000, https://www.npr.org/news/national/election2000/demconvention/speech.agore .html.
36. Gary Younge, "Democratic Convention: Bill Clinton Makes Speech That Obama Needed Most," *The Guardian*, September 6, 2012, https://www.theguardian.com /commentisfree/2012/sep/06/bill-clinton-speech-obama. For more on the failure of Third Way politics, see John Patrick Leary, "The Third Way Is a Death Trap," *Jacobin*, August 3, 2018, https://jacobinmag.com/2018/08/centrism-democratic-party -lieberman-ocasio-cortez; Andy Beckett, "The Death of Consensus: How Conflict Came Back to Politics," *The Guardian*, September 20, 2018, https://www.theguardian .com/politics/2018/sep/20/the-death-of-consensus-how-conflict-came-back-to -politics.
37. Michael Nelson, "How Vietnam Broke the Democratic Party," *New York Times*, March 28, 2018, https://www.nytimes.com/2018/03/28/opinion/vietnam-broke-democratic -party.html.
38. For more on the *Rucho* case, see *Rucho v. Common Cause*, Brennan Center for Justice, June 27, 2019, https://www.brennancenter.org/legal-work/common-cause-v-rucho; Richard L. Hasen, "The Gerrymandering Decision Drags the Supreme Court Further into the Mud," *New York Times*, June 27, 2019, https://www.nytimes.com/2019/06/27 /opinion/gerrymandering-rucho-supreme-court.html.
39. Paul Waldman, "Why Court-Packing Suddenly Looks Appealing to Democrats," *Washington Post*, March 18, 2019, https://www.washingtonpost.com/opinions/2019 /03/18/why-court-packing-suddenly-looks-appealing-democrats/?utm_term= .328c84d2ee9c; Matt Ford, "The Weak Case for Packing the Supreme Court," *New Republic*, March 12, 2019, https://newrepublic.com/article/153286/weak-case-packing -supreme-court.

Chapter 4

1. "President Donald J. Trump's State of the Union Address," February 5, 2019, https:// www.whitehouse.gov/briefings-statements/president-donald-j-trumps-state-union -address-2/.
2. Jeremy W. Peters, "With Polls and Private Meetings, Republicans Craft Blunt Messaging to Paint Democrats as Extreme," *New York Times*, April 13, 2019, https://www .nytimes.com/2019/04/12/us/politics/democrats-republicans-2020.html.
3. Al Smith, "The Facts in the Case," speech at American Liberty League Dinner, Washington, DC, January 25, 1936, American Liberty League Pamphlets, Jouett Shouse Collection, University of Kentucky Libraries, https://exploreuk.uky.edu/catalog /xt7wwp9t2q46_94_2#page/1/mode/1up.
4. Ian Millhiser, "A Brief, 90-Year History of Republicans Calling Democrats 'Socialists,'" *ThinkProgress* blog, March 6, 2019, https://thinkprogress.org/a-history-of-republicans -calling-democrats-socialists-777bcd2b7a6d/.
5. Ronald Reagan, "A Time for Choosing," October 27, 1964, https://www.reaganlibrary .gov/sreference/a-time-for-choosing-speech.

6. Rich Lowry, "Against Socialism: An Introduction," *National Review*, May 16, 2019, https://www.nationalreview.com/magazine/2019/06/03/against-socialism-an -introduction/; David French, "White Progressives Are Polarizing America," *National Review*, February 19, 2019, https://www.nationalreview.com/2019/02/white -progressives-polarizing-america/.

7. Jonathan Chait, "Trump Calls the Democratic Party Socialist. He's Lying," *New York Magazine*, February 20, 2019, http://nymag.com/intelligencer/2019/02/trump-calls -democrats-socialist-lying-bernie-sanders-2020.html; French, "White Progressives Are Polarizing America."

8. Daniel Henninger, "Opinion: The Democrats' Socialist Gene," *Wall Street Journal*, February 20, 2019, https://www.wsj.com/articles/the-democrats-socialist-gene -11550705712.

9. "Democratic Convention 2016," Green Papers, accessed July 15, 2019, http://www .thegreenpapers.com/P16/D; Heather Caygle, Sarah Ferris, and John Bresnahan, "Pelosi and Ocasio-Cortez Clash Drags On, Threatening Democratic Unity," *Politico*, July 11, 2019, https://politi.co/2LfP55r.

10. For all references to polling from PRRI on socialism, see David Tigabu, "Socialism No Longer a Dirty Word in American Political Discourse," PRRI, January 3, 2019, https://www.prri.org/spotlight/socialism-no-longer-a-dirty-word-in-american -political-discourse/; and Alex Vandermaas-Peeler et al., "Partisan Polarization Dominates Trump Era: Findings from the 2018 American Values Survey," PRRI, October 29, 2018, https://www.prri.org/research/partisan-polarization-dominates-trump-era -findings-from-the-2018-american-values-survey/.

11. Harold Meyerson, "How Centrists Misread Scandinavia When Attacking Bernie and Elizabeth," *American Prospect*, July 2, 2019, https://prospect.org/article/how-centrists -misread-scandinavia-when-attacking-bernie-and-elizabeth.

12. For all references to Gallup polling on socialism, see Frank Newport, "The Meaning of 'Socialism' to Americans Today," Gallup, October 4, 2018, https://news.gallup.com /opinion/polling-matters/243362/meaning-socialism-americans-today.aspx.

13. David Weigel, "The Trailer: 'I'm Not a Socialist': What House Democrats Are Saying (and Hearing) Back Home," *Washington Post*, March 19, 2019, https://www.washingtonpost .com/politics/paloma/the-trailer/2019/03/19/the-trailer-i-m-not-a-socialist-what-house -democrats-are-saying-and-hearing-back-home/5c8fecf01b326b0f7f38f1c0/; Anna Giaritelli, "House Democrat Declares Herself 'Proud Capitalist' and Rejects AOC Vision," *Washington Examiner*, April 2, 2019. Murphy later criticized the use of her comments by "the right-wing media beast that ravenously awaits any scent of Democratic infighting," but again defended capitalism in Stephanie Murphy, "I'm a Proud Democrat. I'm Also a Proud Capitalist," *Washington Post*, April 28, 2019, https://www.washingtonpost.com /opinions/2019/04/28/im-proud-democrat-im-also-proud-capitalist/.

14. K. Sabeel Rahman, "The Moral Vision After Neoliberalism," *Democracy Journal*, Summer 2019, https://democracyjournal.org/magazine/53/the-moral-vision-after -neoliberalism/; Bhaskar Sunkara, *The Socialist Manifesto* (New York: Basic Books, 2019), 2–3.

15. Nisha Stickles and Barbara Corbellini Duarte, "Exclusive: Alexandria Ocasio Cortez Explains What Democratic Socialism Means to Her," *Business Insider*, March 4, 2019, https://www.businessinsider.com/alexandria-ocasio-cortez-explains-what-democratic -socialism-means 2019 3.

16. Tim Hains, "Ocasio-Cortez: 'We Should Be Scared Right Now Because Corporations Have Taken Over Our Government,'" *Real Clear Politics*, March 10, 2019, https:// www.realclearpolitics.com/video/2019/03/10/ocasio-cortez_we_should_be_scared _because_corporations_have_taken_over_our_government.html.

17. Andrew Prokop, "Read Bernie Sanders's Speech on Democratic Socialism in the United States," *Vox*, November 19, 2015, https://www.vox.com/2015/11/19/9762028 /bernie-sanders-democratic-socialism.

18. Tara Golshan, "Bernie Sanders Defines His Vision for Democratic Socialism in the United States," *Vox*, June 12, 2019, https://www.vox.com/2019/6/12/18663217/bernie -sanders-democratic-socialism-speech-transcript.
19. Sunkara, *The Socialist Manifesto*, 216–17.
20. "1912 Electoral Vote Tally, February 12, 1913," National Archives, August 15, 2016, https://www.archives.gov/legislative/features/1912-election; John Nichols, *The "S" Word: A Short History of an American Tradition . . . Socialism* (London and New York: Verso, 2011); Christopher Lasch, "Whatever Happened to Socialism?," *New York Review of Books*, September 12, 1968, https://www.nybooks.com/articles/1968/09/12 /whatever-happened-to-socialism/.
21. Mason B. Williams, "Socialism and the Liberal Imagination," *Dissent Magazine*, August 8, 2018, https://www.dissentmagazine.org/online_articles/new-deal-socialism -liberalism-progressive-reform.
22. Adam Kelsey, "Mayor Says Trump's 'Hypocrisy' Regarding 'Christian Values' Needs to Be Called Out," *Good Morning America*, April 4, 2019, https://www .goodmorningamerica.com/news/story/pete-buttigieg-gma-trumps-hypocrisy-called -socialist-criticisms-62153669.
23. Veronica Stracqualursi, "Buttigieg: 'Capitalism Has Let a Lot of People Down,'" CNN, April 16, 2019, https://www.cnn.com/2019/04/16/politics/pete-buttigieg-2020 -socialism-capitalism-cnntv/index.html.
24. John Cassidy, "Why Socialism Is Back," *New Yorker*, June 18, 2019, https://www .newyorker.com/news/our-columnists/why-socialism-is-back; Alexander Burns, "Pete Buttigieg's Campaign Kickoff: Full Speech, Annotated," *New York Times*, April 15, 2019, https://www.nytimes.com/2019/04/15/us/politics/pete-buttigieg-speech.html.
25. See Friedrich A. Hayek, *The Road to Serfdom* (Chicago: University of Chicago Press, 1944).
26. Steven Pearlstein, *Can American Capitalism Survive? Why Greed Is Not Good, Opportunity Is Not Equal, and Fairness Won't Make Us Poor* (New York: St. Martin's Press, 2018), 13–14, 16, 205.
27. Michael Kazin, "Opinion: Whatever Happened to Moral Capitalism?," *New York Times*, June 24, 2019, https://www.nytimes.com/2019/06/24/opinion/democrats-moral -capitalism.html, including Kennedy's remarks.
28. George Gilder, "The Moral Sources of Capitalism," *Imprimis*, December 1980, https://imprimis.hillsdale.edu/wp-content/uploads/2016/11/The-Moral-Sources-of -Capitalism-December-1980.pdf; Gary Langer and Jon Cohen, "Voters and Values in the 2004 Election," *Public Opinion Quarterly* 69, no. 5 (2005): 744–59; Philip Schwadel and Gregory A. Smith, "Evangelical Approval of Trump Remains High, but Other Religious Groups Are Less Supportive," Pew Research Center Fact Tank, March 18, 2019, https://www.pewresearch.org/fact-tank/2019/03/18/evangelical-approval-of-trump -remains-high-but-other-religious-groups-are-less-supportive/; Walter Rauschenbusch, *A Theology for the Social Gospel* (New York: Macmillan, 1917).
29. Robert Kuttner, *Can Democracy Survive Global Capitalism?* (New York: W. W. Norton, 2018), 283.
30. Edward Bellamy, *Looking Backward: 2000 to 1887* (Boston: Ticknor, 1888).

Chapter 5
1. For more information, see William E. Leuchtenburg, "Franklin D. Roosevelt: The American Franchise," University of Virginia Miller Center, accessed July 10, 2019, https://millercenter.org/president/fdroosevelt/the-american-franchise; and Alonzo L. Hamby, "Harry S. Truman: Impact and Legacy," Miller Center, October 4, 2016, https://millercenter.org/president/truman/impact-and-legacy.
2. Adam Clymer, "Textbooks Reassess Kennedy, Putting Camelot Under Siege," *New York Times*, November 10, 2013, https://www.nytimes.com/2013/11/11/us/textbooks -reassess-kennedy-putting-camelot-under-siege.html.

3. For Clinton and Obama operating within the Reagan "consensus," see Jake Sullivan, "The New Old Democrats," *Democracy Journal*, June 20, 2018, https://democracyjournal.org/arguments/the-new-old-democrats/.

4. "Former President Bill Clinton at the 2012 Democratic National Convention," nominating address, September 5, 2012, C-SPAN video, https://www.c-span.org/video/?c3779974/president-bill-clinton-2012-democratic-national-convention.

5. Matthew A. Winkler, "Trump Economy Lags Clinton's, Obama's, Reagan's and Even Carter's," Bloomberg, January 28, 2019, https://www.bloomberg.com/opinion/articles/2019-01-28/trump-economy-lags-clinton-s-obama-s-reagan-s-and-even-carter-s.

6. "Al Gore: 'The Assault on Reason' in America," interview by Michelle Norris, NPR, May 25, 2007, https://www.npr.org/templates/story/story.php?storyId=10440121; Gary L. Gregg II, "George W. Bush: Domestic Affairs," University of Virginia Miller Center, October 4, 2016, https://millercenter.org/president/gwbush/domestic-affairs.

7. For more on the economy, see Randy E. Ilg and Steven E. Haugen, "Earnings and Employment Trends in the 1990s," *Monthly Labor Review* 123, no. 3 (March 2000): 21–33. For the evolution of the "Republican Revolution," see Phil Gailey, "Newtered," *New York Times*, June 2, 1996, https://www.nytimes.com/1996/06/02/books/newtered.html.

8. For more on trade adjustment assistance, see Mark Muro and Joseph Parilla, "Maladjusted: It's Time to Reimagine Economic 'Adjustment' Programs," Brookings Institution, *The Avenue* blog, January 10, 2017, https://www.brookings.edu/blog/the-avenue/2017/01/10/maladjusted-its-time-to-reimagine-economic-adjustment-programs/.

9. Ed Kilgore, "Intelligencer: The End of the Clinton Era of Democratic Politics," *New York Magazine*, November 10, 2016, http://nymag.com/intelligencer/2016/11/the-end-of-the-clinton-era-of-democratic-politics.html.

10. Erica Werner, "Trump Signs Law Rolling Back Post-Financial Crisis Banking Rules," *Washington Post*, May 24, 2018, https://www.washingtonpost.com/business/economy/trump-signs-law-rolling-back-post-financial-crisis-banking-rules/2018/05/24/077e3aa8-5f6c-11e8-a4a4-c070ef53f315_story.html.

11. For more on the legacy of the bailout, see Robert J. Samuelson, "Celebrating the Auto Bailout's Success," *Washington Post*, April 1, 2015, https://www.washingtonpost.com/opinions/celebrating-the-auto-bailouts-success/2015/04/01/67f3f208-d881-11e4-8103-fa84725dbf9d_story.html; Kathryn A. Wolfe and Jessica Meyers, "Auto Bailout May Have Saved Obama," *Politico*, November 7, 2012, https://www.politico.com/news/stories/1112/83511.html.

12. For information on the Recovery Act, see the video "Recovery Is Local: Mayors Speak for the Recovery Act," White House, February 16, 2010, https://obamawhitehouse.archives.gov/featured-videos/video/2010/02/16/recovery-local-mayors-speak-recovery-act. For more on the success of the 2009 stimulus package, see "Estimated Impact of the American Recovery and Reinvestment Act on Employment and Economic Output from January 2011 Through March 2011," Congressional Budget Office, May 2011, https://www.cbo.gov/sites/default/files/112th-congress-2011-2012/reports/05-25-arra.pdf; James Feyrer and Bruce Sacerdote, "Did the Stimulus Stimulate? Real Time Estimates of the Effects of the American Recovery and Reinvestment Act," National Bureau of Economic Research, February 2011, https://www.nber.org/papers/w16759.pdf.

13. For Mitt Romney's comparison of Romneycare to Obamacare, see Jessica Taylor, "Mitt Romney Finally Takes Credit for Obamacare," NPR, October 23, 2015, https://www.npr.org/sections/itsallpolitics/2015/10/23/451200436/mitt-romney-finally-takes-credit-for-obamacare. For approval levels for a public option, see Nate Silver, "Public Support for the Public Option," *FiveThirtyEight*, June 20, 2009, https://fivethirtyeight.com/features/public-support-for-public-option/. For more on public options in health care, see Ganesh Sitaraman and Anne L. Alstott, *The Public Option: How to Expand Freedom, Increase Opportunity, and Promote Equality* (Cambridge: Harvard University Press, 2019), chap. 11.

14. Noam Scheiber, *The Escape Artists: How Obama's Team Fumbled the Recovery* (New York: Simon & Schuster, 2011), 292.

15. For more, see Shauna Shepherd and Ashley Killough, "Perry Stands by Ad, Calls Obama a 'Socialist,'" CNN *Political Ticker* blog, November 18, 2011, http://politicalticker.blogs .cnn.com/2011/11/18/perry-stands-by-ad-calls-obama-a-socialist/; and Branko Marcetic, "How Obama Failed," review of *A Crisis Wasted* by Reed Hundt, *Jacobin*, May 2019, https://jacobinmag.com/2019/05/obama-white-house-financial-crisis -hundt.

16. David Leonhardt, "Opinion: Eliminating All Student Debt Isn't Progressive," *New York Times*, November 18, 2018, https://www.nytimes.com/2018/11/18/opinion/student -debt-forgiveness-college-democrats.html.

17. Sullivan, "The New Old Democrats."

18. Jonathan Cowan, lecture, June 2019, Charleston, SC.

19. Matt Bennett, lecture and interview with author, June 2019, Charleston, SC.

20. David Leonhardt, "Opinion: A Time for Big Economic Ideas," *New York Times*, April 22, 2018, https://www.nytimes.com/2018/04/22/opinion/big-economic-ideas.html.

21. Jacob S. Hacker and Paul Pierson, *Off Center: The Republican Revolution and the Erosion of American Democracy* (New Haven: Yale University Press, 2005), 43.

22. Mason B. Williams, "Socialism and the Liberal Imagination," *Dissent Magazine*, August 8, 2018, https://www.dissentmagazine.org/online_articles/new-deal-socialism -liberalism-progressive-reform; Victor Navasky, "The Left Wing of the Possible," May 28, 2000, https://archive.nytimes.com/www.nytimes.com/books/00/05/28/reviews /000528.28navaskt.html.

23. Robert L. Borosage, "Elizabeth Warren Has the Plans," April 30, 2019, https://www .thenation.com/article/elizabeth-warren-policy-ideas-primary-2020/. For more on the wealth tax debate, see John Cassidy, "Why Elizabeth Warren's Wealth Tax Would Work," *New Yorker*, January 31, 2019, https://www.newyorker.com/news/our-columnists /elizabeth-warrens-wealth-tax-is-an-old-idea-and-its-time-has-come; and Natasha Sarin and Lawrence H. Summers, "A Broader Tax Base That Closes Loopholes Would Raise More Money Than Plans by Ocasio-Cortez and Warren," *Boston Globe*, March 28, 2019, https://www.bostonglobe.com/opinion/2019/03/28/broader-tax-base-that -closes-loopholes-would-raise-more-money-than-plans-ocasio-cortez-and-warren /Bv16zhTAkuEx08SiNrjx9J/story.html.

24. On the rightward shift, see Patrick J. Akard, "Corporate Mobilization and Political Power: The Transformation of U.S. Economic Policy in the 1970s," *American Sociological Review* 57, no. 5 (1992): 597–615.

25. Marco Rubio, "American Investment in the 21st Century," report for the Project for Strong Labor Markets and Capital Development, May, 2019, https://www .rubio.senate.gov/public/_cache/files/9f25139a-6039-465a-9cf1-feb5567aebb7/45 26E9620A9A7DB74267ABEA5881022F.5.15.2019.-final-project-report-american -investment.pdf.

26. The Business Roundtable statement can be found at https://opportunity .businessroundtable.org/ourcommitment/; the organization's press release, which explicitly states that the "Updated Statement Moves Away from Shareholder Primacy," can be found at https://www.businessroundtable.org/business-roundtable-redefines -the-purpose-of-a-corporation-to-promote-an-economy-that-serves-all-americans; David Gelles and David Yaffe-Bellany, "Shareholder Value Is No Longer Everything, Top C.E.O.s Say," *New York Times*, August 19, 2019, https://www.nytimes.com/2019 /08/19/business/business-roundtable-ceos-corporations.html?smid=nytcore-ios -share.

27. See Jerry Taylor, "The Alternative to Ideology," Niskanen Center paper, October 29, 2018, https://niskanencenter.org/blog/the-alternative-to-ideology/; and Samuel Hammond, "The Free Market Welfare State: Preserving Dynamism in a Volatile World,"

Niskanen Center paper, May, 2018, https://niskanencenter.org/wp-content/uploads/2018/04/Final_Free-Market-Welfare-State.pdf.

28. Barack Obama, "For We Were Born of Change," in E. J. Dionne, Jr. and Joy-Ann Reid, eds., *We Are the Change We Seek: The Speeches of Barack Obama* (New York: Bloomsbury, 2017), 253–266.

Chapter 6

1. Michael Harrington, "Visionary Gradualism," in *Socialism: Past and Future* (New York: Arcade Publishing, 1989), 248–278. See also Harold Meyerson, "The (Still) Relevant Socialist," *The Atlantic*, August 1, 2000, https://www.theatlantic.com/magazine/archive/2000/08/the-still-relevant-socialist/378331/.

2. Zack Beauchamp, "Pete Buttigieg's 2020 Presidential Campaign and Policies, Explained," *Vox*, April 3, 2019, https://www.vox.com/policy-and-politics/2019/4/3/18282638/pete-buttigieg-2020-presidential-campaign-policies; Paul Starr, "What Is Hillary Clinton's Agenda?," *American Prospect*, June 20, 2016, https://prospect.org/article/what-hillary-clinton%E2%80%99s-agenda; Laura Meckler, "How Hillary Clinton Shifted Leftward," *Wall Street Journal*, June 8, 2016, https://www.wsj.com/articles/how-hillary-clinton-shifted-leftward-1465345261.

3. K. Sabeel Rahman, "The Moral Vision After Neoliberalism," *Democracy Journal*, Summer 2019, https://democracyjournal.org/magazine/53/the-moral-vision-after-neoliberalism/.

4. Peter Beinart, "Will the Left Go Too Far?," *The Atlantic*, December 2018, https://www.theatlantic.com/magazine/archive/2018/12/democratic-party-moves-left/573946/.

5. Michael Harrington, *Socialism: Past and Future* (New York: Arcade, 1989).

6. Paul Krugman, "Democrats for Family Values," *New York Times*, February 21, 2019, https://www.nytimes.com/2019/02/21/opinion/warren-child-care.html.

7. Paul Kane and Rachael Bade, "'I'm Agnostic': Pelosi Questions Whether Medicare-for-All Can Deliver Benefits of Obamacare," *Washington Post*, April 4, 2019, https://www.washingtonpost.com/politics/im-agnostic-pelosi-questions-whether-medicare-for-all-can-deliver-benefits-of-obamacare/2019/04/04/fe2942c0-56ed-11e9-aa83-504f086bf5d6_story.html.

8. Kane and Bade, "'I'm Agnostic'"; Dylan Scott, "Half of 2018's Democratic Campaign Ads Are About Health Care," *Vox*, September 24, 2018, https://www.vox.com/policy-and-politics/2018/9/24/17897962/health-care-campaign-ads-democrats-2018-midterm-elections-voxcare.

9. Jonathan Martin, "Canceled Fund-Raiser Prompts Question: Can a Democrat Oppose Abortion?," *New York Times*, May 22, 2019, https://www.nytimes.com/2019/05/22/us/politics/dan-lipinski-abortion-cheri-bustos.html; Alan Blinder and Jonathan Martin, "Even a Whiff of Disloyalty to Trump Can Imperil a GOP Incumbent," *New York Times*, June 11, 2018, https://www.nytimes.com/2018/06/11/us/alabama-republican-roby-trump.html; Jonathan Martin and Abby Goodnough, "Medicare for All Emerges as Early Policy Test for 2020 Democrats," *New York Times*, February 2, 2019, https://www.nytimes.com/2019/02/02/us/politics/medicare-for-all-2020.html; "How the Democratic Candidates Responded to a Health Care Policy Survey," *New York Times*, June 23, 2019, https://www.nytimes.com/2019/06/23/us/politics/2020-democrats-health-care.html.

10. Paul Krugman, "Don't Make Health Care a Purity Test," *New York Times*, March 21, 2019, https://www.nytimes.com/2019/03/21/opinion/medicare-for-all-democrats.html.

11. Megan McArdle, "Sorry, Bernie, but Most Americans Like Their Health Insurance the Way It Is," *Washington Post*, May 3, 2019, https://www.washingtonpost.com/opinions/2019/05/03/sorry-bernie-most-americans-like-their-health-insurance-way-it-is/; "NBC News/*Wall Street Journal* Survey," NBC News, September 2019, https://www

.documentcloud.org/documents/6426498-19357-NBCWSJ-September-Registered -Voter-Poll-Final.html.

12. Dhruv Khullar, "What States Can Learn from One Another on Health Care," *New York Times*, November 16, 2017, https://www.nytimes.com/2017/11/16/upshot/what -states-can-learn-from-one-another-on-health-care.html; Paul Krugman, "How Democrats Can Deliver on Health Care," *New York Times*, November 22, 2018, https:// www.nytimes.com/2018/11/22/opinion/democrats-obamacare-states.html; Dylan Scott, "Medicare for America, Beto O'Rourke's Favorite Health Care Plan, Explained," *Vox*, March 18, 2019, https://www.vox.com/policy-and-politics/2019/3/18/18270857 /medicare-for-all-beto-orourke-2020-policies-voxcare.

13. Reid J. Epstein and Astead W. Herndon, "Pete Buttigieg and Kamala Harris Have Made Waves. Some Progressives Remain Skeptical," *New York Times*, July 16, 2019, https:// www.nytimes.com/2019/07/16/us/politics/kamala-harris-pete-buttigieg-2020.html; Dylan Scott, "The 2 Big Disagreements Between the 2020 Democratic Candidates on Medicare-for-All," *Vox*, June 25, 2019, https://www.vox.com/policy-and-politics/2019 /6/25/18691720/2020-presidential-election-democratic-debate-health-care.

14. John Whitesides and Mike Stone, "Biden Healthcare Plan Draws Contrast with White House Rivals," Reuters, July 15, 2019, https://www.reuters.com/article/us-usa -election-biden/biden-healthcare-plan-draws-contrast-with-white-house-rivals -idUSKCN1UA0WV; Paul Waldman, "Joe Biden Proposes Radical Leftist Health-Care Plan," *Washington Post*, July 15, 2019, https://www.washingtonpost.com/opinions /2019/07/15/joe-biden-proposes-radical-leftist-health-care-plan/?utm_term= .7527ba188c4c.

15. Ezra Klein, "Abolish Private Insurance? It Depends," *Vox*, July 8, 2019, https://www .vox.com/policy-and-politics/2019/7/8/20683368/democrats-2020-medicare-private -insurance-single-payer-debate.

16. Paul Starr, *Entrenchment: Wealth, Power and the Constitution of Democratic Societies* (New Haven: Yale University Press, 2019), 174–75.

17. Lilia Vega, "The History of UC Tuition Since 1868," *Daily Californian*, December 22, 2018, https://www.dailycal.org/2014/12/22/history-uc-tuition-since-1868/; Michael Mitchell et al., "Unkept Promises: State Cuts to Higher Education Threaten Access and Equity," Center on Budget and Policy Priorities, October 4, 2018, https://www.cbpp .org/research/state-budget-and-tax/unkept-promises-state-cuts-to-higher-education -threaten-access-and.

18. "Tuition-Free College Is Now a Reality in Nearly 20 States," CNBC, March 12, 2019, https://www.cnbc.com/2019/03/12/free-college-now-a-reality-in-these -states.html.

19. Libby Nelson, "Hillary Clinton's College Affordability Plan, Explained," *Vox*, August 10, 2015, https://www.vox.com/2015/8/10/9125349/hillary-clinton-college; Emily Cochrane, "Bernie Sanders Unveils Education Plan to Eliminate Student Loan Debt," *New York Times*, June 24, 2019, https://www.nytimes.com/2019/06/24/us/politics /bernie-sanders-student-debt.html; Arlie Hochschild, "Opinion: The Coders of Kentucky," *New York Times*, September 21, 2018, https://www.nytimes.com/2018/09/21 /opinion/sunday/silicon-valley-tech.html.

20. Isabel Sawhill, *The Forgotten Americans: An Economic Agenda for a Divided Nation* (New Haven: Yale University Press, 2018), 115–16, 121–23.

21. Edward Luce, "US Higher Education Crisis: Lessons from the Chicago Schools," *Financial Times*, March 17, 2019, https://www.ft.com/content/973340fc-458b-11e9 -b168-96a37d002cd3; Randy Ludlow, "Richard Cordray Ad Promises Help for Blue-Collar Workers," *Akron Beacon Journal*, October 5, 2018, https://www.ohio.com/news /20181005/richard-cordray-ad-promises-help-for-blue-collar-workers.

22. Alan Singer, "Welcome Back! A Brief History of Education in the United States (Part 1)," *HuffPost*, September 7, 2015, https://www.huffpost.com/entry/welcome-back-a -brief-hist_b_8098916.

23. "Climate Change," United Nations Intergovernmental Panel on Climate Change, accessed July 10, 2019, https://www.un.org/en/sections/issues-depth/climate-change/; Jason Samenow, "It Was 84 Degrees Near the Arctic Ocean This Weekend as Carbon Dioxide Hit Its Highest Level in Human History," *Washington Post*, May 14, 2019, https://www.washingtonpost.com/weather/2019/05/14/it-was-degrees-near-arctic-ocean-this-weekend-carbon-dioxide-hit-its-highest-level-human-history/?utm_term=.adedcb8a5b75.
24. Howard Gruenspecht, "The U.S. Coal Sector," Brookings Institution, January 2019, https://www.brookings.edu/research/the-u-s-coal-sector/.
25. Megan Brenan and Lydia Saad, "Global Warming Concern Steady Despite Some Partisan Shifts," Gallup, March 28, 2018, https://news.gallup.com/poll/231530/global-warming-concern-steady-despite-partisan-shifts.aspx; Carrie Dann, "Poll: More Americans See Democrats as 'Mainstream' on Climate, Health Care," NBC News, March 4, 2019, https://www.nbcnews.com/politics/meet-the-press/poll-more-americans-see-democratic-positions-climate-health-care-abortion-n978401.
26. Valerie Volcovici, "Exclusive: Presidential Hopeful Biden Looking for 'Middle Ground' Climate Policy," Reuters, May 10, 2019, https://www.reuters.com/article/us-usa-election-biden-climate-exclusive-idUSKCN1SG18G; Katie Glueck, "Biden Delivers Call for National Unity at Philadelphia Rally," *New York Times*, May 18, 2019, https://www.nytimes.com/2019/05/18/us/politics/joe-biden-philadelphia-rally.html; David Sherfinski, "Joe Biden: I've Never Been 'Middle of the Road' on the Environment," *Washington Times*, May 14, 2019, https://www.washingtontimes.com/news/2019/may/14/joe-biden-ive-never-been-middle-road-environment/; Coral Davenport and Katie Glueck, "Climate Change Takes Center Stage as Biden and Warren Release Plans," *New York Times*, June 4, 2019, https://www.nytimes.com/2019/06/04/us/politics/joe-biden-climate-plan.html.
27. U.S. Congress, House, *Recognizing the Duty of the Federal Government to Create a Green New Deal*, H. Res. 109, 115th Cong., 1st sess., introduced February 7, 2019, https://www.congress.gov/bill/116th-congress/house-resolution/109/text, 7.
28. Jeff Stein and David Weigel, "Ocasio-Cortez Retracts Erroneous Information About Green New Deal Backed by 2020 Democratic Candidates," *Washington Post*, February 11, 2019, https://www.washingtonpost.com/politics/2019/02/11/ocasio-cortez-retracts-erroneous-information-about-green-new-deal-backed-by-democratic-candidates/?utm_term=.f3320d8e6af1; Jessica McDonald, "The Facts on the 'Green New Deal,'" FactCheck.org, February 15, 2019, https://www.factcheck.org/2019/02/the-facts-on-the-green-new-deal/.
29. Avery Anapol, "McConnell Pledges to Be 'Grim Reaper' for Progressive Policies," *The Hill*, April 22, 2019, https://thehill.com/homenews/senate/440041-mcconnell-pledges-to-be-grim-reaper-for-progressive-policies; Dino Grandoni and Felicia Sonmez, "Senate Defeats Green New Deal, as Democrats Call Vote a 'Sham,'" *Washington Post*, March 26, 2019, https://www.washingtonpost.com/powerpost/green-new-deal-on-track-to-senate-defeat-as-democrats-call-vote-a-sham/2019/03/26/834f3e5e-4fdd-11e9-a3f7-78b7525a8d5f_story.html.
30. Michael Grunwald, "The Trouble with the 'Green New Deal,'" *Politico*, January 15, 2019, https://politi.co/2FzUEIk; Anthony Adragna, "Schumer Slams 'Stunt' Green New Deal Vote as Moderates Fret," *Politico*, February 14, 2019, https://politi.co/2IrucUr; Katie Glueck, "Alexandria Ocasio-Cortez and Joe Biden Spar over Climate Policy in Intraparty Spat," *New York Times*, May 14, 2019, https://www.nytimes.com/2019/05/14/us/politics/aoc-biden.html; Alissa J. Rubin and Somini Sengupta, "'Yellow Vest' Protests Shake France. Here's the Lesson for Climate Change," *New York Times*, December 6, 2018, https://www.nytimes.com/2018/12/06/world/europe/france-fuel-carbon-tax.html. For more on a carbon tax, see David Roberts, "The 5 Most Important Questions About Carbon Taxes, Answered," *Vox*, June 27, 2019, https://www.vox.com/energy-and-environment/2018/7/20/17584376/carbon-tax-congress

-republicans-cost-economy; Matthew Yglesias, "The Case for a Carbon Tax," *Vox*, October 10, 2018, https://www.vox.com/2018/10/10/17959686/carbon-tax; Brad Plumer and Nadja Popovich, "These Countries Have Prices on Carbon. Are They Working?," *New York Times*, April 2, 2019, https://www.nytimes.com/interactive/2019/04/02/climate/pricing-carbon-emissions.html.

31. Paul Krugman, "Opinion: Purity vs. Pragmatism, Environment vs. Health," *New York Times*, April 11, 2019, https://www.nytimes.com/2019/04/11/opinion/green-new-deal-medicare-for-all.html.

32. John Cassidy, "The Good News About a Green New Deal," *New Yorker*, March 4, 2019, https://www.newyorker.com/news/our-columnists/the-good-news-about-a-green-new-deal.

33. James Osborne, "Are Republicans Wavering on Climate Change?," *Houston Chronicle*, February 22, 2019, https://www.houstonchronicle.com/business/energy/article/Are-Republicans-wavering-on-climate-change-13635463.php.

34. Harold Meyerson, "Climate Change and the Democrats," *American Prospect*, June 26, 2019, https://prospect.org/article/climate-change-and-democrats.

35. Robert Pear, "Medicaid Expansion Ruling Blunts Health Law's Effect," *New York Times*, July 24, 2012, https://www.nytimes.com/2012/07/25/health/policy/3-million-more-may-lack-insurance-due-to-ruling-study-says.html; Rachel Garfield, Kendal Orgera, and Anthony Damico, "The Coverage Gap: Uninsured Poor Adults in States That Do Not Expand Medicaid," Kaiser Family Foundation, March 21, 2019, https://www.kff.org/medicaid/issue-brief/the-coverage-gap-uninsured-poor-adults-in-states-that-do-not-expand-medicaid/; Paul Krugman, "Self-Inflicted Medical Misery," *New York Times*, June 24, 2019, https://www.nytimes.com/2019/06/24/opinion/republican-states-health-care.html; Steve Dubb, "Medicaid Expansion Campaigns Take 3 Distinct Paths in 3 Southern States," *Nonprofit Quarterly*, June 25, 2019, https://nonprofitquarterly.org/medicaid-expansion-campaigns-take-3-distinct-paths-in-3-southern-states/.

36. John Kenneth Galbraith, *The Affluent Society* (London: Hamish Hamilton, 1958), 200.

37. Jake Sullivan, "The New Old Democrats," *Democracy Journal*, June 20, 2018, https://democracyjournal.org/arguments/the-new-old-democrats/.

38. Alexander Burns, "Joe Biden's Campaign Announcement Video, Annotated," *New York Times*, April 25, 2019, https://www.nytimes.com/2019/04/25/us/politics/biden-campaign-video-announcement.html.

39. Annie Linskey and Michael Scherer, "Democrats Were Said to Be Furious and Hungry for Change. Then Biden Jumped In," *Washington Post*, May 19, 2019, https://www.washingtonpost.com/politics/democrats-were-said-to-be-furious-and-hungry-for-change-then-biden-jumped-in/2019/05/19/6cfe2ad4-78a5-11e9-b7ae-390de4259661_story.html?utm_term=.664ca2bf3c59; Chris Smith, "'A Lot of Bernie's Support Seems to Be Drifting to Warren,'" *Vanity Fair*, June 3, 2019, https://www.vanityfair.com/news/2019/06/as-sanders-reprises-greatest-hits-elizabeth-warren-is-surging; Peter Beinart, "Unlike His Rivals, Biden Sees Trump as an Aberration," *The Atlantic*, April 25, 2019, https://www.theatlantic.com/ideas/archive/2019/04/joe-bidens-announcement-video-has-touch-trump/588001/.

40. Chris Mills Rodrigo, "Trump Accuses Pelosi of 'Racist Statement' for Saying MAGA Means 'Make America White Again,'" *The Hill*, July 15, 2019, https://thehill.com/homenews/administration/453108-trump-hits-pelosi-for-racist-statement-saying-maga-means-make-america; Justin Wise, "Trump Tells Progressive Congresswomen to 'Go Back' Where They Came From," *The Hill*, July 14, 2019, https://thehill.com/homenews/administration/452970-trump-tells-progressive-democrats-to-go-back-and-fix-broken-and-crime; James Poniewozik, "Trump 2016 Returns, This Time as Nostalgia Act," *New York Times*, June 19, 2019, https://www.nytimes.com/2019/06/19/arts/television/trump-rally.html; Edward McClelland, "Perspective: Tariffs Won't Help the Rust Belt. But Trump Thinks He Can Turn Back Time," *Washington Post*,

August 19, 2018, https://www.washingtonpost.com/outlook/2018/08/20/tariffs-wont-help-rust-belt-trump-thinks-he-can-turn-back-time/.

41. "Political Ad: 'The Democratic Party Can Lead Again' Kennedy, 1960," NBC News Learn, https://archives.nbclearn.com/portal/site/k-12/flatview?cuecard=5712.

42. Haley Sweetland Edwards, "'I Have a Plan for That.' Elizabeth Warren Is Betting That Americans Are Ready for Her Big Ideas," *Time*, May 9, 2019, https://time.com/longform/elizabeth-warren-2020/; Katrina vanden Heuvel, "Elizabeth Warren Is Proving Her Doubters Wrong," *Washington Post*, June 11, 2019, https://www.washingtonpost.com/opinions/2019/06/11/elizabeth-warren-is-proving-her-doubters-wrong/.

43. Robert L. Borosage, "Elizabeth Warren Has the Plans," *The Nation*, April 30, 2019, https://www.thenation.com/article/elizabeth-warren-policy-ideas-primary-2020/.

44. Matthew Yglesias, "Elizabeth Warren's 2020 Presidential Campaign and Policy Positions, Explained," *Vox*, June 26, 2019, https://www.vox.com/2019/6/26/18715614/elizabeth-warren-2020-presidential-campaign-policies; Sarah Kliff, "Elizabeth Warren's Universal Child Care Plan, Explained," *Vox*, February 22, 2019, https://www.vox.com/policy-and-politics/2019/2/22/18234606/warren-child-care-universal-2020; Ella Nilsen, "Elizabeth Warren Has the Biggest Free College Plan Yet," *Vox*, April 22, 2019, https://www.vox.com/2019/4/22/18509196/elizabeth-warren-debt-free-college; Elena Schneider, "How Sen. Kirsten Gillibrand Would Address Maternal and Child Health," *Politico*, May 22, 2019, https://politi.co/2JvqJnv; Suzanne Gamboa, "Can Julián Castro Make Education His Issue in the Crowded 2020 Field?," NBC News, March 1, 2019, https://www.nbcnews.com/news/latino/can-juli-n-castro-make-education-his-issue-crowded-2020-n977706.

45. For more on Senator Warren's wealth tax, see "Ultra-Millionaire Tax," Elizabeth Warren campaign website, https://elizabethwarren.com/ultra-millionaire-tax/; Neil Irwin, "Elizabeth Warren Wants a Wealth Tax. How Would That Even Work?," *New York Times*, February 18, 2019, https://www.nytimes.com/2019/02/18/upshot/warren-wealth-tax.html.

46. "Sen. Elizabeth Warren: Making Capitalism Work for All," CNBC, July 24, 2018, https://www.cnbc.com/video/2018/07/24/sen-elizabeth-warren-making-capitalism-work-for-all.html.

47. Paul Waldman, "The 2020 Democrats Are Caught in a Policy Arms Race," *Washington Post*, July 16, 2019, https://www.washingtonpost.com/opinions/2019/07/16/democrats-are-caught-policy-arms-race/?utm_term=.7d928423aab6; 116th Congress, Senate, *S.4: LIFT (Livable Incomes for Families Today) the Middle Class Act*, https://www.congress.gov/bill/116th-congress/senate-bill/4?q=%7B%22search%22%3A%5B%22lift+act%22%5D%7D&s=2&r=1.

48. Christopher Ingraham, "The Top Tax Rate Has Been Cut Six Times Since 1980—Usually with Democrats' Help," *Washington Post*, February 27, 2019, https://www.washingtonpost.com/us-policy/2019/02/27/top-tax-rate-has-been-cut-six-times-since-usually-with-democrats-help/; Dylan Matthews, "Democrats Have United Around a Plan to Dramatically Cut Child Poverty," *Vox*, March 6, 2019, https://www.vox.com/future-perfect/2019/3/6/18249290/child-poverty-american-family-act-sherrod-brown-michael-bennet; Kamala Harris, "Our Teacher Pay Gap Is a National Failure. Here's How We Can Fix It," *Washington Post*, March 26, 2019, https://www.washingtonpost.com/opinions/kamala-harris-our-teacher-pay-gap-is-a-national-failure-heres-how-we-can-fix-it/2019/03/25/8fdd5eaa-4f36-11e9-8d28-f5149e5a2fda_story.html?utm_term=.765ed7b2f063.

49. Matthew Yglesias, "Amy Klobuchar's $1 Trillion Infrastructure Plan, Explained," *Vox*, March 28, 2019, https://www.vox.com/policy-and-politics/2019/3/28/18285343/amy-klobuchar-infrastructure-plan; Elena Schneider, "Klobuchar Details Raft of Policy Plans for First 100 Days," *Politico*, June 18, 2019, https://www.politico.com/story/2019/06/18/klobuchar-100-days-policy-plans-1366757.

50. Arthur M. Schlesinger Jr., *The Politics of Hope* (Boston: Houghton Mifflin, 1963), 81.

51. Colin I. Bradford, "Individual Dignity, Alexandria Ocasio-Cortez, and the Future of American Politics," Brookings Institution *Up Front* blog, July 2, 2018, https://www.brookings.edu/blog/up-front/2018/07/02/individual-dignity-alexandra-ocasio-cortez-and-the-future-of-american-politics/; Michael Sean Winters, "Biden and the Dignity of Work," *America Magazine*, August 28, 2008, https://www.americamagazine.org/content/all-things/biden-and-dignity-work; Benjamin Wallace-Wells, "Sherrod Brown Wants to Bring a Working-Class Ethos Back to the Democratic Party," *New Yorker*, December 13, 2018, https://www.newyorker.com/news/the-political-scene/sherrod-brown-wants-to-bring-a-working-class-ethos-back-to-the-democratic-party; Gene Sperling, "Economic Dignity," *Democracy Journal*, March 11, 2019, https://democracyjournal.org/magazine/52/economic-dignity/.

52. Sperling, "Economic Dignity." For more on inequalities in wages, see Nikki Graf et al., "The Narrowing, but Persistent, Gender Gap in Pay," Pew Research Center *Fact Tank*, March 22, 2019, https://www.pewresearch.org/fact-tank/2019/03/22/gender-pay-gap-facts/; Ariane Hegewisch and Heidi Hartmann, "The Gender Wage Gap: 2018 Earnings Differences by Race and Ethnicity," March 7, 2019, https://iwpr.org/publications/gender-wage-gap-2018/.

53. David Broder, "Dick Armey's Cheat Notes on Good Government," *Chicago Tribune*, June 21, 1995, https://www.chicagotribune.com/news/ct-xpm-1995-06-21-9506220004-story.html.

54. Ganesh Sitaraman and Anne L. Alstott, *The Public Option: How to Expand Freedom, Increase Opportunity, and Promote Equality* (Cambridge: Harvard University Press, 2019), 2–6, 35–36, 40; Elizabeth Bruenig, "The College Admissions Scandal Isn't Fair. Nothing About Our Social Mobility System Is," *Washington Post*, March 13, 2019, https://www.washingtonpost.com/opinions/the-college-admissions-scandal-isnt-fair-nothing-about-our-social-mobility-system-is/2019/03/13/79d4eb30-45ab-11e9-8aab-95b8d80a1e4f_story.html?utm_term=.cf5bc47c8f13.

55. A good account of Warren's evolution on health care is Dan Balz, "Is Elizabeth Warren Looking for Safer Ground in Health Care?" *Washington Post*, November 16, 2019, https://www.washingtonpost.com/politics/has-elizabeth-warren-found-safer-ground-on-health-care/2019/11/16/36a9f0e2-0899-11ea-8ac0-0810ed197c7e_story.html.

Chapter 7

1. "Full Text: Donald Trump Announces a Presidential Bid," *Washington Post*, June 16, 2015, https://www.washingtonpost.com/news/post-politics/wp/2015/06/16/full-text-donald-trump-announces-a-presidential-bid/; Elspeth Reeve, "A Case Study in the Evolution of Birtherism: Donald Trump," *The Atlantic*, May 25, 2012, https://www.theatlantic.com/politics/archive/2012/05/slow-evolution-birther-donald-trump-case-study/327629/.

2. Katie Rogers and Nicholas Fandos, "Trump Tells Congresswomen to 'Go Back' to the Countries They Came From," *New York Times*, July 14, 2019, https://www.nytimes.com/2019/07/14/us/politics/trump-twitter-squad-congress.html; "The Latest: Democrats Plan Vote on Resolution against Trump," AP News, July 16, 2019, https://apnews.com/d83041cd003c4f6b96a192ef53b26623 (including Reagan quotes); Siobhan Hughes and Michael C. Bender, "House Passes Resolution Condemning Trump Tweets as Racist," *Wall Street Journal*, July 16, 2019, https://www.wsj.com/articles/democrats-prepare-vote-condemning-trumps-tweets-about-lawmakers-11563297658; Alana Abramson and Phillip Elliott, "Democrats Vote to Condemn Trump's Racist Tweets. Republicans Use a Rule from 1801 to Defend Him," *Time*, July 17, 2019, https://time.com/5627826/house-trump-racist-tweets-vote/.

3. Jeremy W. Peters, Annie Karni, and Maggie Haberman, "Trump Sets the 2020 Tone:

Like 2016, Only This Time 'the Squad' Is Here," *New York Times*, July 16, 2019, https://www.nytimes.com/2019/07/16/us/politics/trump-election-squad.html.

4. Steven B. Smith, *Modernity and Its Discontents: Making and Unmaking the Bourgeois from Machiavelli to Bellow* (New Haven: Yale University Press, 2016), 270.

5. Nancy Fraser and Axel Honneth, "Social Justice in the Age of Identity Politics: Redistribution, Recognition, and Participation," in *Redistribution or Recognition? A Political-Philosophical Exchange* (London and New York: Verso, 2003).

6. "African Americans and the New Deal: A Look Back in History," Roosevelt Institute blog, February 5, 2010, https://rooseveltinstitute.org/african-americans-and-new-deal-look-back-history/; Fraser and Honneth, "Social Justice in the Age of Identity Politics," 9.

7. "Ethics of the Fathers: Chapter One," Chabad.org, accessed July 12, 2019, https://www.chabad.org/article.asp?aid=2165.

8. Mark Lilla, *The Once and Future Liberal: After Identity Politics* (New York: HarperCollins, 2017), 14.

9. For "coalition of the ascendant," see Ronald Brownstein and *National Journal*, "The Clinton Conundrum," *The Atlantic*, April 17, 2015, https://www.theatlantic.com/politics/archive/2015/04/the-clinton-conundrum/431949/.

10. John Sides, Michael Tesler, and Lynn Vavreck, *Identity Crisis: The 2016 Presidential Campaign and the Battle for the Meaning of America* (Princeton: Princeton University Press, 2018), 214.

11. Amy Gardner, Beth Reinhard, and Lori Rozsa, "Prospect of Another Recount in Florida Sparks Partisan Showdown," *Washington Post*, November 9, 2018, https://www.washingtonpost.com/politics/prospect-of-another-recount-in-florida-provokes-partisan-battle/2018/11/09/b513aa12-e447-11e8-b759-3d88a5ce9e19_story.html; Jordan Pascale, "Virginia Dems Are on a Decade-Long Statewide Win Streak, but Tim Kaine Won't Call the State Blue Just Yet," WAMU/American University Radio, November 7, 2018, https://wamu.org/story/18/11/07/virginia-dems-are-on-a-decade-long-statewide-win-streak-but-tim-kaine-wont-call-the-state-blue-just-yet/; Dan Balz, "The 2020 Electoral Map Could Be the Smallest in Years. Here's Why," *Washington Post*, August 31, 2019, https://www.washingtonpost.com/politics/the-2020-electoral-map-could-be-the-smallest-in-years-heres-why/2019/08/31/61d4bc9a-c9a9-11e9-a1fe-ca46e8d573c0_story.html.

12. Tyler T. Reny, Loren Collingwood, and Ali A. Valenzuela, "Vote Switching in the 2016 Election: How Racial and Immigration Attitudes, Not Economics, Explain Shifts in White Voting," *Public Opinion Quarterly* 83, no. 1 (May 21, 2019): 91–113; German Lopez, "The Past Year of Research Has Made It Very Clear: Trump Won Because of Racial Resentment," *Vox*, December 15, 2017, https://www.vox.com/identities/2017/12/15/16781222/trump-racism-economic-anxiety-study.

13. Sides, Tesler, and Vavreck, *Identity Crisis*, 8, 165, 175–76.

14. Richard Wike and Kat Devlin, "As Trade Tensions Rise, Fewer Americans See China Favorably," Pew Research Center Global Attitudes Project, August 28, 2018, https://www.pewresearch.org/global/2018/08/28/as-trade-tensions-rise-fewer-americans-see-china-favorably/; "The 1992 Campaign: Transcript of 2d TV Debate Between Bush, Clinton and Perot," *New York Times*, October 16, 1992, https://www.nytimes.com/1992/10/16/us/the-1992-campaign-transcript-of-2d-tv-debate-between-bush-clinton-and-perot.html (for "giant sucking sound"); "Presidential Election of 1992," 270 to Win, accessed July 3, 2019, https://www.270towin.com/1992_Election/; "Presidential Election of 1996," 270 to Win, accessed July 3, 2019, https://www.270towin.com/1996_Election/index.html.

15. For references to the 2016 exit polling, see "2016 Election Results: Exit Polls," CNN, updated November 23, 2012, https://www.cnn.com/election/2016/results/exit-polls; for references to the 2012 election, see Scott Clement, "Obama's Problem with Non-College-Educated White Americans," *Washington Post* blog, March 12, 2012, https://www.washingtonpost.com/blogs/behind-the-numbers/post/obamas

-problem-with-non-college-educated-white-americans/2012/03/07/gIQAp8yI7R
_blog.html.

16. For effects of turnout, see Rob Griffin, Ruy Teixeira, and John Halpin, "Voter Trends in 2016," Center for American Progress, November 1, 2017, https://www .americanprogress.org/issues/democracy/reports/2017/11/01/441926/voter-trends -in-2016/. For how voter identification laws in Wisconsin affected turnout, see Michael Wines, "Wisconsin Strict ID Law Discouraged Voters, Study Finds," *New York Times*, September 25, 2017, https://www.nytimes.com/2017/09/25/us/wisconsin -voters.html.

17. Griffin, Teixeira, and Halpin, "Voter Trends in 2016."

18. Mark Muro and Sifan Liu, "Another Clinton-Trump Divide: High-Output America vs Low-Output America," Brookings Institution *The Avenue* blog, November 29, 2016, https://www.brookings.edu/blog/the-avenue/2016/11/29/another-clinton-trump -divide-high-output-america-vs-low-output-america/.

19. Jed Kolko, "Trump Was Stronger Where the Economy Is Weaker," *FiveThirtyEight*, November 10, 2016, https://fivethirtyeight.com/features/trump-was-stronger-where -the-economy-is-weaker/; Ben Casselman, "Stop Saying Trump's Win Had Nothing to Do with Economics," *FiveThirtyEight*, January 9, 2017, https://fivethirtyeight.com /features/stop-saying-trumps-win-had-nothing-to-do-with-economics/.

20. For the essence of the twentieth-century perspective, see Theodore Roosevelt's State of the Union message, December 2, 1902, http://www.let.rug.nl/usa/presidents/theodore -roosevelt/state-of-the-union-1902.php.

21. Lilla, *The Once and Future Liberal*, 76. The *New York Times* piece is "Opinion: The End of Identity Liberalism," November 18, 2016, https://www.nytimes.com/2016/11 /20/opinion/sunday/the-end-of-identity-liberalism.html.

22. Lilla, *The Once and Future Liberal*, 119–20; Quotes in the ensuing two paragraphs from ibid., 111–12, 14, 67.

23. Lilla, "Opinion: The End of Identity Liberalism."

24. The quotations that follow are from Francis Fukuyama, "Against Identity Politics," *Foreign Affairs*, October 2018, https://www.foreignaffairs.com/articles/americas/2018-08 -14/against-identity-politics-tribalism-francis-fukuyama.

25. Beverly Gage, "An Intellectual Historian Argues His Case Against Identity Politics," *New York Times*, August 15, 2017, https://www.nytimes.com/2017/08/15/books/review /mark-lilla-the-once-and-future-liberal.html.

26. Gage, "An Intellectual Historian Argues His Case Against Identity Politics."

27. Arlie Russell Hochschild, "Liberals' Woes Run Deep, but the Way Out Is Murky," *Washington Post*, August 18, 2017, https://www.washingtonpost.com/outlook/liberals -woes-run-deep-but-the-way-out-is-murky/2017/08/18/14d81e3c-7235-11e7-8839 -ec48ec4cae25_story.html?utm_term=.8d8d4950eb02.

28. "Georgia Governor Election Results," *New York Times*, January 28, 2019, https:// www.nytimes.com/elections/results/georgia-governor; P. R. Lockhart, "The Lawsuit Challenging Georgia's Entire Elections System, Explained," *Vox*, November 30, 2018, https://www.vox.com/policy-and-politics/2018/11/30/18118264/georgia-election -lawsuit-voter-suppression-abrams-kemp-race; Stacey Abrams, "Stacey Abrams Debates Francis Fukuyama on Identity Politics," *Foreign Affairs*, March/April 2019, https://www.foreignaffairs.com/articles/2019-02-01/stacey-abrams-response-to -francis-fukuyama-identity-politics-article.

29. Alan Wolfe, "Francis Fukuyama's Shrinking Idea," *New Republic*, January 16, 2019, https://newrepublic.com/article/152668/francis-fukuyama-identity-review-collapse -theory-liberal-democracy.

30. John Sides, Michael Tesler, and Lynn Vavreck, "Identity Politics Can Lead to Progress," *Foreign Affairs*, March/April 2019, https://www.foreignaffairs.com/articles/2019-02-01 /stacey-abrams-response-to-francis-fukuyama-identity-politics-article.

31. Francis Fukuyama, "Fukuyama Replies," *Foreign Affairs*, March/April 2019, https://

www.foreignaffairs.com/articles/2019-02-01/stacey-abrams-response-to-francis
-fukuyama-identity-politics-article.
32. "First Look: Dems Crush GOP in Party Registration," *Axios*, July 10, 2018, https://
www.axios.com/democrats-crush-republican-party-registration-2018-midterms
-872f7ad2-7a3b-4f7c-97b0-8070448e2df4.html; "Presidential Approval Ratings—
Donald Trump," Gallup, accessed July 15, 2019, https://news.gallup.com/poll/203198
/presidential-approval-ratings-donald-trump.aspx.
33. Michael Sandel, *Liberalism and the Limits of Justice* (Cambridge: Cambridge University
Press, 1982), 183.
34. Pauline Maier, "The Debate over Ratification of the U.S. Constitution," *New Republic*,
December 24, 2010, https://newrepublic.com/article/79740/great-american-argument
-ratification; Philip Hamburger, *Separation of Church and State* (Cambridge: Harvard
University Press, 2002), 347–53; Harold Holzer, *Lincoln and the Power of the Press: The
War for Public Opinion* (New York: Simon & Schuster, 2014), 193; Frederick C. Luebke,
"German Immigrants and American Politics: Problems of Leadership, Parties, and
Issues," Faculty Publications, Department of History, University of Nebraska–Lincoln,
1984, http://digitalcommons.unl.edu/historyfacpub/157, 20.
35. Fukuyama, "Against Identity Politics"; Bill Schneider, "The Role of Catholic Voters,"
CNN, April 8, 2005, http://www.cnn.com/2005/POLITICS/04/08/catholic.voters
/index.html.
36. "The King Philosophy," King Center, https://thekingcenter.org/king-philosophy/ (on
"beloved community"); "5 of Martin Luther King Jr.'s Most Memorable Speeches,"
Washington Week, April 3, 2018, https://www.pbs.org/weta/washingtonweek/blog
-post/5-martin-luther-king-jr%E2%80%99s-most-memorable-speeches (on founding documents); March on Washington speech, August 28, 1963, https://www
.naacp.org/i-have-a-dream-speech-full-march-on-washington/ ("tranquilizing drug
of gradualism"); Letter from Birmingham Jail, 1963, rpt. in *Why We Can't Wait*,
King Legacy Series (Boston: Beacon Press, 2010), 85–109; Chris Hayes, "Remem-
bering Why Black Lives Matter with Alicia Garza," *Why Is This Happening?*, pod-
cast and transcript, NBC News, June 11, 2019, https://www.nbcnews.com/think
/opinion/remembering-why-black-lives-matter-alicia-garza-podcast-transcript
-ncna1013901.
37. Shirin Ghaffary, "Voter Suppression Is the Most Existential Crisis in Our Democracy,
According to Stacey Abrams," *Vox*, June 11, 2019, https://www.vox.com/recode/2019
/6/11/18660099/stacey-abrams-voter-suppression-democracy; William J. Barber
II, "America's Moral Malady," *The Atlantic*, King Issue, https://www.theatlantic.com
/magazine/archive/2018/02/a-new-poor-peoples-campaign/552503; Katie Nodjim-
badem, "The Long, Painful History of Police Brutality in the U.S.," *Smithsonian*, July
27, 2017, https://www.smithsonianmag.com/smithsonian-institution/long-painful
-history-police-brutality-in-the-us-180964098/.
38. Corey Brooks, "What Can the Collapse of the Whig Party Tell Us About Today's Politics?," *Smithsonian*, April 12, 2016, https://www.smithsonianmag.com/history/what
-can-collapse-whig-party-tell-us-about-todays-politics-180958729; Glenn Kessler,
"Carly Fiorina's Claim That the GOP Is 'the Party of Women's Suffrage,'" *Washington
Post*, September 15, 2015, https://www.washingtonpost.com/news/fact-checker/wp
/2015/09/15/carly-fiorinas-claim-that-the-gop-is-the-party-of-womens-suffrage/;
Nan D. Hunter, "Varieties of Constitutional Experience: Democracy and the Marriage
Equality Campaign," 64 *UCLA L. Rev.* 1662 (2017), https://www.uclalawreview.org
/varieties-of-constitutional-experience-democracy-marriage-equality-campaign/.
39. Lilla, "Opinion: The End of Identity Liberalism."
40. Gillian B. White, "Not All Money Troubles Are Created Equal," *The Atlantic*, April 21,
2016, https://www.theatlantic.com/business/archive/2016/04/racial-inequality-money
-problems/479349/.

41. Fraser and Honneth, "Social Justice in the Age of Identity Politics," 9, 26–27.
42. Jacob Hacker, "The Institutional Foundations of Middle-Class Democracy," *Policy Network* (2011): 35.
43. Lilla, "Opinion: The End of Identity Liberalism."
44. Fraser and Honneth, "Social Justice in the Age of Identity Politics," 13–19; for quotes for the ensuing three paragraphs see ibid., 36, 47.
45. Fraser and Honneth, "Social Justice in the Age of Identity Politics," 47.
46. Paul Frymer and Jacob M. Grumbach, "Labor Unions and White Racial Politics," 2019 (forthcoming), MS in author's possession, 26.
47. Emily Etkins, "Religious Trump Voters: How Faith Moderates Attitudes About Immigration, Race, and Identity," Cato Institute, Public Opinion Brief no. 2, February 5, 2019, https://www.cato.org/publications/public-opinion-brief/religious-trump-voters-how -faith-moderates-attitudes-about; Eugene Scott, "More Than Half of White Evangelicals Say America's Declining White Population Is a Negative Thing," *Washington Post*, July 18, 2018, https://www.washingtonpost.com/news/the-fix/wp/2018/07/18/more-than -half-of-white-evangelicals-say-americas-declining-white-population-is-a-negative -thing/; Andrew Restuccia, "The Sanctification of Donald Trump," *Politico*, April 30, 2019, https://politi.co/2J4TAhb; "The Trump Era Has Exposed Divisions Among Catholics and Evangelicals," *The Economist*, March 30, 2019, https://www.economist.com/erasmus/2019 /03/30/the-trump-era-has-exposed-divisions-among-catholics-and-evangelicals.
48. Reclaiming Jesus website, http://reclaimingjesus.org; Jim Wallis, *Christ in Crisis: Why We Need to Reclaim Jesus* (San Francisco: HarperOne, 2019); E. J. Dionne, Jr., "Pete Buttigieg Has Broken Through the Noise on Community and Religion," *Washington Post*, March 24, 2019, https://www.washingtonpost.com/opinions/pete-buttigieg-has -broken-through-the-noise-on-community-and-religion/2019/03/24/8fc72084-4ce0 -11e9-93d0-64dbcf38ba41_story.html; Emma Green, "Democrats Have to Decide Whether Faith Is an Asset for 2020," *The Atlantic*, April 5, 2019, https://www.theatlantic .com/politics/archive/2019/04/buttigieg-democrats-religious-left/586492/; Rob Stutzman, "Trump Is a Religious Poser. That Gives Biden an Opportunity," *Washington Post*, May 31, 2019, https://www.washingtonpost.com/opinions/joe-biden-has-god-on-his -side/2019/05/31/c8bd70f4-822e-11e9-bce7-40b4105f7ca0_story.html.
49. Thomas F. Jackson, *From Civil Rights to Human Rights: Martin Luther King, Jr., and the Struggle for Economic Justice* (Philadelphia: University of Pennsylvania Press, 2007), 131, 171.

Chapter 8

1. Robert Sapolsky, "This Is Your Brain on Nationalism," *Foreign Affairs*, June 28, 2019, https://www.foreignaffairs.com/articles/2019-02-12/your-brain-nationalism.
2. Tim Haughton, "It's the Slogan, Stupid: The Brexit Referendum," *Perspectives*, University of Birmingham (UK), June 24, 2016, https://www.birmingham.ac.uk/research /perspective/eu-ref-haughton.aspx.
3. Yascha Mounk, *The People vs. Democracy: Why Our Freedom Is in Danger and How to Save It* (Cambridge: Harvard University Press, 2018), 208; William A, Galston, *Anti-Pluralism: The Populist Threat to Liberal Democracy* (New Haven: Yale University Press, 2018), 63.
4. Jill Lepore, "Opinion: Don't Let Nationalists Speak for the Nation," *New York Times*, May 25, 2019, https://www.nytimes.com/2019/05/25/opinion/sunday/nationalism -liberalism-2020.html.
5. Greg Sargent, "'The Squad's' Defenders Argue for a Better America Than Trump Does," *Washington Post*, July 17, 2019, https://www.washingtonpost.com/opinions/2019/07 /17/squads-defenders-represent-better-america-than-trump-does/.
6. Chris Prosser, Jon Mellon, and Jane Green, "What Mattered Most to You When Deciding How to Vote in the EU Referendum?," British Election Study, November 7,

2016, https://www.britishelectionstudy.com/bes-findings/what-mattered-most-to-you
-when-deciding-how-to-vote-in-the-eu-referendum/#.XTIQOuhKjcs.

7. "Immigration," Gallup, accessed July 3, 2019, https://news.gallup.com/poll/1660
/Immigration.aspx; John Gramlich, "How Americans See Illegal Immigration, the
Border Wall and Political Compromise," Pew Research Center *Fact Tank*, January 16,
2019, https://www.pewresearch.org/fact-tank/2019/01/16/how-americans-see-illegal
-immigration-the-border-wall-and-political-compromise/.

8. D'Vera Cohn, "How U.S. Immigration Laws and Rules Have Changed Through History," Pew Research Center *Fact Tank*, September 30, 2015, https://www.pewresearch
.org/fact-tank/2015/09/30/how-u-s-immigration-laws-and-rules-have-changed
-through-history/; see Seung Min Kim, "Senate Passes Immigration Bill," *Politico*,
June 27, 2013, https://www.politico.com/story/2013/06/immigration-bill-2013-senate
-passes-93530.html.

9. John B. Judis, *The Populist Explosion: How the Great Recession Transformed American
and European Politics* (New York: Columbia Global Reports, 2016), 14; quote in ensuing paragraph from ibid, 17.

10. John B. Judis, *The Nationalist Revival: Trade, Immigration, and the Revolt Against Globalization* (New York: Columbia Global Reports, 2018), 35.

11. John B. Judis and Michael Lind, "For a New Nationalism," *New Republic*, March 27,
1995, https://newrepublic.com/article/104783/new-nationalism.

12. Judis, *The Nationalist Revival*, 31 (quoted), 81–85, 115–16.

13. Judis, *The Nationalist Revival*, 144–45; Dani Rodrik, *The Globalization Paradox: Democracy and the Future of the World Economy* (New York and London: W. W. Norton,
2011); Dani Rodrik, *Has Globalization Gone Too Far?* (Washington, DC: Institute for
International Economics, 1997); Fletcher Cox, *Democracy and Inequality: A Resource
Guide* (Stockholm: International Institute for Democracy and Electoral Assistance,
2017), https://www.idea.int/gsod/files/IDEA-GSOD-2017-RESOURCE-GUIDE
-INEQUALITY.pdf.

14. Judis, *The Nationalist Revival*, 147. Quotes in ensuing four paragraphs from ibid., 34,
16.

15. George Orwell, "Notes on Nationalism," *Polemic*, May 1945, http://orwell.ru/library
/essays/nationalism/english/e_nat; Isaiah Berlin, *The Sense of Reality: Studies in Ideas
and Their History*, ed. Henry Hardy (Princeton and Oxford: Princeton University Press,
2019), 315; Madeleine Albright, *Fascism: A Warning* (New York: HarperCollins, 2018).

16. Jason Lange and Yeganeh Torbati, "U.S. Foreign-Born Population Swells to Highest in
over a Century," Reuters, September 13, 2018, https://www.reuters.com/article/us-usa
-immigration-data-idUSKCN1LT2HZ; Judis, *The Nationalist Revival*, 76–80; Ronald
Brownstein, "Places with the Fewest Immigrants Push Back Hardest Against Immigration," CNN, August 22, 2017, https://www.cnn.com/2017/08/22/politics/immigration
-trump-arizona/index.html.

17. For Judis on "cosmopolitans" and Goodhart on "Somewheres" and "Anywheres," see
Judis, *The Nationalist Revival*, 44–46.

18. I make the case that Americans have been torn from the earliest days of our country's
existence between our devotion to individualism and our love of community in *Our
Divided Political Heart: The Battle for the American Idea in an Age of Discontent* (New
York: Bloomsbury, 2012).

19. Greg Sargent, "How Democrats Can Defeat Trump and His Ugly Ideas, According to
Pete Buttigieg," *Washington Post*, March 19, 2019, https://www.washingtonpost.com
/opinions/2019/03/19/how-democrats-can-defeat-trump-his-ugly-ideas-according
-pete-buttigieg/?utm_term=.a5905017a6c8; Timothy Carney, *Alienated America: Why
Some Places Thrive While Others Collapse* (New York: HarperCollins, 2019), 46 and 111.

20. On postliberalism, see Patrick Deneen, *Why Liberalism Failed* (New Haven, CT: Yale
University Press, 2018).

21. Jackson Diehl, "In a Month, Trump has Destroyed 'America First,'" *Washington Post*,

October 13, 2019, https://www.washingtonpost.com/opinions/global-opinions/in-a
-month-trump-has-destroyed-america-first/2019/10/13/0fa390cc-eb6e-11e9-9306
-47cb0324fd44_story.html.

Chapter 9

1. I wrote my sentence about Trump's "America First" foreign policy being "Trump First"
before my *Washington Post* colleague Dana Milbank wrote an excellent column on
the same theme, and I use this footnote to acknowledge our agreement. Dana Milbank, "It Was Never About 'America First.' It's Always Been Trump First," *Washington
Post*, October 4, 2019, https://www.washingtonpost.com/opinions/it-was-never-about
-america-first-its-always-been-trump-first/2019/10/04/8c26f132-e6c0-11e9-a6e8
-8759c5c7f608_story.html.
2. Robert Wright, "American Foreign Policy Has an Empathy Problem," *The Nation*,
December 21, 2016, https://www.thenation.com/article/american-foreign-policy-has
-an-empathy-problem/.
3. Joseph S. Nye Jr., "American Soft Power in the Age of Trump," *Project Syndicate*, May 6,
2019, https://www.project-syndicate.org/commentary/american-soft-power-decline-under
-trump-by-joseph-s-nye-2019-05; Heather Hurlburt, interview with author, July 2019.
4. Adam Serwer, "What Americans Do Now Will Define Us Forever," *The Atlantic*, July 18,
2019, https://www.theatlantic.com/ideas/archive/2019/07/send-her-back-battle-will
-define-us-forever/594307/.
5. For more on interventionism, see Michael White, "Iraq, Syria and the Cost of Intervention (and Non-intervention)," *The Guardian*, May 16, 2016, https://www.theguardian
.com/world/blog/2016/may/16/iraq-syria-and-the-cost-of-intervention-and-non
-intervention; Stephen M. Walt, "Could We Have Stopped This Tragedy?," *Foreign
Policy*, September 21, 2015, https://foreignpolicy.com/2015/09/21/could-we-have
-stopped-this-tragedy-syria-intervention-realist/.
6. Michael Kinsley, "'The Tragedy of 'Foreign Policy Elites,'" *Washington Post*, April 17,
2016, https://www.washingtonpost.com/blogs/post-partisan/wp/2016/04/17/the
-tragedy-of-foreign-policy-elites/?utm_term=.1d2b993c4249.
7. Alex Ward, "Democrats Want to Challenge Trump's Foreign Policy in 2020. They're
Still Working Out How," *Vox*, April 24, 2019, https://www.vox.com/policy-and-politics
/2019/4/24/18510844/2020-election-trump-democrats-foreign-policy; Richard Haass,
Foreign Policy Begins at Home (New York: Basic Books, 2013).
8. "Former Vice President Joe Biden Speech on Foreign Policy," C-SPAN video, July
11, 2019, https://www.c-span.org/video/?462515-1/vice-president-joe-biden-speech
-foreign-policy.
9. Pete Buttigieg, "America and the World in 2054: Reimagining National Security for
a New Era," Pete for America, June 11, 2019, https://peteforamerica.com/national
-security-for-a-new-era/.
10. Kamala Harris, "Our America: American Leadership at Home and Abroad," Kamala
Harris for the People, https://kamalaharris.org/issue/american-leadership-at-home
-and-abroad/.
11. Bernie Sanders, "Future of the International Left: A New Authoritarian Axis Demands
an International Progressive Front," *The Guardian*, September 13, 2018, https://www
.theguardian.com/commentisfree/ng-interactive/2018/sep/13/bernie-sanders
-international-progressive-front.
12. Elizabeth Warren, "A Foreign Policy for All," *Foreign Affairs*, June 21, 2019, https://www
.foreignaffairs.com/articles/2018-11-29/foreign-policy-all; Franklin D. Roosevelt, "On
U.S. Involvement in the War in Europe," speech, Washington, D.C., March 15, 1941),
American Rhetoric, https://www.americanrhetoric.com/speeches/fdrwarineurope.htm.
13. John B. Judis and Michael Lind, "For a New Nationalism," *New Republic*, March 27,
1995, https://newrepublic.com/article/104783/new-nationalism.

14. Ganesh Sitaraman, "The Emergence of Progressive Foreign Policy," *War on the Rocks*, April 15, 2019, https://warontherocks.com/2019/04/the-emergence-of-progressive-foreign-policy/.
15. John Halpin et al., "America Adrift," Center for American Progress, May 5, 2019, https://www.americanprogress.org/issues/security/reports/2019/05/05/469218/america-adrift/.
16. Phone interview with author, May 2019.
17. Samuel Moyn, "Economic Rights Are Human Rights," *Foreign Policy*, April 9, 2018, https://foreignpolicy.com/2018/04/09/the-freedom-america-forgot-populism-human-rights-united-nations/; John Cassidy, "The New World Disorder," *New Yorker*, October 18, 1998, https://www.newyorker.com/magazine/1998/10/26/the-new-world-disorder.
18. Ethan B. Kapstein, "Workers and the World Economy: Breaking the Postwar Bargain," *Foreign Affairs*, May/June 1996, https://www.foreignaffairs.com/articles/1996-05-01/workers-and-world-economy-breaking-postwar-bargain.
19. Peter Beinart, "America Needs an Entirely New Foreign Policy for the Trump Age," *The Atlantic*, September 16, 2018, https://www.theatlantic.com/ideas/archive/2018/09/shield-of-the-republic-a-democratic-foreign-policy-for-the-trump-age/570010/.
20. Interview with author, July 2019.
21. "President Obama Farewell Address: Full Text," CNN, January 11, 2017, https://www.cnn.com/2017/01/10/politics/president-obama-farewell-speech/index.html.
22. Robert Wright, "'Progressive Realism,'" *New York Times*, July 18, 2006, https://www.nytimes.com/2006/07/18/opinion/18iht-edwright.2231959.html; Michael Mandelbaum, "The New Containment," *Foreign Affairs*, March/April 2019, https://www.foreignaffairs.com/articles/china/2019-02-12/new-containment: See also Mandelbaum's *The Rise and Fall of Peace on Earth* (New York: Oxford University Press, 2019).
23. Robert M. Gates, "Landon Lecture (Kansas State University)," November 26, 2007, https://archive.defense.gov/Speeches/Speech.aspx?SpeechID=1199. For more on civilian agencies, see Jena McGregor, "A Disturbing Look at Personnel Issues Inside Federal Agencies," *Washington Post*, August 3, 2015, https://www.washingtonpost.com/news/on-leadership/wp/2015/08/03/a-disturbing-look-at-personnel-issues-inside-federal-agencies/?utm_term=.e068ce4450bb; Editorial Board, "Donald Trump's Nasty Budget," *New York Times*, February 12, 2018, https://www.nytimes.com/2018/02/12/opinion/trump-budget-cuts.html.
24. David L. Roll, "The Key to Avoiding a New Cold War with China," *Washington Post*, July 10, 2019, https://www.washingtonpost.com/outlook/2019/07/10/key-avoiding-new-cold-war-with-china/?utm_term=.909ef6feaf35; Ed Pilkington, "Julián Castro: The US Should Launch a Marshall Plan in Central America," *The Guardian*, March 14, 2019, https://www.theguardian.com/world/2019/mar/14/julian-castro-interview-central-america-marshall-plan; Jennifer Harris, "Making Trade Address Inequality," *Democracy Journal*, Spring 2018, https://democracyjournal.org/magazine/48/making-trade-address-inequality/.
25. Kurt M. Campbell and Jake Sullivan, "Competition Without Catastrophe: How America Can Both Challenge and Coexist with China," *Foreign Affairs* (September/October 2019); 96–111; Martin Wolf, "How the US Should Deal with China," *Financial Times*, November 13, 2019, 9.
26. David Ignatius, "Democrats Need to Stop Running Scared on Foreign Policy," *Washington Post*, August 13, 2019, https://www.washingtonpost.com/opinions/global-opinions/democrats-need-to-stop-running-scared-on-foreign-policy/2019/08/13/92c525c2-bde4-11e9-9b73-fd3c65ef8f9c_story.html.
27. James Reston, "The Kissinger Appointment: A New Approach to Conduct of Foreign Policy Is Seen," *New York Times*, August 23, 1973, https://www.nytimes.com/1973/08/23/archives/the-kissinger-appointment-a-new-approach-to-conduct-of-foreign.html.

Chapter 10

1. For more on unrepresentative institutions, see Jamelle Bouie, "The Electoral College Is the Greatest Threat to Our Democracy," *New York Times*, February 28, 2019, https://www.nytimes.com/2019/02/28/opinion/the-electoral-college.html; David Leonhardt, "The Senate: Affirmative Action for White People," *New York Times*, October 14, 2018, https://www.nytimes.com/2018/10/14/opinion/dc-puerto-rico-statehood-senate.html.
2. Tom Malinowski, "What America Stood For," *The Atlantic*, March 25, 2017, https://www.theatlantic.com/international/archive/2017/03/trump-human-rights-freedom-state-department/520677/.
3. Bill Barrow, "In Democratic Response, Abrams Sharply Rebukes Trump," Associated Press, February 6, 2019, https://www.apnews.com/4873a7e9c9b740b59864a44287e5e38e.
4. Peter Baker, "Onset of Woes Casts Pall over Obama's Policy Aspirations," *New York Times*, May 15, 2013, https://www.nytimes.com/2013/05/16/us/politics/new-controversies-may-undermine-obama.html.

INDEX